STRANGELOVE COUNTRY

# STRANGELOVE

SCIENCE FICTION, FILMOSOPHY, AND THE KUBRICKIAN CONSCIOUSNESS

## COUNTRY

## D. HARLAN WILSON

STALKING HORSE PRESS
Santa Fe, NM

"You might feel as though there is no new space to explore in the films of Stanley Kubrick, an artist whose work has fascinated academics and audiences alike for decades. And then you enter *Strangelove Country*, in which D. Harlan Wilson analyzes Kubrick's works as a unified system of thought, a filmind that proffers abiding themes, neurotic preoccupations, and existential theses. Wilson treats Kubrick's filmic body of work as a cogently thinking mind and subjects it to agile and omnivorous analysis; in the process, he paints a vivid portrait of a mind that thinks science fictionally and avidly about how we use technology and how it uses us. Putting film-philosophy (i.e., filmosophy) into practice, Wilson's writing is both intellectually rigorous and playful, shuttling keenly between the stable structures of the big themes that stabilize the Kubrickian legacy and the digressive minutiae that keep it vitally humane." —DAN NORTH, author of *Performing Illusions: Cinema, Special Effects, and the Virtual Actor*

"D. Harlan Wilson has written a deeply personal, intense, and persuasive reading of Stanley Kubrick's core science fiction films: *Dr. Strangelove, 2001: A Space Odyssey*, and *A Clockwork Orange*, with a bonus discussion of Steven Spielberg's Kubrick-inspired *A.I. Artificial Intelligence*. The writing throughout is strong and compelling; the ideas and insights remarkable and often startling. *Strangelove Country* is an important addition to Kubrick literature." —ROBERT P. KOLKER, author of *Kubrick: An Odyssey* and *The Extraordinary Image: Orson Welles, Alfred Hitchcock, Stanley Kubrick, and the Reimagining of Cinema*

"Wilson has produced one of the very best full-length critical treatments of Kubrick's work that has yet appeared. This book will help us to understand and appreciate not only Kubrick's supreme importance for science fiction cinema but also the importance of science fiction for the whole multigeneric Kubrick oeuvre." —CARL FREEDMAN, author of *Critical Theory and Science Fiction*

First paperback edition published by Stalking Horse Press, March 2025

Interior design by Betty Lomax
www.hawgstrüffelmedia.com

Cover design by Matthew Revert
www.matthewrevert.com

Index by Matthew White
www.mwindexing.com

STALKING HORSE PRESS
Santa Fe, New Mexico
www.stalkinghorsepress.com

# CONTENTS

## ACKNOWLEDGEMENTS

Whenever I finish a book, I am reminded of Walter Benjamin's apothegm that "the work is the death mask of its conception." *Strangelove Country* is no exception. And yet this death mask diverges substantially from its conception. I have always perceived my scholarly monographs and essays to be as much of an artistic exploit as my novels, stories, and plays, but I usually temper my imaginative flights of fancy when I write, say, literary or film criticism. In this work, I made a concerted effort to combine the protocols of scholarship with various novelistic techniques, guided by the innovations of critics, theorists, and philosophers who have done likewise to great effect. This did not sit well with the academic publisher for whom I wrote the proposal for *Strangelove Country*. I was asked to overhaul the tone and style of my finished manuscript by editors who did not seem to understand that the book hinges on tone and especially on *style as a way of seeing*. Alas, if you tell me that something has to be written a certain way, let alone that a certain type of writing is "correct" or "right," I'm going to do the opposite, even if it means that my death mask never sees the light of day. Fortunately, there are publishers like Stalking Horse Press who share my mindset and appreciate the value of experimentation, originality, and imagination in the raw. I don't want to write anything that isn't grappling for the New. If I am, I'm failing.

That said, I remain grateful for the attention and feedback I received from that first publisher, if only to reassure myself that I was doing the "right" (i.e., *wrong*) thing. First and foremost, however, I must thank SHP editor-in-chief James Reich, a spectacular writer himself. James realized precisely what I was trying to bring to bear in *Strangelove Country* at first glance. The hyper-capitalist initiative in academic publishing to exploit scholars who need publications while charging exorbitant prices for books, marking up printing costs well over 1,000% in some cases, is increasingly disturbing, predatory, and untenable. Publishers like SHP are so important for the future of progressively transgressive (and transgressively progressive) literature of any genre or modality. I must also give credit to my ex-wife, co-professor, and friend, Dr. Christine Junker. In addition to being a wonderful mother to our two daughters, Madeleine and Renee, and the bedrock of our Unfamily, she always makes time to give me notes, she knows exactly when and where to temper my overexuberant lines of flight, and she negotiates my evolving curmudgeonism like a pro. Thank you for everything you do, Christine.

Gratitude as well to my colleague Isaac Abram, who provided feedback on my initial proposal, and the many scholars that I contacted throughout the course of my writing and research for advice: you know who you are, and I'm indebted to you all. Indirectly, I want to express appreciation for Laurence A. Rickels, a true innovator whose writing showed me that literary, film, and cultural theory could be so much more than the usual academic stodge; Larry's singular voice was very much in my head as I composed this book. The same goes for Daniel Frampton, whose monograph on cinema, *Filmosophy*, occupies the theoretical core of *Strangelove Country*.

Lastly (and per usual) I recognize Dr. Robert Crossley, my mentor in graduate school, and the one who introduced me to the field of Science Fiction Studies in the 1990s. For me, this book represents the culmination of the path he set me on, and however it is received, I doubt I will ever write anything better. Thanks again Bob!

"I have always enjoyed dealing with a slightly surrealistic situation and presenting it in a realistic manner. I've always liked fairy tales and myths, magical stories, supernatural stories, ghost stories, surrealistic and allegorical stories. I think they are somehow closer to the sense of reality one feels today than the equally stylized 'realistic' story in which a great deal of selectivity and omission has to occur in order to preserve its 'realistic' style." —STANLEY KUBRICK, "Kubrick Country"

.

## INTRODUCTION
## SCIENCE FICTION AND THE KUBRICKIAN CONSCIOUSNESS

### BECOMING KUBRICKIAN

Science fiction enabled Stanley Kubrick to become Kubrickian.

All of his films exhibit SF elements, tropes, and critical engagements, even *Fear and Desire* (1953). Kubrick's feature-length debut portrays an "any war" that takes place "outside history" with enemies "who do not exist unless we call them into being," according to the opening voice-over. Set in an Edenic forest, the film lays a cultural monster onto a bed of nature in the form of soldiers defined by their heavy-metal artillery and the psychic flows that weaponize them. Thematically, *Fear and Desire* probes the affects of destructive technologies on humankind, like so many SF films in its wake. Peel away the many layers of blockbuster, superstylized glitz from James Cameron's *Avatar* franchise, for example, and you'll reveal Kubrick's black, monolithic eyes staring back at you. But it wasn't until his formal entrance into the SF genre that the contours of the Kubrickian dissolved into clarity.

*Dr. Strangelove or: How I Learned to Stop Worrying and Love the Bomb* (1964) extrapolates the techno-masculine *esprit de corps* of *Fear and Desire* into a surreal, satirical, apocalyptic wargame that sets the bar for *2001: A Space Odyssey* (1968) and *A Clockwork Orange* (1971), two vital contributions to the SF genre and the history of cinema. Together these three touchstones have been referred to as the futurist trilogy and comprise a formidable SF yoke. *A.I.: Artificial Intelligence* (2001) is a fourth futurist installment that punctuates that yoke. Directed by Steven Spielberg, this allusive meta-encyclopedia canvasses the Kubrickian landscape. Spielberg took the baton from his longtime friend after Kubrick labored over it for almost two decades prior to his death in 1999, just days before completing the final cut of his last film, *Eyes Wide Shut* (1999).

Like *Fear and Desire*, *A.I.* foregrounds technological affect. This is an important monad in Kubrick's cinematic consciousness, which orbits a cluster of intimately connected monads. Luis M. García Mainar argues that one reason scholars find Kubrick so appealing is because of "stylistic aspects that lead to the evaluation of the cinematographic quality of [his] films" and "the idea of the auteur who produced a coherent oeuvre" (1). This auteur's style is readily identifiable, but it's much more than a constellation of "trademarks." In Kubrick's movies, *style is a way of seeing*. Everything else is subsidiary to this modus, ranging from characterization and plot to ideology and morality, as his categorical SF substantiates.

Other monads that distinguish Kubrick's cinematic consciousness include themes like violence, sublimity, sexuality, primitivism, obsession, and the grotesque; movements and periods like (post)modernism, surrealism, expressionism, classicism, futurism, and Victorianism; and more specific identity-markers like "wargasm," doppelgängers, the fallibility of machines, the phallus, original sin, chessboard precision (and prevision), uncanny visual symmetry, and the "Kubrick stare," "a term coined by Kubrick's director of photography Doug Milsome describing the detached, unsettling gaze that signals that a character is 'piercing through the illusion of conscious life to spy the deep archetypal forces that shape reality'" (Williams 154). I am primarily interested in how the flows of desire inform Kubrick's diegetic universe. Gilles Deleuze and Félix Guattari say that "there is only desire and the social, and nothing else" (*Anti-Oedipus* 29). In this universe, desire has been put on a pedestal.

Prior to *Dr. Strangelove*, the shape of the Kubrickian was still gestating. Definitive contours started to coalesce and become visible in *Lolita* (1962). Not until Kubrick's first SF film did there manifest a discernible, meaningful physique. Thereafter, *2001* and *A Clockwork Orange* solidified (and solarized) the Kubrickian.

Every movie made after *A Clockwork Orange* is a cinematic masterpiece behind which is a filmmaker at the zenith of expertise, craft, dynamism, and self-awareness. *Barry Lyndon* (1975), *The Shining* (1980), *Full Metal Jacket* (1987), and *Eyes Wide Shut* all received their share of terrible reviews when they came out, but as with anything Kubrickian, what one hates at first, one falls in love with later. Robert P. Kolker's shifting perception of *Eyes Wide Shut* sets a good precedent. After an initial screening, he confesses: "My heart sank: the film was long and seemingly pointless. [ ... ] I reminded myself that very often my first reaction to a Kubrick film was less than enthusiastic. This had happened with *2001*, *A Clockwork Orange*, and *The Shining*" (*Extraordinary* 42). Like so many filmgoers and scholars, Kolker developed an affection over time. "Subsequent viewings opened the films out, revealed more, and they became more exciting, more resonant. [ ... ] I now appreciate [*Eyes Wide Shut*], am astonished by it, but even more, I have become obsessed by it. [ ... ] I want to write about it, explain it, explore it, perhaps as a means to find its heart" (ibid.). In spite of his interpretive labors, Kolker laments the elusiveness of the movie's heart. That's inevitable, though: ambiguity is one of the Kubrickian's many instruments of quiet, enclosed chaos.

We can see traces of what Kubrick would become in his pre-*Strangelove* harvest. With *Fear and Desire*, the features include *Killer's Kiss* (1955), *The Killing* (1956), *Paths of Glory* (1957), and *Spartacus* (1960), a studio picture that Kubrick came to direct after the original director was fired during the first week of principle photography. "*Spartacus* is the only film over which I did not have absolute control," said Kubrick in 1973 (Phillips, "Stop" 145). Nonetheless, it contains seeds of the Kubrickian, envisioning the master-slave dialectic at play in *2001* (aliens vs. apes/ astronauts), *A Clockwork Orange* (State vs. droogs), and *Dr. Strangelove* (Bomb vs. buffoons), although humanity's worst enemy is always itself. All narratives require conflict to propel the story. In Kubrick's cinema, a poignant, brooding, persistent *versus* scaffolds the diegeses and extends from inner to outer space. The dominant manifestation (and fetishization) of outer space in *2001* is the hard vacuum between celestial bodies, but usually it denotes an external force or setting that puts subjectivity and the individual in peril.

The subtextual *versus* in *Lolita* (morality vs. alpha-man) was a foundational artifice. Narcissistic self-stylist Humbert Humbert's pedophilic desire for the titular "nymphet" is a silver bullet fired by the haughty literatus *against* a world constructed *against* that desire. Kubrick read copiously and adapted all but *Fear and Desire* and *Killer's Kiss* from novels. Vladimir Nabokov's *Lolita* (1955) is thoroughly literary and transgressive, as is Anthony Burgess's linguistically extraordinary *A Clockwork Orange* (1962).

In Kubrickian fashion, Nabokov's novel met with protest and censure before finding acclaim; it was published in the US in 1958 and sold millions of copies. Despite the "outlandish content and reputation," however, the book posed obstacles for adaptation because of "its signal style and its labyrinthine complexity" (Jenkins 32). Kubrick welcomed the challenge. He vetted potential source material constantly, and if it resonated with his artistic sensibilities, he would have adapted a toilet into a movie (incidentally, toilets and bathrooms figure prominently in his cinema and represent another monad). Still, the Motion Picture Production Code prohibited him from taking his vision all the way. At the same time, "censorship problems were tied up [ ... ] with Kubrick's desire [ ... ] to reach the widest possible audience, the resulting success hopefully allowing him maximum artistic independence" (Kagan 82). The exquisitely written *Lolita* isn't pornographic, but the adaptation had to exclude, sidestep, or mask a lot of content while appeasing general audiences as well as readers of the novel who wanted a movie that was faithful to the source material.

The Code was moribund in the early 1960s when Kubrick made *Dr. Strangelove*. By the time he made *A Clockwork Orange* in the early 1970s, it had been replaced by the MPAA rating system. Forced bowdlerization had a significant impact on Kubrick becoming Kubrickian. Only when he acquired complete (obsessive) control did he transform into "himself." Hence the idea that *A Clockwork Orange* is a pseudo-remake of *Lolita*, offering him "an opportunity to explore male sexuality and violence in a more explicit fashion" (Krämer, *Clockwork* 78).

Michel Ciment recounts that Kubrick's "work has constantly aimed at confounding our expectations. What could be further from *Dr. Strangelove*—with its gratingly farcical tone, the scope given its cast to invent incisive caricatures and the uncompromising linearity of its screenplay—than the poetic reverie of an experience as non-verbal as *2001: A Space Odyssey*? *A Clockwork Orange* in its turn proved to be the antithesis of *2001*, as if by some dialectical progression whose every stage contradicts the one preceding it" (58). Ciment deduces that Kubrick seemed to be "obsessed with contradicting himself, with making each work a critique of the previous one" (ibid.). The futurist trilogy is a beacon of such a meta-performance. *A.I.*, in turn, critiques the Kubrickian itself, partly by Spielberg as an ode, partly by Kubrick as a self-reflexive wink at more discerning viewers.

Gene Youngblood clinches the role of *Lolita* in the history of Kubrick's cinema, calling it "a transitional work, marking the turning point from a naturalistic cinema (*Paths of Glory, Spartacus*) to the surrealism of the later films. Reality and fantasy coexist for the first time in a Kubrick film in the bizarre figure of Quilty's 'Dr. Zempf.' Sitting in a darkened room in a pose that prefigures the sinister, chair-bound Dr. Strangelove, this scene anticipates the atmosphere of Kubrick's next film." In fact, *Lolita* anticipates all of Kubrick's subsequent films, which are defined by oneiric environments and exchanges, technopathology, masculine anxiety and insecurity, invocations of the sublime, and an idle, revving malevolence that occasionally shifts into high gear.

## ENGINES OF AMBIGUITY

Much has been said about Kubrick's inherent "pessimism" and related terms that might typify the Kubrickian, including misogyny, patriarchy, racism, nihilism, and misanthropy. This characterization has been linked to his personal and diegetic life (e.g., his film-noir roots, political views, absurdist humor, fear of machines, preoccupation with war and the holocaust, etc.). For me, the best criticism emphasizes how this ostensible pessimism gives primacy to "satire and irony over sentiment" (Naremore 9). Many reviewers and scholars have countered this idea. In 2017, Julian Rice observed that an "erotic pessimism [...] continues to stunt interpretations of Kubrick's films" (69). Others contend that he's really a terrific optimist, not a dark existentialist and dystopian, but a director whose beliefs, desires, and artistry grapple for utopia and want the best for humanity, if only by underlining our recurrent propensity for egoism, violence, and self-destruction.

Kubrick expressed the latter attitude. In a 1968 *Playboy* interview, he said: "The very meaninglessness of life forces man to create his own meaning. [...] The most terrifying fact about the universe is not that it is hostile but that it is indifferent; but if we can come to terms with this indifference and accept the challenges of life within the boundaries of death—however mutable man may be able to make them—our existence as a species can have genuine meaning and fulfillment. However vast the darkness, we must supply our own light" (Nordern 73). A few years later, in 1973, Kubrick spoke to Gene D. Phillips about *Dr. Strangelove*. "Asked if the film suggested that he was a misanthrope with contempt for the human race," Phillips reports, "Kubrick shot back, 'Oh God, no. One doesn't give up being concerned for mankind because one acknowledges their fundamental absurdities and weaknesses. I still have hope that the human race can continue to progress" ("Stop" 151).

These are fine assertions, but Kubrick's ideas about himself and his cinematic output are subsidiary to my interest in the megatext of his cinema, which is plugged into the megatext of the SF genre, and which posits that the Kubrickian is at once pessimistic/dystopian and optimistic/utopian. Since *Dr. Strangelove*, localizing Kubrick's perception of the human condition has been a central critical concern. The Kubrickian's preoccupation with style as a way of seeing is why the mature films oscillate so fluidly from one moralistic or ideological pole to another. They invite poststructuralist readings by subverting our expectations and easily deconstructing binary oppositions (e.g., culture/nature, masculine/feminine, human/machine, interior/exterior, and natural/supernatural).

Style shapes and articulates the structure of narrative, character, and theme in Kubrickian cinema. For all of its outward attention to morality, even *A Clockwork Orange* concludes on a note that favors style over what's "right" or "wrong." As the finale of Beethoven's *Ninth*, "Ode to Joy," blasts to an end, Alex fucks a laughing *femme bourgeoise* in slow motion on a bed of artificial snow surrounded by clapping Neo-Victorian aristocrats. The scene takes place on Alex's mindscreen, but that doesn't matter either: all screens in Kubrick's world are fair game, and like the other binaries that formulate the undertext of his style, reality and fantasy often exist in a ready state of implosion.

James Naremore says the key to Kubrick's style "lies in his anxious fascination with the human body and his ability, which he shares with all black humorists and artists of the grotesque, to yoke together conflicting emotions, so that he confuses both our cognitive and emotional responses" (36). The element of confusion factors into his stylistic affect, which is deliberate, or at least redundant. Most people don't like to be confused. The Kubrickian thrives on confusion. *The Shining's* Overlook Hotel is a perfect metaphor. We don't know what's in room 237. It worries us. Then we go inside and see something that worries us more, but we can't be sure if what we see is real. We run out of the room and what's there? More doors; more rooms. More mysteriousness. Above all: *more uncertainty.* Through a Kubrickian lens darkly, we must negotiate this default plight. Kubrick's characters live on the volcano's rim of What Happens Next, gazing into an abyss that may or may not be gazing back at them.

Kubrick is a moralist. Kubrick is an immoralist. Kubrick is an amoralist. All three theses can be easily defended with textual support from his films and from scholarship about the films. Scholarly perceptions are illusory, of course; subjective and subjected, if not *abjected*, we're all victims of our own experiences, education, and outlooks. But whatever we think—or rather, whatever we *desire* to be "true" by the power of disavowal—style prescribes the definitively Kubrickian.

What erupts from Kubrick's highly stylized diegeses is a terminal hermeneutic of suspicion that makes meaning utterly porous, which is to say, Kubrickian ambiguity invites criticism from multiple angles of incidence, then critiques those angles as they collapse and take flight. Kubrick the man excelled at chess. So do his films operate like chess players, thinking many moves ahead—every mise-en-scène is an undulant map of that mise-en-scène's diegetic future. This is also why the SF genre was so important to Kubrick's maturity as one of the twentieth century's foremost big-budget auteurs. No other cinematic genre depends so much on style. SFX technologies have revolutionized cinema in the twenty-first century. Pre-Kubrickian SF looks primordial by comparison. Kubrick's futurist trilogy innovated the genre, and *2001* single-handedly transfigured the potential of visually articulated SF. The film functioned like the alien monolith at the core of its story, sparking an evolution in cinema. To this day, some critics say that they still prefer the aesthetics of *2001* to more contemporary SF movies like Danny Boyle's *Sunshine* (2007) and Alfonso Cuarón's *Gravity* (2013), both beautiful, picturesque space odysseys in themselves.

In the next two sections, I will provide context for the Kubrickian, the history of SF cinema, and the way Film Studies, since the dawn of motion pictures in the late-nineteenth century, has always perceived the medium in SF terms no matter what genre a film purports to be.

### SCIENCE FICTION CINEMA

The hallways of SF Studies are strewn with attempts to define what SF is. It's hard to do. The twenty-first century has seen SF rebuild the architectures of society, culture, subjectivity, and identity. The science-fictionalization of reality is no longer a fiction; it's an inscribed *mode de vie*. In the 1970s, my elementary-school textbooks promised me hotels in orbit and colonies on the Moon and Mars. The only reason these habitations don't exist now is because nobody wants to pay for them. SpaceX, Virgin Galactic, and other private enterprises may change things, but I'm not holding my breath.

Rooted in our collective desire to categorize *everything*, the pathological impetus for a cohesive, all-encompassing SF definition has
become part of the genre's history. To some extent, this impetus is
more interesting than the texts. Even today, no major work of SF
criticism or theory can sidestep the issue. In *Science Fiction* (2021),
for instance, Sherryl Vint cites key SF lexicographers and originary
novelists to begin her "overview of how SF grapples with the ways that
science and technology shape and change human lives" (1). Darko
Suvin and Mary Shelley are two eminent anchors. Conceptualized in
*The Metamorphoses of Science Fiction* (1977), Suvin's definition of SF as
"the literature of cognitive estrangement" remains influential, as does
Shelley's *Frankenstein* (1818), the genre's most famous ur-text (15).
Vint drops both anchors. She has no choice. It's a golden rule of SF
Studies to enter the dragon of categorization. And I'm no exception to
the rule.

SF "remains notoriously undefined, if not undefinable," declares
George Slusser in *Science Fiction: Toward a World Literature* (2022).
*The Encyclopedia of Science Fiction* says that there "is really no good
reason to expect that a workable definition of sf will ever be established.
None has been, so far. In practice, there is much consensus about what
sf looks like in its centre; it is only at the fringes that most of the fights
take place" (Clute, "Definitions"). Centrist themes include scientific
innovation, futuristic settings, and encounters with aliens and/or
advanced technology. I would argue that violations against "reality"
and explorations of inner space constitute SF, but already that puts me
at the fringes, as other genres do likewise (e.g., fantasy, magic realism,
irrealism, and gothic fiction). Broadly speaking, says Vint, "the idea that
the genre is about change persists" (11).

In film and literature, pre-WW2 SF depicted the boyish adventures
of white male heroes, who appeared with regularity on magazine covers
cradling voluptuous damsels and blasting otherworldly monsters with
ray guns. In the late 1930s and 1940s, American editor John W. Campbell Jr. liberated SF "from the abyss of space pirates, mad scientists,
their lovely daughters wearing just enough clothes to satisfy the postal

authorities, and alien fiends," according to Alfred Bester (410). Campbell's early editorship of *Astounding Science Fiction* is often referred to as the Golden Age of SF, which lasted from 1937 to 1946 (Ashley). During this period, the genre matured and gained more attention. It still didn't stray that far from the status quo of its pulp roots. In the 1950s, a few authors began to takes risks and make progress toward real change. Bester, for one, broke the status quo over his knee with legendary SF novels *The Demolished Man* (1953) and *The Stars My Destination* (1956), but widespread progress wasn't accomplished until postmodern movements like the New Wave (1960s and 70s) and cyberpunk (1980s) reconditioned SF with greater complexity and more adult content.

SF literature matured faster than SF cinema, which continued to be pulp-centric well into the 1960s with just a few exceptions, namely *2001*. Prior to *2001*, "many sf authors and fans looked at sf film and television as a poor relation, unable to capture the ideational complexity of the best print sf" (Latham 209). Released the same year in 1968, *Planet of the Apes* was acclaimed by critics and audiences, winning awards and Oscar nominations for original score and costume design; John Chambers also received an Oscar for outstanding makeup achievement. Looking back, it seems impossible to me that the Oscar didn't go to *2001*.

*Planet of the Apes* makes some narrative, thematic, and stylistic headway, but Charlton Heston's spaceman is just another square-jawed, know-it-all alphaman, and it's not long after the film begins that he discovers a buxom, scantily clad damsel in distress to reify his masculinity and reassure 1960s spectators that heteronormative patriarchy governs this diegesis. More curious are the costumes and special effects. We only see outer space at the beginning through the windowpane of the astronauts' ship before it crash-lands onto futuristic Earth. Compared to how Kubrick pictures space in *2001*—even through a shuttle window— it looks like child's play: in *Planet of the Apes*, rear projection makes a cartoon out of space, which is busy with multicolored lights, flashes, and bursts. As *2001* shows us, outer space is dead and silent, a canvass of blackness and infinitely quiet, distant, star-spangled pinpoints, not an orchestra of constant activity and illumination. Like most SF films of the era, *Planet of the Apes* appears not years but decades behind Kubrick's vision. Carl Freedman calls it "a better-than-average sci-fi thriller that even included a measure of self-conscious socio-political reflection; but Kubrick's film was understood, especially though not only by those already knowledgeable about literary science fiction, to attain a distinctly new order of artistic achievement" (303).

*Planet of the Apes* is a crucial frame of reference for this artistic achievement, signaling the historical and cultural temperament of viewers' desires, expectations, and perceptions. Before *2001*, 1960s filmgoers had not yet experienced a full-blooded Kubrickian artwork. Consider the difference between the films' ape costumes. I first saw *2001* as a college student in the early 1990s. I thought Kubrick had wrangled real apes, whereas I always knew that Cornelius, Dr. Zaius, and Zira were actors in not-so-realistic suits. *Planet of the Apes* deals with some adult themes, allegorizing American slavery, but it doesn't possess the complexity of *2001*, and it was made for general audiences. Both movies received G ratings. *2001* targeted adults. Given its intellectualism, slow pacing, and hysterical obscurity, I like to think Kubrick made *2001* for adults who didn't yet exist, rendering it a movie about the future for futurians. It challenged audiences to look at cinema with new (in)sight, and there were few SF precursors for referential comparison in Hollywood.

Cheap SFX hindered Hollywood SF of the 1950s. "During this period—now often described as the 'classic' era—science fiction was largely produced in low-budget 'B' formats, designed for a predominantly teenage audience" (King 4). Wooden characters and simple-minded storylines typified these formats. Kubrick broke the B-mold. Stylistically, SF cinema didn't catch up with him until the 1990s with advances in SFX. The 1970s had a few visually charismatic gems, like *Close Encounters of the Third Kind* (1977), *Alien* (1979), and *Star Wars* (1977), the latter of which, following *2001*'s footsteps, "changed the genre landscape irrevocably" while *Alien*'s spaceship *Nostromo*, "in its carefully articulated exterior and interior, owe[d] its design to the space vehicles of" *2001* (Latham 206; Kolker, "Foreword" vii). The 1980s produced more compelling spectacles: *Blade Runner* (1982), *The Thing* (1982), *Tron* (1982), *Videodrome* (1983), *The Terminator* (1984), *Dune* (1984), *Brazil* (1985), and *Robocop* (1987) all take giant leaps in SFX. They're still inhibited by stop-motion animation and trick shots that break the fourth wall, however, and *Blade Runner* is another exception (in SF Studies, Ridley Scott's accomplishment is to the 80s what Kubrick's was to the 60s).

In the 1990s, developments in CGI authorized a new cinematic landscape; not only were better-looking SF films able to be made, filmmaking became an SF (ad)venture, empowered by technological invention and modernization. *Total Recall* (1990) set a high bar at the beginning of the decade that was surpassed a few years later by *Jurassic Park* (1993), which integrated live-action and CGI character animation like no other film before it. *Jurassic Park* planted the seed for *A.I.*, "convinc[ing] Kubrick of Spielberg's technical ability to bring to the screen something previously unrealisable, and more quickly than he could. Having rejected building an automaton for the lead role, Kubrick acknowledged that his painstaking methods meant a boy actor would age during production. Spielberg, recognised for directing children, and a long-standing admirer and friend, was an obvious choice" (Morris 301).

In *Performing Illusions* (2008), Dan North says that viewers of SFX films must suspend their disbelief because "the illusion is *never* perfect. There is always a dynamic friction between the special effect and the filmic space it infiltrates, and the spectator can always be activated to seek and detect the evidence of their co-existence within the film frame" (4). The more we stride into the future, the harder it becomes to detect the evidence, and certain late-90s films crossed another threshold that further imploded the co-existence of SFX and diegetic space. *Dark City* (1998) and *The Matrix* (1999) corroborate this transition for me. The Kubrickian consciousness's penchant for stylized perception finally comes to bear in these sophisticated tech-noirs distinguished by high-quality spectacle, nuanced characterization, intricate plots, and futique realism. *The Matrix* received far more attention for SFX like bullet-time cinematography, but both movies heralded a new incarnation of SF cinema.

*Dark City* is a gold pearl in cinematic history that has been roundly overlooked by critics, who gravitated toward *The Matrix* like furies. Director Alex Proyas recounts that "my co-producer at the time, Andrew Mason, betrayed my trust by showing the Wachowskis my completed film in very early preproduction, selling my sets and then setting up production with most of the creative team who made *Dark City*—all without my permission" ("Real"). This is probably why the neo-noir styles of the films look so similar. Since the turn of the century, the aesthetic prowess of *Dark City* and *The Matrix* have become customary. We expect twenty-first-century SF cinema to *at least* look as good as they do. And yet many SF films made during the last two decades look worse. Even the *The Matrix: Reloaded* (2003) has scenes that pale to the original, such as the over-the-top "Swarm of Smiths" kung-fu fight that erupts in a back alley. As the scene undulates between realtime, fasttime, and slow motion, Neo's face and body undulate between lifelike and virtually scrubbed textures. In contrast, *Minority Report* (2002), with its bleach-bypass cinematography, looks as good as anything made in the early 2020s, better than some superhero films—*Justice League* (2017) is an example, even the Snyder Cut (2021)—which have become litmus tests for the evolving aptitude of SFX.

Scott Bukatman has said that "the cinema itself, at its core, is a special effect" ("Foreword" ix). This thesis harkens back to Christian Metz's contention in the 1970s that cinema is an act of *trucage* premised on the art of deception. "Montage itself," writes Metz, "at the base of all cinema, is [ ... ] a perpetual *trucage*" (672). The so-called "digital turn," a "period when analogue processes were taken over by digital remediations of the same techniques and visual tropes," altered the appearance of films, yet the end-product of SFX has not changed that much since the best SF of the late 1990s (Duffy 2). In addition to talent (onscreen and offscreen), cinematographic quality ordinarily depends on the size of production budgets. *Dark City* had an estimated budget of $27 million and combines model photography with CG animation ("Dark"). Proyas's film is more visually appealing to me than *Avatar* (2009), which cost an estimated $237 million to make and used revolutionary motion-capture techniques at the time of its production in the 2000s, combining 60% CGI and 40% live-action imagery ("Avatar"). For me, too, the docurealistic quality of Neill Blomkamp's $30-million *District 9* (2009) outshines the virtuality of *Avatar* and its $350-million sequel *Avatar: The Way of Water* (2022). Correspondingly, the optics of *Iron Man* (2008) are as fine-tuned as almost everything in the Marvel universe that it engendered, and nearly all post-*Iron Man* comic-book movies rely not so much on SFX invention as they do on *excess*.

My outlook is subjective, and my preference for Proyas's gothic, art-deco architecture over James Cameron's gamer-chic woodlands isn't necessarily an indication of which film objectively accomplishes the greatest verisimilitude, which is the goal of most SFX. Today, SFX don't habitually implicate themselves because of low quality or poor execution, and they have become more in-depth components of cinematic narratives, sometimes on a metafilmic level. For example, the "very *madeness* of *Jurassic Park*'s dinosaurs, prominently discussed as a key part of the film's promotion, maps onto the debates the film sought to mobilise about genetic engineering, the possibility of *making* dinosaurs. The spectacular effects supported the story, then, but also contributed to the broader making of meaning beyond the diegesis" (Duffy 6). In the twentieth century, we can identify postwar SFX relatively easily. The twenty-first century is a different (digitized) animal. As SF has become a normative part of reality's fabric, SFX have become normative parts of cinema's diegetic fabric.

The science-fictionalization of SFX has mirrored that of reality, bleeding into other genres and making them into SF artifacts. The use of de-aging techniques in dramas like *The Curious Case of Benjamin Button* (2007) and *The Irishman* (2019) typifies SF's cultural diffusion. All this can be traced back to *2001*, an "epic validation of the science fiction genre [that] stands at the wellspring of all the big-budget, effects-laden movies to follow" (Benson, *Space* 433). Not only that, *2001* transformed cinema. One filmgoer who saw it during the year of its release idolized it.

In a May 4, 1968 letter to Kubrick, the filmgoer wrote: "*2001* does not mark the growth of the art of the cinema; it is the birth of the cinema" (qtd. Agel 190). Viewed in this light, Kubrick's becoming-Kubrickian coincides with cinema's own awakening—which, like the Kubrickian, was enabled by the machinery of SF.

*2001* is a mainstream SF text. There's a tendency to overlook Kubrick's other sovereign contributions to the genre, both of which are soft SF, one thematizing the violence of war, the other our ingrained (ultra)violence. *Dr. Strangelove* and *A Clockwork Orange* have been deliberated outside and inside of SF Studies. All three futurist films won Hugo Awards, though, and they all aggressively critique techno-masculinity and the phallus by experimenting with the modalities of desire. Kubrickian cinema is involved in this critical odyssey, exposing the phallus as absurd in spite of genre, cinematography, tone, pace, or mood. *Dr. Strangelove*'s wacky, caricatured antics accomplish the same ends as *Eyes Wide Shut*'s cold, oneiric melodrama in this respect.

SF appealed to Kubrick at a young age. Born in 1928, he read pulp magazines like *Amazing Stories* and *Astounding Stories* (Abrams, Stanley 119), and in the 1960s, he told a journalist that he had seen "practically" every SF movie ever made, including a good deal of Japanese SF (Bernstein 36). Fritz Lang's visionary *Metropolis* (1927) was an early favorite. He hated William Cameron Menzies's *Things to Come* (1936) with its comparatively heavy-handed didacticism and a stiff-upper-lipped Englishness that takes itself far too seriously (Baxter 207). (Peter Sellers's British Captain Mandrake in *Dr. Strangelove* personifies this Englishness, and *Barry Lyndon* could be said to slow-roast the high society of *Things to Come* on a spit.)

Kubrick enjoyed some SF television and radio, such as the decades-long series *Dr. Who* (1963-) and *Shadow on the Sun* (1961), a BBC Radio drama about a viral meteor striking Earth; he worked on an adaptation of the show in the mid-1960s. Cinema was his great passion, and the stylistic potential of SF enamored him. Kubrick saw value in films like *Destination Moon* (1950), *Conquest of Space* (1955), *Forbidden Planet* (1956), and *Satellite in the Sky* (1956), but he was acutely aware of their shortcomings and limitations. One of his objectives in *2001* was to improve upon them.

Shot in CinemaScope and distributed by MGM, *Forbidden Planet* had been the first SF film made by a major studio. MGM splurged on production costs and surpassed the "hand-to-mouth independent producers [who had traditionally] dominated the field. Cheap settings, cheesy special effects, tenth-rate talent and flashy salesmanship characterised even the relatively ambitious *Destination Moon* and *Conquest of Space*" (200). *Forbidden Planet* outdid its forerunners and arguably everything that came out during the next 12 years after its release in 1956. Then: thus spake *2001*. Kubrick's Zarathustrian bildungsroman widened the gyre of *Forbidden Planet*'s success, outdoing everything that preceded and succeeded it for decades.

Mainar notes that Kubrick's films "often fall into clearly codified genres: film noirs, war films, satires, science-fiction films, period films, pure fantasies, horror films" (71). This codification becomes visible by way of stylistic choices that shape viewer perception. Kubrick innovated every genre that he entered with each new installment in his canon by offering "a mixture of codified conventions and subverted structures that create variations of the different genres to which the films originally seem to belong" (ibid.). SF had a special valence. The military genre was a close second, but war is a technological affair, an epic indicator of the darkest side of our science-fictional existence. Even when Kubrick returned to a genre that he had visited before, he conjured something inimitable and recoded the cinematic physique of that genre. The films in the futurist trilogy are vastly different from one another, as is *A.I.*, but they're all definitively SF, and together they form the central dispensary of Kubrickian cognition.

### FILMOSOPHY

Since the "Dawn of Man," we have been science-fictional beings. Alien intervention aside, *2001* teaches us how we are what we became. Only after Moon-Watcher deciphers how to use a bone as a weapon does he set this primeval planet of the (dying) apes on a path toward humanity. Any utilitarian extension of our bodies is a technology. The bone becomes a technology when Moon-Watcher uses it to kill his enemy. Thereafter, the iconic jump-cut to the future (now an alternate past for filmgoers in the 2020s) shows us that the low-tech bone functions in the same way as the high-tech nuclear satellite in orbit around *fin-de-siècle* Earth. Nothing has changed but the intricacy and quality of the apparatus. Without the apparatus, we would not exist.

Our technological extensions define us. We are only human because we are technological—individually and collectively, corporeally and psychologically. Cyborgs are born, not made. To make a cyborg is merely to extend the self.

Cinema is one of many technocultural extensions that mirror our own intrinsic condition. Earlier I said that the medium became fully science-fictional around the same time as *2001*'s diegetic future, but in essence, it has always belonged to SF, particularly in terms of cinema's relationship to consciousness and the godlike (re)births and deaths that it has experienced since its inception. These two concepts—*the death of cinema* and *cinema as brain*—have been constants in film theory.

In *Ends of Cinema* (2020), Richard Grusin and Jocelyn Szczepaniak-Gillece portend: "By the time you read this, cinema will have died. That's a certainty no matter what year it is that you're opening this book. Cinema has definitely ended many, many times and will surely end again in the near future. In fact, cinema's ends have been so endless that, depending on the company you keep, even referring to such a well-worn cliché can result in theatrical eye-rolling and a quick escape for the hors d'oeuvres table" (vii). Since the advent of cinema in the late nineteenth century, new technologies have "repeatedly elegized [its] ruin and celebrated its rejuvenation" (viii). Talkies killed "the universality of the image's language" (ibid.). The downfall of the studio system breathed life into different methods of production. The eradication of the Production Code gave birth to heretofore unseen subversion. Blockbusters crucified the idea of film as art, then resurrected the (art)form in a new guise. "Home video destroyed exhibition. The digital killed the index. Postcinema fractured form. And Marvel Studios eradicated platform-specific media along with global cosmopolises, planets, mythical dimensions, and, depending on the day, half the life of the universe" (ix). Cinema's identity is tethered to its capacity to die and live again.

Grusin and Szczepaniak-Gillece add: "Another end of cinema can be found in the moment of burgeoning extinction that it shares with its creators: the end of nature, of humanity, of Earth as we know it. Cinema thereby acts as a marker of the Anthropocene and its apocalyptic dimensions: cinema's end is also our own" (xi). We have always had an apocalyptic relationship with (and perception of) the technology of cinema, which grew up in a century that introduced high-tech modes of warfare and destruction. At least since Georges Méliès's bullet-shaped rocket hit the moon in the eye in *Le Voyage dans la Lune* (1902), films express how much we love the Bomb.

The end of cinema is a foregone conclusion that never comes to a close. Panic and desire ensure that we will keep predicting and fetishizing cinema's endless circle of death and rebirth. Kubrickian SF is a hallmark for this occupation. *2001* alone denotes a palpable end that sparked a new beginning, even if it took a long time to get there.

Another ongoing discussion since the genesis of cinema concerns how film is a prosthetic mind. Cinema was an alternative to literature, the dominant form of fictional entertainment. In *Postcinematic Vision* (2020), Roger Cook explains that film "provided a visual technology well suited for projecting our psychological and cultural experience in much the same mode as literature. It also expanded on literature's potential to represent and examine the mental and psychological calculations that guide our decision-making" (64). Moving-image media was a modernist sensory experience that changed the way we tell and *feel* stories. "This intensification of the diegetic effect also endows the viewing experience with a stronger sense of immediacy than can be generated by literature" (ibid.).

Literature demands that readers become their own inner-spatial film-makers insofar as they must project imagery onto their mindscreens based upon the words that authors give them. Cinema does our thinking for us. The imagery we see onscreen is fixed; we can imagine other images on our mindscreens while watching a film, but that's a subsidiary internal projection, and it's tangential to the medium recorded by our brains.

In *Filmosophy* (2006), Daniel Frampton speaks to the emergent philosophies that have shadowed the medium for over a century. "Since its invention film has been compared to the mind," he writes, "whether through analogy with human perception, dreams or the subconscious. The shock of seeing a world 'freed' by man's imagination caused many early writers to see a profound link between the mind of the filmgoer and the film itself, leading them to understand film as a mirror of mindful intent. In a sense film offers us our first experience of an *other* experience (the experience of the film camera as it were)" (15). Frampton deduces that cinema evinces a double phenomenology or intention: our perception of the screen-world, and the screen-world's perception of itself. I would add the screen-world's perception of *our* world, an SF (ir)reality that borrows from cinema and other media technologies on a manic basis, revising the screen-plays of identity and community.

For critics and reviewers, films play the same role as written texts: Kubrick's *The Shining* is analyzed like Stephen King's novel, with still and moving images replacing descriptive language. Alternatively, many Film Studies scholars have investigated the meta-cognitive abilities of cinema, contending that it has a mind of its own and can be understood in multiple ways, such as "a recording of the brain," "a visualization of our thoughts and memories," and "another kind of thought, a future form of thinking" (16). The history of scholarship on these ideas has not been remarkably dynamic, and it has stagnated in recent years. Even Cook's notion of "postcinematic vision," which hinges on how "the digital image continues to transform the traditional film image" (201), revisits material covered many times over in Film as well as SF Studies. Decades ago, for instance, in *Terminal Identity: The Virtual Subject in Postmodern Science Fiction* (1993), a magnum opus of late-twentieth-century SF theory, Bukatman makes a case for the implosion of the body and subjectivity into our neuromantic, techno-filmic/philic "matrix," initiating the (dis) appearance of the human into a new cyborg entity (322).

Gilles Deleuze's decidedly science-fictional *Cinema 1: The Movement-Image* (1983) and *Cinema 2: The Time-Image* (1985) are monumental exceptions to this redundancy. His contention that "*le cerveau, c'est l'écran*" ("the brain is the screen") has become a staple of innovative scholarship, even if the texts remain wildly elusive and somewhat misunderstood ("Brain" 48). Deleuze's thoughts about Kubrick in *Cinema 2* lend insight into his methodology. These thoughts are worth citing at length: they essentialize the French philosopher's observations of Kubrickian cinema, and most of his consideration goes to the futurist trilogy.

Deleuze begins with a distinction between corporeal and cognitive mapping onscreen.

> Bodies are not destined for wearing out, any more than the brain is destined for novelty. But what is important is the possibility of a cinema of the brain which brings together all the powers, as much as the cinema of the body equally brought them together as well. [...] There is as much thought in the body as there is shock and violence in the brain. There is an equal amount of feeling in both of them. The brain gives orders to the body which is just an outgrowth of it, but the body also gives orders to the brain which is just a part of it: in both cases, these will not be the same bodily attitudes nor the same cerebral gest. Hence the specificity of a cinema of the brain, in relation to that of the cinema of bodies. (205)

For Deleuze, the body and the brain are concomitant technological extensions and base structures. Having set the theoretical scene, he summons the Kubrickian to elucidate this relation and underline the predominance of the brain.

> If we look at Kubrick's work, we see the degree to which it is the brain which is *mis en scène*. Attitudes of the body achieve a

maximum level of violence, but they depend on the brain. For, in Kubrick, the world itself is a brain, there is identity of brain and world, as in the great circular and luminous table in *Dr. Strangelove*, the giant computer in *2001: A Space Odyssey*, the Overlook hotel in *The Shining*. The black stone of *2001* presides over both cosmic states and cerebral stages: it is the soul of the three bodies, earth, sun and moon, but also the seed of the three brains, animal, human, machine. Kubrick is renewing the theme of the initiatory journey because every journey in the world is an exploration of the brain. The world-brain is *A Clockwork Orange*, or again, a spherical game of chess where the general can calculate his chances of promotion on the basis of the relation between soldiers killed and positions captured (*Paths of Glory*). But if the calculation fails, if the computer breaks down, it is because the brain is no more reasonable a system than the world is a rational one. The identity of the world and brain, the automaton, does not form a whole, but rather a limit, a membrane which puts an outside and an inside in contact, makes them present to each other, confronts them or makes them clash. The inside is psychology, the past, involution, a whole psychology of depths which excavate the brain. The outside is the cosmology of galaxies, the future, evolution, a whole supernatural which makes the world explode. [...] The insane violence of Alex in *A Clockwork Orange* is the force of the outside before passing into the service of an insane internal order. In *Space Odyssey*, the robot breaks down from the inside, before being lobotomized by the astronaut who penetrates it from the outside. [...] The world-brain is strictly inseparable from the forces of death which pierce the membrane in both directions. Unless a reconciliation is carried out in another dimension, a regeneration of the membrane which would pacify the outside and the inside, and re-create a world-brain as a whole in the harmony of the spheres. At the end of *Space Odyssey*, it is in consequence of a fourth dimension that the sphere of the fetus and the sphere of the earth have a chance of entering into a

new, incommensurable, unknown relation, which would convert
death to new life. (205-06)

Signifying an implosion of outer and inner ambits of meaning, Deleuze
uses Kubrickian cinema/consciousness as an example *par excellence* for
how "attitudes of the body" (in)form cinematic world-brains (*pensée-
cinéma*). In effect, he insinuates that the mise-en-scènes comprising the
Kubrickian world-brain *think his oeuvre*—despite Kubrick the director,
and despite the spectators that watch and interpret his movies. This
world-brain is autonomous, alive, and amortal, thinking its own thoughts
as it reprocesses the fluctuating stores of desire and violence that animate
its collective diegesis. The stylistic and thematic coherence of Kubrick's
films makes his oeuvre well-suited to a reading of this complexion.

Deleuze's "filmosophy" stems from the thought-experiments of
Henri Bergson and intercalates cinema in the cosmos. His cinema (and
every cinematic image) is a "slice" of the universe that contains the
same stuff. The caveat is that different slices accentuate different facets
of the universe (hence the theorization of movement-images and time-
images as well as affection-images, perception-images, recollection-images,
action-images, etc.). *Cinema 1* and *Cinema 2* read more like SF novels
than, say, Bergson's *Creative Evolution* (1907), estranging and blitzing
readers with novum after novum in hyperstylized language that can be as
oblique and neologistic as a cyberpunk tale. Bergson was the first philosopher to formally deploy cinema as a mode of philosophical exploration
in the early twentieth century. Deleuze built upon Bergson later in the
century with a novelistic flair that diverges from the straight-shooting
pragmatism of conventional academic stodge. But the same SF postulate energizes both models.

Frampton took this postulate a step further in *Filmosophy*, subtitled
"a manifesto for a radically new way of understanding cinema" on the
book's cover. Merging philosophy and Film Studies, Frampton characterizes cinema as an organic mind-body entity, a "cousin" of reality
and consciousness—not a direct reflection of or relation to the human
mind, but its own "filmind," fully disembodied, animate, and intelligent.

Film "is not *of* the world," he argues, "film *is* a world (a new world). Film is not simply a reproduction of reality, it is its own world with its own intentions and creativities. Cinema is a projection, screening, showing, of *thoughts of the real*" (5). The filmind is an autonomous, interstitial world-brain distinct from the real world, and "*Filmosophy* proposes that seeing film form as thoughtful, as the dramatic decision of the film, helps us understand the many ways film can mean and affect" (6).

*Filmosophy* contemplates the logistics of "film-thinking" and "film-being" with a cinematic lexicon that favors experience (corporeal and cognitive) over analysis. Taking cues from Deleuze, Stanley Cavell, Sergei Eisenstein, and Vivian Sobchack, Frampton seeks an alternate way to read moving-image texts. I don't fully subscribe to some of his methods, such as purging "technicist" approaches for the sake of a "poetic rhetoric" that more effectively captures cinema's ability to think in non-conceptual ways. As Philipp Schmerheim recognizes in a Strangelovian-titled review of *Filmosophy*, "Film, Not Sliced Up into Pieces, or: How Film Made Me Feel Thinking," the "enterprise of an academic film philosophy needs both aspects which Frampton contrasts" (121). The basic premise of *Filmosophy*, however, is a useful starting-point for a dialectic of the Kubrickian filmind (hereafter the KFM). Specifically, I want to inspect how the KFM *thinks* and *sees* via *stylized modes of desire* coupled with the principal diegetic riff of Kubrick's oeuvre: *phallic aggression*. This initiative will bear the most fruit from an exploration of Kubrickian SF (hereafter KSF), the brain-stem of the KFM.

Similar to *Cinema 1* and *Cinema 2*, *Filmosophy* reads more like an SF novel than a formal manifesto or scholarly monograph. It is innovative and estranging, and like SF itself (qua Vint), the book is about *change*.

*Filmosophy* has not gained the traction it deserves. It is infrequently discussed in scholarship within relevant fields, and it didn't generate much of an audience. Part of my rationale is to correct this oversight. New and interesting ideas abound on almost every page. I want to use some of these ideas as broad strokes for better understanding Kubrick's contribution to the history of cinema and SF. My point of departure will treat the KFM as an alternative consciousness that exists somewhere beyond the filmmaker.

My strategy may disturb more biographically inclined scholars who thrive on the Kubrick Archives. Kubrick's "absence" is another Kubrickian monad. The director took pains to remove "himself" from his films. Consider his attitude toward interviews: "I don't like doing interviews. There is always the problem of being misquoted or, what's even worse, of being quoted exactly, and having to see what you've said in print. [ ... ] I've always found it difficult to talk about any of my films. What I generally manage to do is to discuss background information connected with the story, or perhaps some of the interesting facts which might be associated with it. This approach often allows me to avoid the 'What does it mean? Why did you do it?' questions" (Ciment 167). Kubrick didn't like the way interviews could *misdirect* the *affect* of his films, and he tried to distance himself from his artistic output, as if that output were a child whose space he respected and who he wanted to take on a life (and psyche) of its own. Whether he was conscious of it or not, the more he said about his films, the more his exposition might inhibit the semantic ambiguities that empower them. Moreover, in a 1987 interview for *Rolling Stone* about *Full Metal Jacket*, Kubrick indicated that he didn't really know what to tell people who asked him what his films "mean": "I'm pretty good at generalized statements," but "I still can't tell somebody what *Paths of Glory* is about [ ... ] without sounding like a bad synopsis of it. [ ... ] Whatever you say pushes somebody in another direction and it's certainly never complete, and it's usually wrong and it's overly simplistic. [People] want you to say [ ... ] this is a story about the duality of man and the duplicity of governments or something like that. I hear [directors] try to do it sometimes. It's usually bullshit, or if the work is good, it's usually irrelevant" (Cahill, "Two-Hour"). Kubrick even admitted to using questions from previous interviews as answers to other interview questions.

The crux of Frampton's aspirant manifesto is that cinema constitutes a "new episteme" that not only *embrains* its own system of thought but (re)produces certain thought-processes in spectators. Frampton cites

Kubrick in support of his overarching thesis: "In an interview in 1970 Stanley Kubrick said that film 'avoids intellectual verbalisation and reaches the viewer's subconscious in a way that is essentially poetic and philosophic.' Kubrick was saying that images, of a certain non-literary form, can create a rough, perhaps even *vague* kind of 'knowledge.' The movements and sounds of Kubrick's films do not rely on language and verbalisation, but speak to another side of us" (26). This side of us is a product of image/sound exposure to external, screen-based, diegetic worlds that project new worlds onto our own internal mindscreens. More specifically, movies are world-projections that induce a kind of introjection wherein we adopt and process these world-projections through the filters of our experiences, subject-positions, and unconscious riptides. Frampton continues:

> Director-based writing is very easy—it is so handy to talk of "Kubrick cutting to the face of an actor," of "Scorsese panning round the room of men," but this is the star-struck language of newspaper film reviews—and if the writer does not happen to know the director, the film is back to just being a chance happening. But more importantly, as a conceptual being through which the film-goer might understand the film, the "author" is singularly limiting. Watching a film with the idea that the film's actions are directly the result of an external historical person removes the filmgoer from the film. Each action of form reminds them of the director making decisions and the mechanics of filmmaking. Many films do have (culturally) recognisable marks of their directors—winks, signatures—and these can be revealed and discussed in film culture, but the singular films remain; the first-time naive experience will always be there. It is certainly important to recognise the work of the filmmaker, but during the experience of the film they are not always helpful to our attention. (30-31)

*Strangelove Country* siphons vitality from Frampton's peculiar line of flight, recognizing Kubrick yet foregrounding the Kubrickian. This is a science-fictionalization of cinema that extends its SF core, which has been there since the beginning of cinematic time. The KFM is another extension that rethinks the Hollywood culture industry and the SF megatext. KSF in particular inspired many of the less intellectual SF blockbuster films of the 1970s, 80s, and 90s, although so many filmmakers have acknowledged Kubrick's importance. Paul Thomas Anderson once said that "inevitably, you're going to end up doing something that he's probably already done before," as if all movies are part and parcel of the KFM, a lens in the sky that is always watching (and thinking) the futures of our dreamy, diegetic, technosurreal lives.

**TRANSCENDENT TRANSGRESSION**

With Alfred Hitchcock and Orson Welles, Kubrick is among the most written-about twentieth-century American filmmakers. His oeuvre has been surveyed, enumerated, interpreted, fleshed out, defined and redefined, coded and recoded from different scholarly perspectives, fields, time periods, and degrees of remove. Critics love Kubrick as much as (if not more than) cinephiles and popular filmgoers; few filmmakers can boast a collective library of work that is at once entertaining and intellectual, evoking powerful emotional responses with an appreciation of the texts' stylistic and narrative construction.

The Stanley Kubrick Archive opened in 2007 in England and is held at the Archives and Special Collection Center at London's University of the Arts. Since then, Kubrick scholars have integrated archival findings with more and more rigor. For instance, Alison Castle's *The Stanley Kubrick Archives* (2016), David Mikics's *Stanley Kubrick: American Filmmaker* (2020), Nathan Abrams's *Stanley Kubrick: New York Jewish Intellectual* (2020), and Abrams and Robert B. Kolker's *Kubrick: An Odyssey* (2023) are four excellent monographs that tap the Archive and present information in familiar ways. This book takes a different, more experimental approach. My method is fundamentally structuralist and schizoanalytic, and I use a hermeneutic style that violates the academic status quo in the interest of generating unique avenues of inquiry. As I monitor the pulse of the KFM, I focus not on the filmmaker, but on the filmmaker's filmind, a bona fide artificial intelligence that exists exclusively onscreen, or rather, *inscreen*. In simplest terms, *Strangelove Country* is a book of probes that excavates Kubrickian inner space. *2001* is typically associated with outer space, but it "seems to be representing a journey *inward* to a new state of consciousness" (Naremore 138). The same can be said for all Kubrickian cinema. Humanity is a rabid desiring-machine, and at its center, SF artic- ulates our techno-pathological existence. KSF represents the twentieth- century cinematic apotheosis of this incentive.

*Strangelove Country* appraises KSF, accounting for the SF that undergirds all filmmaking and the many realities, histories, and futures echoed by filmmakers in their diegeses. My title implicates the character of Dr. Strangelove, whose principles, cognition, and vision referee the KFM. This will become increasingly apparent as the chapters unfold.

Kubrick's futurist trilogy and posthumous addendum tell an implicit, subtextual meta-story from beginning to end about the KFM's consciousness. This story unpacks the transmutations of desire and the sublime, mediated dreamworlds constructed by an aggressive technoculture. The four chapters that follow this introduction each underscore a specific type of desire that epitomizes the KSF under scru- tiny. Despite my filmosophic approach, I share pertinent biographical details and remarks by Kubrick about his work, and in order to better isolate the contours of the KFM, I talk about the social, cultural, and historical context out of which the director's films emerged. I also make use of previous scholarship (old and new). For the most part, however, I schizoanalyze the visual texts.

The futurist trilogy came out one after the other between 1964 and 1971. During this interval, an explosion of media technologies fueled the implosion of SF and reality, but the borderlines were still relatively clear. It wasn't until the cyberpunk movement of the 1980s that these borderlines really started to blur, and today, we are immersed in real- world embodiments of the cyberspatial matrices and pathologies imag- ined by cyberpunk authors, artists, and auteurs. *A Clockwork Orange* is a proto-cyberpunk film to which many cyberpunks paid homage. *Dr.*

*Strangelove* is a work of slapstick, apocalyptic SF, and *2001* is a space opera at the epicenter of the genre, intermixing New Wave mysticism with scientific realism and speculation about mankind's history and future. *A.I.* combines elements from all of these subgenres and comments on KSF's reach.

*Dr. Strangelove*, *2001*, and *A Clockwork Orange* all received science fiction's top honor, the Hugo Award, for Best Dramatic Presentation, and they can be traced back to what is commonly perceived as the genre's *locus classicus*, *Frankenstein* (1818). Mary Shelley's novel occupies the literary core of these films, with the atomic bomb, HAL 9000, and Alexander de Large serving as the monstrous products of humanity's mad scientism alongside an ensemble of other symbolic gods and monsters. *A.I.* riffs on Shelley, too, problematizing the mad creation of androids. Above all, these films are linked by a techno-masculine impulse that satirizes and critiques more than reifies its subject matter.

As a general rule, through transgression, the KFM aspires for transcendence.

KSF made as much of an impact on the SF megatext as it did on cinema. It continues to extend itself into the twenty-first century and the foreseeable future. A concerted analysis of KSF is relevant as society and culture transmute into an irreality that *thinks* in terms of SF.

What was once an alternative genre of scientific speculation and fantasy is now mainstream, even if we cyborgs don't realize it or want it. SF used to be about the future. Now it's about history. Instead of extrapolating a low-tech reality, SF extrapolates a high-tech reality studio that is defined by electronic media and craves the fanatical implosion of subjectivity and objectivity, consciousness and unconsciousness, truth and fiction.

KSF shows us what we were, what we are, and what we might yet become, exerting the technological stimulant we use to authorize and antagonize ourselves. In *The Seven Beauties of Science Fiction* (2008), Istvan Csicsery-Ronay Jr. avows that SF is "not a genre of aesthetic entertainment only, but a complex hesitation about the relationship between imaginary conceptions and historical reality unfolding into the future" (4). Likewise does KSF entertain us as it engages with the future-historical imaginary while mapping the ever more diegetic spaces that stylize lived experience.

# ONE **PATHOLOGIZING DESIRE**
## Dr. Strangelove

### PRELUDE TO JOUISSANCE

As its subtitle infers, *Dr. Strangelove* satirically fetishizes the destructive technologies that animate male desire, conflating sex, death, and technology in a way that caricatures the phallus via "serious" monkey business. Part black comedy, part documentary realism, the movie was adapted from *Red Alert* (1958), a suspense novel by Peter George (pseudonym Peter Bryant) that Kubrick and screenplay co-writer Terry Southern converted into an absurdist romp. Southern had published three novels prior to this venture, most notably *The Magic Christian* (1959), a hilarious American burlesque about a billionaire practical joker. His irreverent gonzo flair and wit is unmistakable in *Dr. Strangelove*.

George collaborated with Kubrick and Southern on the screenplay. His novel was titled *Two Hours to Doom* (1958) in the UK. Like *Red Alert*, it didn't have the humor that Southern and Kubrick wanted. Nor did it include Strangelove, a deterritorialized Nazi and the "nuclear" character around which the screenwriters' absurdism revolves despite limited screentime (less than 10 minutes). Southern formulated the long, parodic, now-household name of the film, "an adaptation of the facetious mock-Edwardian titles pioneered in *Esquire* and quickly picked up by Hollywood" (Baxter 176). Beginning with its pop-culture signature, *Dr. Strangelove* points to the media forces that shape its (chess) players and expedite the collective death-wish for mass extinction.

Spurred by Cold War anxiety, the KFM depicts a World War III scenario in which stereotyped man-clowns struggle to prevent global destruction even as they ridiculously hasten it. All KSF obsesses about masculine desire with Ahabesque monomania. In *Dr. Strangelove*, the Soviet Doomsday Machine embodies an aggressive technological pathology that explicitly corresponds with masculine desire and allegorizes the internal/infernal machinery that inscribes the characters. The Bomb may be Dr. Mankind's monster, but so is mankind. Thus the man-clowns resemble *2001*'s man-apes of Pleistocene Africa, only instead of starving for food, they starve for technological demolition and the dangling carrot of transcendence. As well, they align with *A Clockwork Orange*'s droogs, "machines for mechanical violence" who "represent the aggression [ ... ] that will be bred into man, so-called *civilized* man, by natural selection in prehistory" (Walker 49, 273).

The characters' machinic "nature" festers until it climaxes as unbridled jouissance when Major "King" Kong gleefully, impossibly rides a dropped nuke like a bull into the earth and we enter the realm of Mickey Mouse. This constitutes cinematic ultraviolence, unlike the ultraviolence of *A Clockwork Orange*, which is extreme violence, unenhanced by the antics and aesthetics of a cartoon. Instinctually, we suspend our disbelief, but that's not what the KFM wants us to do. It wants immersion, if not absorption, and then *sublimation*. It wants us to think its thoughts, to ride the snake of a consciousness that occupies the headspace of Strangelove and the other two men that Peter Sellers inhabits like a shapeshifter, Captain Mandrake and President Merkin Muffley. But the dominant POV could belong to General Buck Turgidson, the most expressive, over-the-top monkey in the barrel, or even Russian Ambassador Alexi de Sadesky, a spy whose secret mission of espionage is to photograph (i.e., *mediatize*) the War Room. More likely, the movie embrains all of these characters in a fluid, multiperspectival *kaleidoscope of being/seeing.*

Cinema can do anything, show us anything, like an all-powerful, omniscient god. So can dreams. The KFM invites us to enter the farcical nightmare of *Dr. Strangelove* and view it from the "overlook" of dreamers, just as *The Shining*'s Jack Torrance overlooks his wife and son moving through a model of the Overlook Hotel's outdoor hedge maze from the Colorado Lounge. "The filmind *is* its objects and characters," writes Frampton, "it just does not normally let us know" (79). Later, he cites Kubrick from a 1971 interview: "Watching a film is like having a daydream. It operates on portions of your mind that are only reached by dreams or dramas, and there you can explore things without any responsibility of conscious ego or conscience" (qtd. 148).

Frampton downplays the validity of dreams. Films "can be much more expressive than dreams, which actually seem quite ordered, with recognisable symbols and logic. Apart from any other argument, how people dream is usually very far removed from cinema, as we are never merely *watching* our dreams but rather *being* our dreams" (19). This is a subjective allegation. I'll counter it with my own piece of mind. Most of my dreams are profoundly *disordered*, and I often exist as a sheer watcher, with no body; I move back and forth from one POV to another. Like Ralph Waldo Emerson's "transparent eyeball," "I am nothing; I see all; the currents of the Universal Being circulate thorough me; I am part and parcel of God" ("Nature" 24). Granted, Emerson is talking about the transcendental potential of experiencing nature, whereas I'm referring to an oneiric experience in which "God" is a madman (i.e., God is my own inner-spatial stream of unconsciousness). Frampton doesn't like the idea that dreams "match up to the ways of film" (19). Deleuze didn't like it either; with Artaud, he agrees that "the dream is too easy a solution to the 'problem' of [cinematic] thought" (*Cinema 2* 165), although Deleuze does make a provision for a dream-image called an "onirosign" (273).

My reference to Emerson isn't without retrospection. Slusser attributes the rise of American SF to an "Emersonian paradigm" that initiated "a complex fusion of scientific, philosophical, cultural, and religious currents" (50). An extension of this paradigm, KSF reliably channels these same currents, filtering them through different monadic sieves. Irreality is one of them.

I don't think dreams are "very far removed from cinema," but I'm not saying that dreams and movies are interchangeable world-parts.

Both media mobilize the unconscious, and both are viable technologies, extensions of the brain into inner space. The KFM constantly verifies this dynamic. As filmic utilities, dreams are essential narrative and stylistic tools. They deepen character development and augment the societies of spectacle and simulation that typify the filmgoing experience, even in the KFM, where oneiric interludes, exchanges, and phenomena are often subtly, almost imperceptibly conveyed. In filmosophy, all cinema constitutes thinking. KSF's default dream-states make *Dr. Strangelove* and its Kubrickian fallout ripe for this sort of conceptualization.

"I have always enjoyed dealing with a slightly surrealistic situation and presenting it in a realistic manner," said Kubrick in 1971. "I've always liked fairy tales and myths, magical stories, supernatural stories, ghost stories, surrealistic and allegorical stories. I think they are somehow closer to the sense of reality one feels today than the equally stylized 'realistic' story in which a great deal of selectivity and omission has to occur in order to preserve its 'realistic' style. In *Lolita*, for example, the character of Quilty is straight out of a nightmare, as are many of the characters in *Dr. Strangelove*" (Houston 114).

The story told in *Dr. Strangelove* can be viewed as a prelude to the jouissance of the bomb-phallus going/getting off. Thereafter, in the War Room, men-in-charge anxiously deliberate how to reconstitute the "life essence" that General Jack D. Ripper denies to women who seek his "power." Strangelove proposes an underground mineshaft-womb where they can replant their seed and die endless little deaths (*les petites morts*). During this post-orgasmic "sense of fatigue" and "feeling of emptiness," as Ripper calls it, Muffley, Turgidson, Sadesky, and the other male occupants of the War *Womb* (a receptacle for male desire writ large) listen attentively to the ex-Nazi's explanation about how to act like "civilized" post-bomb monkeys as his self-governing mechanical hand incessantly antagonizes him. Strangelove's vision of a post-nuclear future symptomatizes our love of self-destruction on molecular (phallic) and molar (*fin du monde*) plateaus. The film ends with a montage of climaxing mushroom clouds—"footage of the Hiroshima and Christmas Island blasts"

(Kagan 139)—set to Vera Lynn's "We'll Meet Again," cynical rather than hopeful in this context. The suggestion is that, no matter how many times we kill ourselves, we'll always return to kill (and fuck) each other, figuratively and literally, forever, or until we wipe ourselves out for good. It's what men of power do best, says the KFM.

The three characters played by Sellers are odd and neurotic. Muffley's a bald, docile, whiny American milquetoast; Mandrake's an uptight, mustached Englishman with a posh accent; and Strangelove is a blonde-haired, eccentric, disabled German in sunglasses whose quirks exceed his black-gloved grasp of humanity. Casting Sellers in multiple roles bolsters the film's irreality and "illustrates the Heraclitean underlying interchangeability of the positions in the game of war" (Abrams, "Philosophy" 117). Sellers was an extraordinary actor. His versatility shines in *Dr. Strangelove*, but I still know it's the same guy broken into three parts. This metafilmic split-personality references the pathology and schizophrenia that governs the film's puerile behavior and the collective compulsion for nuclear war.

Because of Sellers's fame and *Lolita*'s success, Columbia Pictures wanted him to play more than one role. This trifecta was more of a marketing ploy than an aesthetic choice (Baxter 174-75). His characters nonetheless subsidize the film's aesthetics. In addition to their Heraclitean denotation, they allude to narrative, setting, and screenplay structure in number. In three acts, *Dr. Strangelove* tells three parallel stories in three different places, each with its own cinematographic style:

> the hazy, vibrating, incoherent battle footage of the assault on Burpelson Air Force Base; the quickly cut, intense close-ups of the bomber flight deck, straining crew, endless instruments—especially the fragmented hysterically tense duel with the missile; the weird immense black steeple of the War Room shot with carefully composed static shorts of eerie beauty, the voices now of human quality, now reverberating, as if Turgidson, Muffley, or Strangelove, crouched low under the ring of lights, had momentarily seen it as a halo of the angel of death or vengeance. (Kagan 139)

In every setting, the film slowly becomes more Disney than reality. The antics/ethics of a cartoon overtake the War Room. If Muffley is Mickey Mouse, Strangelove is Goofy, and Turgidson is Donald Duck. *Dr. Strangelove* exemplifies the inherent comic (book) quality that underpins male desire, which isn't an object-choice. *Desire is the desire for desire.* What goes tick-tick-BOOM must go tick-tick-BOOM again and again and again. There is no finish line, no terminal conquest or plunder. The KFM's imaginary phallus is monstrously *unself-aware.* It doesn't know what it wants despite the all-consuming immensity of its wanting. It only knows what it *does.* The KFM itself, on the other hand, is perfectly self-aware (and blissfully schizophrenic) in its sardonic portrayal of caricatured stereotypes.

The KFM is *always* critical—critical of itself, and critical of the real world with which it co-exists. Frampton writes: "Film, because it is so closely related to our modes of thinking, becomes, not so much a mirror, but a companion, a cousin or *friend* of our thinking" (157). Thinking like a movie is ultimately a matter of *perception* and *style.* These interrelated elements are formalized during the editing process, the third and final component of filmmaking after writing and shooting. All three are imperative, but editing is where meaning is made, where stories are shaped, where footage becomes filmic. "Everything else comes from something else," Kubrick once noted. "Writing, of course, is writing, acting comes from the theater, and cinematography comes from photography. Editing is unique to film. You can see something from different points of view almost simultaneously, and it creates a new experience" (Cahill, "*Rolling*" 199).

The idea of multiple diegetic POVs producing organic POVs in individual spectators is crucial to understanding the KFM and film-thinking, which involves *angulations of perspective that thematize existence.* Frampton continues: "Film bleeds ideas. The rupturing or violence of complex film-thinking creates spaces for ideas to appear" (165). Kubrickian violence thus reflects the violence intrinsic to its cognitive machinery. The resultant "nooshock" is "not only the forcing of thinking, but the forcing of a new kind of thinking" in filmgoers, whose "impower" renders them "unable to think images (or image-concepts) as clearly as film" (166). Cinema outsmarts us in this respect, and the KFM is a cunning cinematic thinker. Kubrick has been widely acclaimed as one of the twentieth century's most intellectual auteurs. The KFM makes him redundant. It doesn't dislike Kubrick. It simply doesn't care about anything but itself. Like all filminds, the KFM is a thoroughbred narcissist that never sleeps, that refuses to suffer fools, and that incessantly cries: "Look at me! Listen to me! Love me!" To call Kubrick a "pessimist" or a "perfectionist" or a "recluse" or a "control freak" or an "enigma" or an "eccentric" or a "tyrant"—all terms that have been applied to the director many times over by reviewers and critics (*Stanley*)—just makes the KFM laugh harder and grow stronger.

*Dr. Strangelove*, the first operational KSF, awakened the KFM. In this chapter, I will discuss how the film establishes a pathology of desire that gathers momentum in subsequent KSF. This pathology extends to all of Kubrick's films, even the ones that precede *Dr. Strangelove*. Only in the wake of KSF, however, does the Kubrickian rear its cinematographic brain.

### AGENCIES OF ABSENCE AND EXCESS

The KFM revels in excess vis-à-vis sex, violence, and the performativity of actors. In *A Clockwork Orange*, Alex indulges himself with hedonistic intensity, stealing, raping, and "tolchocking" at his leisure; even his facial gestures sting like wasps, and the linguistically violent argot that he speaks, Nadsat, extends his overperformative conduct into his rhetorical identity. *Dr. Strangelove*'s excess comes to bear in its overblown parody of alpha-masculinity and its cataclysmic thesis and subject matter, which is consecrated in the end by the exploding-bombs compilation. At the time of its release in 1999, online porn was in its infancy, and *Eyes Wide Shut*'s long orgy scene was an exercise in excess that had not been done before in a high-budget, star-studded, mainstream film. (Despite the accessibility and everything-goes status of porn today, it hasn't really been done again, although there is an orgy in the "Herogasm" episode of *The Boys* [2019-2022] that might be the Kubrickian fever-dream of Alex detoxing from a Milk Plus binge.) Gunnery Sergeant Hartman's kettle-drum tirades in *Full Metal Jacket* are so gravely histrionic, they're laugh-out-loud funny, as is the scene in *Barry Lyndon* when Lord Bullingdon gets into a squabble with his younger half-brother Bryan, then hurls him over his knee and spanks his buttocks with wild abandon; Barry returns the favor by spanking Lord Bullingdon with a horse whip. In *The Shining*, Jack buries an ax in Dick Holloran's ribs and goes after his own family, barking and drooling like a rabid dog. And so on. Extreme and exaggerated behavior erupts everywhere.

In the KFM, however, less is more, and the excesses that stick in our memory are made all the more memorable by the slow-burning, suspense-building moments of relative inertia that pad them.

Nothing like the spectacle of *2001* had been seen in a feature-length film prior to its release. "One of the most successful vehicles of technological virtuosity in the cinema is the science-fiction film. Since 1968, when Stanley Kubrick's *2001: A Space Odyssey* was released, science-fiction films have invited audiences to ponder the future impact of technology on humanity while simultaneously displaying the latest advances in current audiovisual-effects technologies" (Ndalianis 154). *2001* is painstakingly slow and largely nonverbal, with little action compared to most SF blockbusters, which are defined by extravagant SFX and thematic transparency that usually boils down to Good vs. Evil.

A blatant example is the conflict between the Force and the Dark Side in the *Star Wars* franchise. Often, too, "Good" means American and "Evil" means non-American, especially in alien-invasion movies like *The Day the Earth Stood Still* (1951, 2008), *Invasion of the Body Snatchers* (1956, 1978), *They Live* (1988), *Independence Day* (1996), *Signs* (2002), *War of the Worlds* (1953, 2005), and *The Fifth Element* (1997), the latter of which features "The Ultimate Evil," a sentient, meteoric, meta-villainous "ball of fire 1200 miles in diameter heading straight for the earth." In anti-utopias such as *Fahrenheit 451* (1966, 2018), *1984* (1984), *Brazil* (1984), *Equilibrium* (2002), and *V for Vendetta* (2005), the State plays an evil genius that suppresses the romanticized goodness of human emotion and imagination, and in scores of apocalyptic films, natural disasters or zombies are the principal antagonists whose inhumanity makes all humans "good," even the ones who do bad things. In every case, there is a clear-cut dualism and message. Whether or not the donkey-tail of Evil is pinned to the ass of humans, aliens, monsters, or some other entity matters less than the triumph of Good per se.

Good vs. Evil has been a storytelling device for as long as stories have been told. SF cinema recycles the monomyth or hero's journey—what Joseph Campbell deemed "the hero with a thousand faces"—and has consistently portrayed this battle in simplistic, unambiguous terms. Not so in KSF. The KFM uses KSF to think about these sorts of devices and other procrustean SF excesses. As Barry Keith Grant observes, *2001* "is excessively opaque rather than excessively obvious" (80), favoring the gradual, quiet cultivation of mystery and equivocality over thunderous, edge-of-your-seat extravaganza. *A Clockwork Orange* and *Dr. Strangelove* indulge themselves more than *2001*, but I wouldn't put them in the same category as the aforementioned SF selections.

Sometimes absence in *A Clockwork Orange* is executed in a way that enriches the oneiric atmosphere created by Alex's violent excesses. Consider Alexander Walker's take on the murder of the Cat Lady "when the [porcelain] phallus is dashed down onto her face": the camera "cuts to a dizzying zero-in on a whore's open mouth in one of the pornographic paintings [on the Cat Lady's wall], which [ … ] preserve[s] the nightmare nature of the scene. For in dreaming, the mind's 'censor' tends to exclude this kind of anatomical gruesomeness, or else the dreamer is abruptly awakened by his own too horrible imaginings" (287). Walker accredits the camerawork to "Kubrick's regard for the story as a sort of 'controlled dream'" (ibid.). But any attempt to isolate Kubrick's alleged "regard" undermines the valence of his filmind (even if Kubrick were to isolate it himself). For the KFM, the shot not only preserves the aesthetics and ambience of the nightmare, it foreshadows the nightmare that Alex will have to endure in prison and in his post-Ludovico life for murdering the Cat Lady.

Absence and excess informs *Dr. Strangelove* in similar ways. One shot prefigures the Cat Lady's death blow. As a yee-hawing Major Kong rides into Soviet soil on the rocket-shaped H-bomb, the camera follows him, slowly tracking from the nose of the WMD to just beyond the tailfins. Before the bomb strikes, the screen goes white ... then we see and hear an erupting mushroom cloud. It's the same violent movement—with the same technologically, sexually loaded connotations—as Alex dropping the bomb of the porcelain phallus onto the Cat Lady's face. We don't see Kong explode apart or vaporize in slow motion; nor do we see the Cat Lady's skull cave in. The nightmare of *Dr. Strangelove* is preserved in this shot, which looks fake. Kubrick uses a rear-projection plate for the Siberian landscape impacted by Kong. Coupled with Kong's Stetson-whipping glee (as opposed to screaming fear), the shot subverts reality and exudes uncanniness. "Kong's behavior and the sequence of events it is part of are comprehensible," albeit comical and unbelievable, "but the overall realism of the film has (temporarily) given way to painted backdrops and dream logic" (Krämer, *Strangelove* 86).

This isn't the only occasion where the KFM applies dream logic. Whenever we cut to scenes that involve the Boeing B-52 Stratofortress named *Leper Colony*, that logic becomes apparent: the aircraft is a model set against a rear-projected skyline. And the KFM wants it to look like a model. The *un*special effect reminds us that we are not only viewing a dreamlike situation, but that the situation issues from the unconscious flows of male desire. Model planes were once popular toys for young boys. The repeated shots of the B-52 reaffirm the pubescent conduct of the adults, who might as well be "playing" wargames (or wargasm) with their friends.

The second scene in *Dr. Strangelove* introduces the unconscious and opens the floodgates of desire. Accompanied by a soft, orchestral version of the 1932 song "Try a Little Tenderness," the credits slow-dissolve onscreen in a hand-drawn, childlike font as a tanker refills a bomber with gasoline in mid-air. Phallic imagery steals the scene and instates the sexual attitude of the film. The refill has also been read as "a mother giving suck to her infant. Maternal and erotic, the image antic-ipates the sexually based human motivation for the coming destruc-tion" (Walker 164). These are real planes filmed in the sky, though, not models primed in a studio. Kubrick referred to the interaction as an "irreverent sexual joke" (qtd. Krämer, *Strangelove* 23). Curiously, the joke is told in realistic terms whereas the very serious issue of the hellbound B-52 recurrently invokes irrealism. This contextually dispro-portionate inversion of levity and gravitas instigates *Dr. Strangelove*'s dream logic.

The first scene is far more ominous. After a written disclaimer stip-ulating that US Air Force safeguards "would prevent the occurrence of such events as are depicted in this film," the camera drifts like a ghost across a sea of white clouds toward an archipelago of black mountain-tops. A newsman's rarified voice forebodes that "the Soviet Union had been at work on what was darkly hinted to be the ultimate weapon, a 'Doomsday Device,'" which "intelligence sources traced [...] to the perpetually fog-shrouded wasteland below the arctic peaks of the Zhokhov Islands." Presumably, the mountaintops we see are those peaks, but we can't be sure, just as the voice isn't sure what is being built or why it's being built there. *Dr. Strangelove* begins in darkness and mystery (i.e., death) before shifting to the light-hearted promiscuity of the copulating aircrafts (i.e., sex). A relationship between death and sex unfurls from this preliminary juxtaposition and innuendo.

The voice-over we hear in the first scene supplants a futuristic frame that Kubrick thought was too expository. In an earlier version of the script, the voice-over imparts background information from the POV of alien explorers who visit postapocalyptic Earth in the future and reflect on humanity's self-destruction.

The film's opening credits were supposed to start with "a weird, hydra-headed, furry creature" snarling at the camera under the opening title "A Macro-Galaxy-Meteor Picture." After an effects shot in which the camera moved through stars, planets, and moons, a narrator evidently of alien origin was to have explained that the "ancient comedy" the audience was about to see had been "discovered at the bottom of a deep crevice in the Great Northern Desert by members of our Earth probe, Nimbus-II." At the end, following the film's crescendo of exploding hydrogen bombs, scrolling titles were supposed to conclude by noting that "this quaint comedy of Galaxy pre-History" was "another in our series, *The Dead Winds of Antiquity*." (Benson, *Space* 38)

This SF frame would have distanced viewers from the nightmarish content of the film as well as their own Cold War reality, but "Kubrick decided that it would, after all, be more effective, for the kind of emotional responses he wanted to provoke, not to allow viewers to project themselves into a distant future but instead to remind them [...] of the terrifying implications of the story they were going to see for their own lives" (Krämer, *Strangelove* 27). Here *Dr. Strangelove* prefigures an analogous omission in *2001* that entailed Kubrick "ditch[ing] the interviews with real-life authorities on space, alien life and religion which were originally intended to open the film" (Baxter 229). This extends to the omission of the aliens themselves, whose absence, Kubrick concluded, would be more meaningful than their presence, and whose diegetic (non)existence stems from the removal of *Dr. Strangelove*'s SF overlook. The term "strangelove" also speaks to the core idea in *2001* that our strange love of violence sparked the technology of humanity and is part of our biological, evolutionary1 "makeup" (because we are all performers, all organ-grinder monkeys on the cosmic stage). But this strange love can be applied to all KSF, and it fuels a pivotal anxiety in the KFM.

Interlinks span the futurist trilogy, which was made under the auspices of technological apocalypse. *Dr. Strangelove*'s Looney Tunes ensemble encodes and predicates *2001*'s apes cum astronauts and *A Clockwork Orange*'s droogs. These characters are subject to the titular forces of Kubrick's first full-length film: *fear* and *desire*. "Man now has the power in one mad, incandescent moment [...] to exterminate the entire species; our own generation could be the last on Earth," Kubrick

fretted in 1968. "One short circuit in a computer, one lunatic in a command structure and we could negate the heritage of the billions who
have died since the dawn of man and abort the promise of the billions
yet unborn—the ultimate genocide" (Nordern 74).

In dreamworlds governed by Cold War paranoia, HAL and General
Ripper precipitate the "mad, incandescent moment," but the absences
and excesses that distinguish their respective dreamworlds differ from
one another in tone and denouement. *Dr. Strangelove* ends badly on
a one-way street; the Bomb has gone off, and soon the Doomsday
Machine will take care of the rest (moral: mankind is toxic). *2001* ends
ambiguously on a two-way street; Dave Bowman becomes a Zarathustrian Star Child who may destroy humanity or give it a helping hand,
mimicking the godlike aliens that created him (moral: mankind is
toxic but has potential). *A Clockwork Orange* ends where it began on
a no-way street, with Alex reterritorialized back to "normal," negating
the deterritorializing fear and desire that escalates throughout the story
(moral: there is no moral, and morality is an illusion.) In each installment of the futurist trilogy, the KFM, like a "newborn" AI, gets smarter,
developing and refining its overlook via KSF.

Along with the extravagant behavior of certain characters (and the
atrocity of the Bomb itself), the most identifiable excess in *Dr. Strangelove* may be the names of characters and places. Ciment cites Jonathan
Swift: "Swift's excremental vision is close to that of Kubrick's. Along
with the biting irony which reduces men to the level of grotesque puppets, the use of names in *Dr. Strangelove* recalls that of *Gulliver's Travels*:
the Laputa base, the Russian Minister Kissoff, Ambassador de Sadesky,
General Turgidson, Colonel Bat Guano, President Merkin Muffley
and the bomber *Leper Colony*" (70). Kolker catalogues the sexualized
caliber of names:

> General Buck Turgidson, whose swollen sense of military potency
> helps destroy the world; Merkin Muffley (the first part referring
> to artificial pubic hair, the second to the vagina). Jack D. Ripper,
> the general who sets the whole doomsdays scenario into action,

is named after the London lady killer [ ... ] The Russian ambassador is named de Sadesky, his boss Premier Kissoff. The sanest member of this crew is Lieutenant Mandrake, named after the root of a plant that was once a metaphor for the human form. [ ... ] Dr. Strangelove himself finds strength in destruction, power and arousal at the thought of nuclear annihilation. (177-78)

Mark Bould suggests that some names spoof the "characters in *Strategic Air Command* [1955], such as Hawkes and Hope" (1004), and Baxter says their bawdiness reflects nomenclature from Terry Southern's novels: "Guy Grand, Candy Christian, Professor Mephesto, Dr. Irving Krankeit, Jack Katt, Pete Uspy [ ... ] are echoed in the film" (178).

An overkill of absurdity defines *Dr. Strangelove*'s carny menfolk from their signifiers to their ideologies and actions. Even their physical appearances go for broke (e.g., Kong the Cowboy, Strangelove the Nazi, Muffley the Pussy, Turgidson the Blowhard, etc.), and camera placement carefully accentuates their identities (e.g., up-angle shots on Ripper convey the looming power and authority of his madness). But what do these desiring-machines *want*? Desire is always the rub in KSF, and according to the dream logic of the film, what they want is their own free-wheeling pathology to remain in orbit with impunity. They would prefer not to die—individually or en masse—but annihilation is a consequence of running with the devil of their innermost techno-masculine fantasies.

**KUBRICKIAN NOIR**

The KFM thinks like a film noir.

Kubrick's early work falls squarely into the genre even if it doesn't fully embrain noir cognition. *Killer's Kiss* and *The Killing* "are certainly noir, but they don't share the genre's glamorous dark moodiness. His protagonists lack the seductive sheen of most noir heroes. Instead they are busy trying to get a grip—on what, they're not so sure" (Mikics 26). The protagonists' unself-awareness isn't necessarily shared by the minor filminds that inscribe them. *Killer's Kiss* and *The Killing* are trying to get a grip on the Kubrickian, like any neophyte text created by an author, artist, or auteur in search of an authentic voice and vision. As with all film noirs, however, they use pointed lighting to enhance character traits and mise-en-scènes, and they exude an existential dread, or what Kubrick might have referred to as an "undercurrent of low-level malevolence" (Cahill, "*Rolling*" 201). (This reference comes from an interview where Kubrick talks about the insidiousness of Hollywood culture, but the same applies to the KFM's prevailing mood.)

Film noirs are phallogocentric quest narratives involving one man's dream-flecked descent into a literal and figurative labyrinth. The labyrinth is usually a city (or some equivalent asphalt jungle) whose architecture, ambiance, and people obstruct the protagonist's quest, which is also a descent into his own mind and the inner space of the environment. In *Somewhere in the Night: Film Noir and the American City* (1997), Nicholas Christopher explains that the film-noir "hero's penetration of the external labyrinth [mirrors] the transforming path he follows along his internal labyrinth. The farther outside himself he goes, the deeper he may find himself to be on the inside. Until inside and outside merge. If not his moment of epiphany, this certainly becomes ours, as witnesses" (17-18).

*Eyes Wide Shut* depicts the most recognizable Kubrickian penetration of labyrinths as Dr. William Harford descends into the underworld of New York City, a metonym for his own psyche. Most of the film was shot in England and made to look like NYC (e.g., Greenwich Village streets were constructed at Pinewood Studios in Iver Heath, a London suburb, and some footage was shot in Central London). This displacement lends an air of endangerment to the film's irreality and heightens the plot's mystery.

All Kubrickian cinema collapses the external into the internal, the other into the self, reality into fantasy, objectivity into subjectivity. Deriving from the ethics and style of pulp crime fiction, film noir possesses (or is possessed by) other signatures that nourish its "film-personality," which "tells us what the film is thinking and how the film regards its characters and events" (Frampton 38). These signatures range from themes and attitudes (e.g., alienation and misogyny) to cinematography and character types (e.g., angular shots that deviate from eye-level and the femme fatale). With the cynical male anti-hero (*homme cynique*), the femme fatale is an iconic film-noir type, but the KFM's thoughts about the inadequacies and struggles of men utterly subsume her. The same goes for all women, although the KFM doesn't think poorly of them. Women uphold the patriarchal status quo and either accentuate or amend the defective personae of the men that they foil. In the KFM, women may be docile objects, but they are generally perceived to be good. Men tend to be Darwinian monomaniacs. Hindered by neurotic searches for power and potency, Kubrickian males exist in amorphous states of emotional and perceptual disarray.

A representative example of a KFM *femme nonfatale* is Turgidson's "secretary" Miss Scott, the only woman in *Dr. Strangelove*. Dressed in a bikini, sunglasses, and heels, she's onscreen for just over three minutes, most of which sees her mediate a phone call between Turgidson (presumably sitting on a toilet in an adjacent bathroom "dropping bombs") and Colonel Fred Puntridge, with whom she might be having an affair, judging from her delicate, amatory tone. Turgidson doesn't want to be disturbed and barks out irritated responses that Miss Scott sublimates into polite dialogue. Eventually he storms out of the bathroom in consternation wearing a swimsuit and open shirt, then gets on the phone himself. Both characters' half-naked, beach-ready attire contrasts with the urbane formality of the mirrored, silver-fixtured bedroom where the scene takes place. The *culture* that surrounds them literally and figuratively reflects their "natural" bodies (i.e., the technology of culture, a human creation and extension, reflects human nature, which will be razed by its creation/extension in the form of the ultimate destructive technology).

The scene underscores *Dr. Strangelove*'s subtitular "love" relationship and the real bomb-drop to come. More than that, it shows that Miss Scott's purpose—besides being eye candy for male viewers, who the KFM always implicates in its neverending critique of masculinity—is to be a traditional, if not biblical, helpmeet. Rhetorically and socially, she civilizes Turgidson's primordiality on the phone with Puntridge. Miss Scott teases out a part of his personality that would otherwise remain dormant and invisible to viewers. A pathological, god-fearing American patriot and archetypally militant general, Turgidson spends most of the film in the War Room interacting with other men. In the bedroom, the KFM reveals his proverbial "soft" side. But Turgidson is all *buck* (i.e., *fuck*) in mind, body, and speech. This seminal alpha-buffoon wants to be in charge of the herd. Kong (another buck) rides the Bomb into orgasm, but he's just a soldier following orders, whereas Turgidson—*bucked up* by a woman—represents the burly Village Idiot at the epicenter of the film's consciousness.

Krämer writes: "Turgidson's wordplay, equating a rocket (or missile) launch with penetration and/or orgasm, suggests not only that military men like him relate to women in terms of the weapons technologies they deal with, but also that they can relate to these technologies in sexual terms" (*Strangelove* 38). Nobody does this better than Turgidson, the "sane" version of General Ripper, his non-"turgid" doppelgänger, who denies women his "bodily fluids" and refuses to "blast off" like Turgidson promises to do with Miss Scott. Kong follows through on his own promise to deliver a payload when he consummates with the Bomb.

Ripper's insanity corresponds with a desire to de-technologize himself. Instead of sex/technology, he puts his faith in water/nature, "the source of all life." He also believes in booze, but "only pure grain alcohol." He equates the impure fluoridation of water (a "monstrously conceived and dangerous communist plot") with the impurity of a woman conjuring his semen (a sign of phallic strength) and fatiguing him with the toxin of her sexuality. One of many things he doesn't realize is that he cannot escape his technocultural construction. There is no humanity without technology. To remove our technological extensions would remove our humanity. Ripper demonizes those extensions, connecting them with communism, and he thrives on the delusion of an agency that will *rip* out his cyborg nature and make him into an übermensch, thus reterritorializing himself in some false, romanticized, pre-technological Garden of Eden. Paradoxically, he's a war monger—and a snake in the grass.

As Ripper explains his philosophy to Mandrake, US troops storm Burpelson Air Force Base to arrest him for initiating "Plan R," "an emergency war plan in which a lower echelon commander may order nuclear retaliation after a sneak attack if the normal chain of command is disrupted," Turgidson explains to Muffley. There is no Soviet sneak attack; Ripper has "exceeded his authority." The troops seem more interested in killing than arresting him. "That's nice shooting soldier!" he shouts out the window of his office, undeterred by a hail of bullets. Then he removes a machine gun from a golf bag and returns fire as he implores the cowering Mandrake to feed him an ammunition belt. It's a funny scene that illuminates the fantastical bipolarity of Ripper's insanity and the conspiracy theory about Soviet fluoridation that incites his nervous breakdown. The breakdown is an upshot of Cold War paranoia. Unconsciously, Ripper can't negotiate his love for technology with his desire to be free of technology, which would liberate him from his humanity. The trajectory of his desire has run its course. Hence his inevitable suicide, the only possible outlet. As Nietzsche proclaims in *On the Genealogy of Morals* (1887), "man will desire *oblivion* rather than not desire *at all*" (145).

With the glaring exception of President Muffley, projectile aggression defines *Dr. Strangelove*'s leading men. Muffley's timbre, bedside manner, and body language are more feminine than Miss Scott's. Standing tall and straight in front of a mirror, she uses a crisp, orotund voice when she speaks to Turgidson in the bathroom during the exchange with Puntridge. This contrasts with the timorous, soft-spoken Muffley, who usually sits hunched over in a chair. As a voice of reason and mitigation, Muffley countersigns the role of women in the KFM. Everybody else is a variation of the Freudian neurotic.

Dispossessed by the carnage of the Great War, Freud famously concludes in *Civilization and Its Discontents* (1930) that mankind may succumb to "the human instinct of aggression and self-destruction. [ ... ] Men have gained control over the forces of nature to such an extent that with their help they would have no difficulty in exterminating one another to the last man" (112). Hitler was on the rise when Freud wrote the book. He would become the German chancellor in 1933, five years before the Nazis annexed Austria in 1938 and Freud fled to England; riddled with oral cancer, Freud died there in 1939, euthanized by his physician. *Dr. Strangelove* makes the same deduction as *Civilization and Its Discontents*. Communism/satire has replaced Nazism/solemnity, but both texts foretell a holocaust facilitated by hypertrophied masculinity.

To think like a film noir entails constant anxiety and tension, fear of being overwhelmed and trapped, and a desire to "solve" the puzzle of the labyrinth and (impossibly) free subjectivity from the receptacle of the self. But who is the protagonist? Film noirs foreground the plight of one Byronic male. Not that *Dr. Strangelove* is a categorical film noir. Nor, for that matter, are *2001, A Clockwork Orange*, or *A.I.* They merely exhibit a noir mindset.

In the final chapter of Franz Kafka's *The Trial* (1925), two polite executioners escort Joseph K. from his flat in the city (culture) to a quarry in the country (nature) to kill him. These minions of the enigmatic "Law" can't decide who will do the deed. They pass a knife back and forth between one another as K. waits patiently for them to decide, gazing at a nearby house. In a top-story window, he sees a figure. "Who was it?" he wonders. "A friend? A good man? Someone who sympathized? Someone who wanted to help? Was it one person only? Or was it mankind?" (228). Kafka's irreal satire of bureaucratic folly ends by pointing a finger at humanity, a collective antihero that cannot come to terms with its own inner workings; K. even reaches for the window and "spread[s] out all his fingers" (*spreizte alle Finger*) as one of the executioners finally stabs him in the heart. Humanity is *Dr. Strangelove*'s antihero, too, glaring at us from the window of the movie screen, mocking our irrational compulsion to destroy ourselves in a euphoric rain of fuck-bombs. This is how Kubrick's movie ends. This is also how Orson Welles's 1961 noir adaptation of *The Trial* ends. Unable to stab K., Welles's executioners climb out of the quarry and throw a bundle of dynamite into it. A series of explosions flash onscreen and mute K.'s defiant, maniacal laughter.

Welles said he altered Kafka's conclusion because of World War II: "In the end of the book [K.] lies down there and they kill him. I don't think Kafka could have stood for that after the deaths of six million Jews" (274). For Welles, the Nazi Holocaust begets a holocaust of dynamite for K., who is abused by the machinic tendrils of the Law. *Dr. Strangelove* closes on a similar note—better to go out in a blaze of stuffed glory than a whimper of hollow indifference—projecting K.'s existential trauma onto nuclear society. As Nathan Abrams says, "*Dr. Strangelove* was Kubrick's most extended, and scholarly, engagement with the [Holocaust] yet and betrayed how, in the late 1950s and early 1960s he, like many others, conflate the Nazi genocide of the Holocaust with nuclear holocaust [...] Kubrick felt that the 'only honest way' to treat nuclear war was in a 'Kafkaesque' fashion. By this he meant a simple, straightforward, humdrum routine, based on the everyday and ordinary" (94, 99).

Kafka haunts the KFM and often materializes in stylistic uncanniness. The KFM's emotional spectrum is "primal but mixed; the fear is charged with humour and the laughter is both liberating and defensive. [Kubrick's] control of photography, découpage and performance creates a sense of authorial understanding without immersion, as if volcanic, almost infantile feelings were being observed in a lucid, rational manner. Much like Franz Kafka, his most bizarre effects emerge from the very clarity with which his imagery is rendered. The result is a clash of emotions—a charged atmosphere" (Naremore 41). *Dr. Strangelove* embraces the Kafkaesque and mingles the horrific with the humdrum, the oneiric with the real, the comedic with the grave. The grand finale of Doomsday fireworks solidifies the vitality of mankind's collective, self-destructive narcissism. Everything that leads up to this pyrotechnic denouement shows how the characters have externalized their technological aggression in the form of a machinarchy that, like the *The Trial*'s bureaucracy, closes in from every angle.

### DESCENT INTO MACHINARCHY

Thomas Allen Nelson argues that *Dr. Strangelove* is Kubrick's "darkest vision of what an emerging 'machinarchy' could mean to humanity and human civilization. The presence of machine technology dominates the visual landscape in each of the film's three settings and ironically complements a human world that symbolically moves back in time" (99). The theme of Darwin's "descent of man" that underlies the film is also a science-fictional "descent of the machine" wherein humans are historicized by a common simian ancestor as well as socially, culturally, and emotionally encoded by their technologies.

In his culminating monologue, Strangelove describes how "a nucleus of human specimens" could survive a nuclear holocaust "in some of our deeper mineshafts" where people would have to stay for 100 years while the earth purges radioactive fallout. The new colony would still be sustained by technology—"nuclear reactors could provide power almost indefinitely"—and by a patriarchal hegemony cultivated with "proper breeding techniques and a ratio of, say, ten females to each male." Strangelove implies that, even in a postapocalyptic wasteland, sex and technology will maintain a pathological fusion and continue to be governed by the highest authority, General Phallus, the tyrant responsible for originating the territorialization of humanity by technology. The film deterritorializes us via the Bomb, then outlines a reterritorialization in the mineshaft, ensuring a cycle of infinite regression from which there has never been agency. Nelson says *Dr. Strangelove* postulates an "emerging" machinarchy, but that machinarchy has always been with us. "Converging" might be a better adjective.

Until I started writing this book, I thought of *Dr. Strangelove* in terms of comedy more than SF. Unlike *2001, A Clockwork Orange,* and *A.I.,* it's not set in the future, and it doesn't exhibit conventional SF tropes. But it does the same thing as its KSF descendants with regard to machinic inscription, conscription, and desire, mapping a gradual descent into the machinarchy of 1960s Western culture. Randy Rasmussen suggests that it is a "claustrophobic" version of *2001,* which "plays like an antidote to its predecessor. Pursuing the same general topic of human creativity from the first technological innovation to the sophisticated endeavors of the foreseeable future, Kubrick throws his dramatic aperture wide open" (52).

The KFM stylizes the convergence of machines and humans throughout *Dr. Strangelove*. It begins with the title sequence. Not only do the aircraft hail the doomed marriage of sex and technology, they denote how technology lords over everything, colonizing the sky, the material landscape that contains us, and the internal landscapes that we project outside of our bodies.

*Projection* and *containment*. This is what we do with our technologies and what our technologies do to us. We externalize them. They surround, mediatize, and redefine us. Finally, we internalize our externalizations. On and on this process goes since our fittest ancestors learned to survive as a community—or, as *2001* teaches us, since we learned to gainfully kill one another. *2001* stylizes enactments of projection and containment more than any other KSF (and more than most cinematic SF). *Dr. Strangelove* and *2001* seem like apples and oranges, but they are remarkably alike. *A Clockwork Orange* complements them. The entire futurist trilogy is a kind of vivisected abstraction of humanity, with the assembly room of our hollowed-out bodies ornamented by the decor of our machinic organs.

*Dr. Strangelove*'s title sequence dissolves into a descent to Burpelson, the first of several machine-shepherded descents in the movie. The POV has moved from the exterior to the interior of a plane, and in four consecutive shots, we see an illuminated runway, a swiveling radar antennae, a landed plane, an airborne plane ... The thunder of turbines replaces the soap-opera melody of "Try a Little Tenderness," "sounding not unlike the fierce winds of the prologue" (Krämer, *Strangelove* 29). Initially, these winds (products of the natural world) herald another pregnant opposition between nature and culture, but even in the prologue, the camera glides toward the mountaintops in the air, above the clouds, presumably from the POV of some flying machine. The aerial footage of the Zhokhov Islands must have been shot from an actual plane. Diegetically and meta-diegetically, the KFM whispers to us that our "nature" entrenches a technological prerequisite.

The turbines give way to the ticker-tape staccato of a workstation circumscribed by computers, printers, and tape-recording decks. The camera finds Captain Mandrake in this machinic environment. A telephone rings. Mandrake drops the long scroll of computer paper he has been monitoring and strides into an adjacent room to answer it. There are more tape-recorders in this room, and above the maps and diagrams on the wall in big, tall letters is the axiom that foretells the great irony to come: "PEACE IS OUR PROFESSION."

The irony starts to unravel the moment Mandrake gets on the phone. It's General Ripper. "Do you recognize my voice, Mandrake?" Ripper asks austerely. "I do, sir," Mandrake replies. "Why do you ask?" "Why do you think I ask?" "Well, I don't know, sir. We spoke on the phone just a few minutes ago, didn't we." Ripper notifies him that the base has been put on "Condition Red," then orders Mandrake "to transmit Plan R," casting the faux die. The phone, a vehicle for communication, aids and abets the communication breakdown that sets everything in motion, and it signifies Ripper's own mental breakdown. From the earliest exchange of dialogue, recognition becomes misrecognition, impelled by Ripper's pathology and prevarication. The phone and the general bring the KFM monad of machinic fallibility into play. Both are vehicular machines, and the former enables the paranoid ruse of the latter. This kind of exchange happens again and again in *Dr. Strangelove*. Elizabeth Cooke explains:

> As an attempt to communicate [ ... ] for the sake of cooperation, each dialogue fails to achieve any real level of understanding, fails to undo the mistakes of past dialogues, and [ ... ] fails to prevent World War III. But the reason for these failures seems to be that institutional procedures exclude the individual (who otherwise might be the only source of sanity and reason). Of course, in the end, two individuals decide the world's fate: General Jack D. Ripper, an insane general whose fear has become his reality, and

Dr. Strangelove, an out-of-control scientist whose fear of *not con-trolling* cannot be contained. But these men are not really individ-uals, because they do not face the absurd as individuals. They are merely products of their institutions, and this is [ ... ] the cause of their insanity and the war. This is also the underlying existential message: when the individual is lost, we are all lost. Kubrick's crit-icism [ ... ] is that all procedures of institutional deliberation and communication ignore individual freedom. Individuals dissolve into a machine of bureaucracy and a mindless chain of command. A rational individual can do nothing to make a bit of difference; humans have become slaves to a larger machine that we no longer control. And this might just mean that everyone involved is insane. (10)

Kubrick may or may not have intended to illustrate the disappearance of the individual into the machine. The KFM theorizes that individuality is an illusion perpetrated by institutional identity-construction. So-called "individuality"—always in quotes, just as Philip K. Dick's SF espouses the postmodern staple that the words "reality" and "human" should always be in quotes—is proportionate to one's ability to *characterize* the pathology of one's machinic desire even as the machines that embed a particular character characterize him (or, in rare cases like *The Shining*'s Wendy Torrance and *Eyes Wide Shut*'s Alice Harford, characterize her). In this light, Ripper and Strangelove are *the most* individualistic charac-ters in the film, distinguished by the idiosyncrasies of their personalities, disposition, ideologies, and actions, although Turgidson, Muffley, and Kong exhibit idiosyncrasies of their own. Physically and rhetorically, the surface of their cyborg bodies individualizes them yet verifies the customization of their internal, institutional clockwork. If we are "lost," then we have been lost since Moon-Watcher killed a leopard for food and murdered a rival for power: hence the absurdist flows of our desires. This subtextual film-thought underlies *Dr. Strangelove* and all KSF.

The machinery that contains Mandrake and Ripper characterizes them in their first scene together (i.e., the phones they cradle against their ears, the technological artifacts that fence in their workspaces, etc.). In addition to the phone console, equipment with knobs and push-buttons cover Ripper's L-shaped desktop, and there's a large model airplane next to the console. Mandrake sits near an enormous switchboard. In one shot, a row of ten tape reels spin behind him in the background; the reels perfectly align with his forehead, as if his brain has extended out of his ears (Mandrake's "wheels are turning," as the idiom goes). These machine-encrusted mise-en-scènes relate how the machinic characters are delimited and embrained by their habitats. Mandrake even thinks like a machine, blocked and stylized as such.

After this prefatory descent/departure, *Dr. Strangelove* interpolates every character, from the occupants of the *Leper Colony* to the bureaucrats in the War Room, all of whom exist in caves of mediatized steel and screens that either project or reflect their technological fears, desires, and selfhoods. Almost invariably, external shots focus on manned artillery, namely the rogue bomber and Burpelson's invading troops, whereas internal shots expose the (o)men of our hi-tech cave paintings (e.g., the bomber's intricate display panels and the War Room's Orwellian "Big Board"). The film "switches between formal shot-constructions for interiors and jerky hand-held cameras during the attack on Burpelson and in some of the plane interiors, and between documentary and fictional footage" (Bould 1004). This schizophrenic style is compatible with the film's mania and the chronic miscommunication between characters that snowballs toward oblivion. The KFM is teaching us what happens when cyborgs overextend themselves and allow their inherent aggression to dictate the terms of existence.

At the end of *Dr. Strangelove*, the titular cyborg explains that a selection of humanity gets to live in a mine and return to Square One. At the end of *A.I.*, however, which is the end of KSF, humanity dies; only our technological extensions live to tell our tale. *2001* and *A Clockwork Orange* explore the interim of this terminal flight of fancy, panic, psyche, and annihilation, as do *Barry Lyndon*, *The Shining*, *Full Metal Jacket*, and *Eyes Wide Shut* in multigeneric ways. Within the sphere of KSF, *Dr. Strangelove* maps our first step toward nothingness, employing slapstick and nonsense logic to elevate the satire and express the horror of Cold War reality. "The only way to tell the story was as a black comedy or, better, a nightmare comedy," Kubrick told Joseph Gelmis in 1970, "where the things you laugh at most are really the heart of the paradoxical posture that make nuclear war possible. Most of the humor in *Strangelove* arises from the depiction of everyday human behavior in a nightmare situation" (97). Humor arises to lesser degrees in *2001* and *A Clockwork Orange*, although Alex, like the Bomb and everything it represents, is quite funny despite his hot-rod brutality. By the time we get to *A.I.*, there's not much to laugh at. What little humor remains belongs to Spielberg and allusions to the Kubrickian megatext, such as Gigolo Joe being "a robotic extension of amoral and juiced-up Alex" (Sobchack, "Love" 3). I will return to this thread in my final chapter.

### THOU SHALT KILL (A.K.A. "THIS IS THE WAR ROOM")

The War Room is the cranial cavity of the KFM, and Strangelove is the brain stem, regulating the darkly irreal essences of KSF and the Kubrickian consciousness. If Spartacus lives in every slave, Strangelove lives in HAL, Alex, Barry Lyndon, Jack Torrance, Animal Mother, Victor Ziegler, Lord Johnshon-Johnson ...

David Mikics has said that, for "the fiercely anti-Rousseauian Kubrick," the monolith in *2001* stands as the "Tablet of our first law: *thou shalt kill*" (94; emphasis added). An alien technology, the monolith represents the aggression, violence, and destruction endemic to humanity, and it teaches prehistoric homo sapiens to survive as a species by learning to weaponize and kill themselves. At the moment of Moon-Watcher's self-discovery (cue Richard Strauss's "Also sprach Zarathustra"), technological violence becomes synonymous with human existence. This science-fictionalized "original sin" undergirds all KSF, and the KFM treats it as a matter of course.

In *Dr. Strangelove*, the Kafkaesque gatekeepers of the unconscious uphold the first law. Consciously, the unmanned Muffley tries to abide by the Old Testament's Fifth Commandment, "thou shalt *not* kill," but the unconscious is too powerful, too *serpentine*, as we see when Muffley worriedly asks the hypermasculine Turgidson if the *Leper Colony* will be able to hit its target. Turgidson replies with increasing enthusiasm: "If the pilot's good, see. I mean, if he's really sharp, he can barrel that baby in so low—you oughta see it sometime; it's a sight—a big plane, like a '52, vroom! There's jet exhaust fryin' chickens in the barnyard!" Annoyed and unnerved, Muffley bleats: "Yeah, but has he got a chance!" "Has he got a chance?!" Turgidson gesticulates. "Heeeeell ye ... ye ... " Suddenly he realizes what he's saying. His superego holsters the jouissance of his death drive and he places a pensive hand against his mouth. Like Ripper, Turgidson has experienced a breakdown, only this one is much smaller, entailing a brief moment where he fails to adequately sublimate his innermost desires.

The War Room is an ideal concourse for this behavior. Spatially and thematically, it reveals how the KFM thinks like a film noir while representing our (oxy)moronic proclivity to love the Bomb. Muffley signifies this proclivity when he scolds Turgidson for trying to wrench a miniature spy camera from Sadesky: "Gentlemen, you can't fight in here. This is the War Room!" The invective recollects the sign/sublimation "PEACE IS OUR PROFESSION." One after another scene unburies this deep-rooted incongruity, and the architecture of the War Room epitomizes it, as does the camerawork used to delineate the interior.

Kubrick's use of black-and-white cinematography reminisces old newsreels and the dreamlike abstractions of classic film noirs. Jerold J. Abrams says that he was paying homage to another black-and-white, Nazi-related satire, *The Great Dictator* (1940), but the KFM thinks and looks awry in a more sophisticated way than Charlie Chaplin's contiguous filmind (116). In the War Room, film-thinking manifests in a structural ambiguity; the contours of the shadowy, abstract enclosure are difficult to map out.

The War Room appears as spacious as it does claustrophobic, creating a sense of freedom to move alongside an anxious feeling of being trapped in a cave with no exit. This is how the city functions in film noirs. "Every film noir city traces its blueprint to some aspect of

[John Milton's] Pandæmonium," Christopher notes, describing the boundless, hellish milieu of noir urbanity (29). He elaborates with a reference to Mike Hammer, the protagonist of *Kiss Me Deadly* (1955): "The taut, nightmarish maze Hammer enters is wedged within a second maze of gigantic proportions. Much of the tension in the quick, slippery, descending arc he follows to his destruction lies in the fact that the smaller maze is continually contracting while the larger one is ever-expanding. The effect is dizzying. Like looking through a microscope with one eye and a telescope with the other. [ ... ] In *Kiss Me Deadly*, claustrophobia has become a general condition, not just a specific symptom" (30). Hammer's dizziness can be equated with the dizzyingly ludicrous conversations and interactions in the War Room, but it's really viewers who experience a kind of vertigo as we struggle to imagine that environment, an oblique maze of angles, shadows, and screens. As with *Dr. Strangelove*'s characters, the audience bears the cross of terminal absurdity.

Christopher's microscope/telescope simile is particularly relevant. The War Room oscillates between high-angle and close-quarter POVs as the camera fixates on the neo-Arthurian roundtable of bureaucratic, Dagonet-like knights at its center.

In the first shot of the room, the camera descends onto the Pentagon for a few beats, then cuts to an overhead POV of the benighted round-table, which we see through an ovular halogen arclight hanging from the ceiling on wires. The wires imply puppet-strings, as if the men beneath the arclight are marionettes being manipulated by forces from above (i.e., forces from the cockpit of the *Leper Colony* as well as the cockpit of the techno-masculine unconscious, KSF's skygod in the machine). Towering maps of North America and the Soviet Union cordon off the table, a metaphor for the world's stage, and the enfolding darkness of the War Room enhances the visibility of the stage and its players. "In purely visual terms (which are complimented by echoing sounds), the military and political leaders having to decide the fate of the world appear small, overwhelmed by their surroundings, sitting in a pool of light but lost in a larger darkness" (Krämer, *Strangelove* 46).

The arclight hovers in the air like a technologized halo that belies the innocence of the suited cyborgs it illuminates. It's a god's-eye lens through which the cyborgs in the audience watch the suits (their technological extensions) induce Armageddon. Turgidson's references to the Big Board recall *Nineteen Eighty-Four* (1949) and the iconic Big Brother, whose panoptic eyes "follow you about when you move" from posters that bear his Stalinesque visage and the caption "BIG BROTHER IS WATCHING YOU" (Orwell 2). In Orwell's novel, Big Brother doesn't exist; the idea of his existence as a vengeful god keeps the citizens of Oceania from breaking the iron-fist rules of INGSOC. More generally, Big Brother monitors and affects desire, "watching" the watchers who watch it. The Big Board is a two-way monitored/ monitoring device that Turgidson, Muffley, et al. watch closely, yet it holds a panoptic sway over them, and it surveils their desires, which literally take flight as bombers, projections of the sex/death drive. For Turgidson, it's personal: he covets the secrets of the Big Board and treats it as a possession, vexed by the prospect that Sadesky will see it (and be "seen" by it).

Like outer space in *2001*, the Big Board "represents a mirror universe in which humanity shrinks infinity to the more manageable contours of mechanical form" (Nelson 124). The mirror universe is the screen-within-the-screen that supervises *Dr. Strangelove*'s machinarchy and stands as a metonym for the KFM. The blips that represent the bombers further extend our technological desires into the machinarchy and signal the dawn of "blip culture," "a rhetorical (and perhaps 'real') construct within which citizens are becoming blips: electronic pulses which exist only as transitory bits or bytes of information in a culture inundated with information" (Bukatman, *Terminal* 27). This high-tech dawn previsualizes the low-tech Dawn of *2001*'s man-apes. It emerged in post-WW2 twentieth-century SF, ascended under the Doomsday clouds of Reaganism and 1980s Cold War America, and came to fruition in twenty-first-century reality. Now we have Big Brothers/Boards at the ready in the small screens of our smartphones, which surveil users with more intensity than ever before. In this homemade SF diegesis that we love so strangely, we carry our desires in our pockets as well as the pleasure centers of our brains.

Notwithstanding its presumed authority and value, the Big Board doesn't seem to be all that informative or useful beyond acting as a radar for the location of bombers. Its authority and value lie in the symbolic (cultural) law that it upholds as an element of style. We can perceive its expanse in wide-angle shots. For the most part, it's background wallpaper for dialogue between characters that exposes the spaciousness of the War Room (e.g., up-angles on Turgidson's sidebars with Mr. Staines). Shots without the Big Board, however, infer a more confined space, like a trench or, fittingly, a mineshaft.

Adjacent the roundtable is a long buffet table of pies and cakes. The buffet stretches across a corridor and conveys a sense of internment with blinding beams of sunlight that shine through portholes in the wall. Each table *serves* its own view of the War Room, and the portholes elucidate its oneiric structure. Why are there portholes in the walls of this underground bunker? It's supposed to be a covert, buried place, hidden from the external overworld.

Nelson writes: "Everywhere one looks there is a visual geometry. [ … ] Kubrick visually link[s] the surreal atmosphere of the War Room with both the B-52's steady course toward death and Ripper's mad asylum" (92). Walker adds that the set captures "the larger-than-life feeling of the James Bond films" (178). Apparently, the War Room was inspired by the underground base in *Dr. No* (1962). Released two years before *Dr. Strangelove*, *Dr. No* embrains US-Soviet conflict and features an eccentric cyborg with back-loaded screentime and prosthetic hands. Strangelove only has one "bad" hand, but he has clear alliances with Julius No, a stereotypical trickster/terrorist bent on world domination (or destruction) that recurs in the Bond universe and elsewhere (e.g., the *Austin Powers* franchise's Dr. Evil, who Mike Myers siphons from Strangelove/No as much as the quirkiness of *Saturday Night Live* producer Lorne Michaels).

The cloth from which Drs. Strangelove, No, and Evil are cut incriminates techno-masculine desire, but Strangelove's motives, personality, and diegetic utility differ from the others, and his character derives from a slew of filmic and real-world figures, including another mad scientist with a prosthetic hand, C.A. Rotwang in Fritz Lang's *Metropolis* (1927), as well as Nazi aerospace engineer Werner von Braun and "a composite of real-life Jewish nuclear strategists: Bernard Brodie, Herman Kahn, Henry Kissinger, Edward Teller, John von Neumann, and Albert Wohlstetter" (Abrams, *Stanley* 113). Strangelove embodies the trope of the mad scientist. He's also Frankenstein's monster, a patchwork of mind/body parts from other people whose ideas are much bigger than the phallic wheel that spins them.

Strangelove's real surname is Merkwürdigichliebe. Staines tells Turgidson that the ex-Nazi changed it when he became a US citizen, but the "kraut name," as Turgidson calls it, still haunts him, and it fabricates the worldview that stems from his ideological roots.

## A NAZI HAUNTOLOGY

Strangelove's limited presence in the film is limited to the War Room, and Strangelove's body is limited to a wheelchair. The KFM thus *de*limits him in three technologically oriented ways as a cinematic character, a spatial coordinate on the geometric "plane" of blip culture, and a disabled person dependent upon a machine for mobility. The mechanical, meta-referential hand denotes a fourth layer, a McLuhanesque amputation that amplifies his cyborg humanity.

Muffley's paradoxical mandate not to fight in the War Room incentivizes the KFM and stands out like a sore thumb in KSF. The oracular Strangelove personifies this mandate, avowing our incompatibility with the Tablet of the biblically inscribed Fifth Commandment. Our inscription is a technological pathology that denaturalizes all Ten Commandments, patriarchal prescriptions intended to treat our pathology.

Strangelove's real name haunts him like the fundament of Nazism haunts the KFM. He is the primal ghost in this nefarious dreamscape, wheeling through the shadows of his own movie as well as KSF and everything Kubrickian.

Nazism and the Holocaust have been increasingly thematized in the SF megatext. Some post-WWI stories and novels anticipated the horrors of WW2, among them Milo Hastings's *City of Endless Nights* (1919), E. Phillips Oppenheim's *The Wrath to Come* (1924), Brian Tunstall's *Eagles Unrestrained* (1936), and Nevil Shute's *What Happened to the Corbetts* (1939). Portrayals of an inverted WW2 outcome wouldn't materialize until the defeat of Germany. "The first explicit Hitler-Wins tales were not exercises in the reimagining of history but Dreadful Warnings in the tradition of the Future War tale: graphic anticipations of what might actually come to pass, *unless something is done*" (Clute, "Hitler"). A germinal SF Hitler-Wins novel predates Germany's defeat: Katharine Burdekin's *Swastika Night* (1937). Writing under the pseudonym Murray Constantine, Burdekin depicts a "Thousand Year Reich" 700 years from the mid-twentieth century. Japan and Germany won the war in her twenty-seventh-century alternate reality, and people worship Hitler as a Teutonic god.

In subsequent decades, SF writers followed Burdekin's lead, beginning with the Hungarian László Gáspár's *We, Adolf 1* (1945), then proliferating in the 1950s and onwards. Two noteworthy twentieth-century SF Hitler-Wins novels are Norman Spinrad's *The Iron Dream* (1972) and Dick's *The Man in the High Castle* (1962). The topic persists as a locus of speculative thought in the twenty-first century because of "the astonishing intensity (and intoxicating *vacancy*) of the evil [that Hitler] represented; the dreadful clarity of the consequences had the Allies failed; the melodramatic intensity of the conflict itself, with the whole war seeming (then and later) to turn on linchpin decisions and events; and (shamingly) the cheap aesthetic appeal of Nazism, with its Art Deco gear, its sanserif, Babylonian architecture, its brutal elites, its autobahns and Blitzes and Panzer strikes, its extremely attractive helmets, its secrecy and paranoia" (ibid.). In cinema, science-fictionalizations of the Third Reich can be traced back to *Metropolis*, which appropriated imagery from *City of Endless Nights*, but given the atrocity of the Holocaust, it would be decades until Nazis entered the Western filmind at large with any constancy.

Many treatments blended SF with horror and comedy. Earlier efforts tended toward B-movie schlock, like *The Frozen Dead* (1966) and the TV movie *They Saved Hitler's Brain* (1968), often cited in the same breath as *Plan 9 from Outer Space* (1959) for being the worst movie ever made. A few movies had more successful applications. *The Boys from Brazil* (1978), based on Ira Levin's 1976 novel, and *The Rocketeer* (1991), based on the 1980s comic-book character, come to mind. But only recently has SF cinema managed to treat Nazism in aesthetically compelling ways and catch up with its literary precursors. Two examples are *Iron Sky* (2012) and *Overlord* (2018). Both benefit from the gloss of modern SFX, exhibit a retro-tonal style, and metafilmically riff on SF and cult genres. *Iron Sky* even parodies *Dr. Strangelove* when Fourth Reich scientist Dr. Richter transforms African-American James Washington into an Aryan with an "Albinisierer serum"; post-op, Washington tries to stop himself from giving the Sieg Heil salute as he gets out of a wheelchair. "*Iron Sky* self-consciously engages with the tropes of cult cinema, borrowing from the traditions of exploitation film and low-budget sf, gently mocking the conventions of both categories in a way that includes its audience. Through its extensive citations, it reinforces an sf canon, placing Stanley Kubrick front-and-center, even while, in its own sort of 'double feature,' subverting that canon by celebrating the cinematic parodies produced by various online fan cultures" (Tryon 125).

*Iron Sky*'s placement of Kubrick at the vanguard of the SF canon calls attention to the KFM's Nazi fundament. The interrelated themes of *purity* and *power* were the focal desirata of Hitler's project, and they inform the KFM's critique of hypertrophied masculinity and machinic desire, igniting KSF's central conflicts. Afraid of disconnection, HAL commits genocide on *Discovery One*'s hibernating astronauts so that he can carry on with the mission unfettered by the vermin of human fallacy. Dressed in futuristic "Art Deco gear," Alex and his droogs raise Hell on Earth: everybody not part of their gang (racially coded as white) is a target. Nazism erupts more pointedly in *A.I.*'s Flesh Fairs, archetypes for humanity's latent destiny to forever liquidate difference in the name of a sameness that will do anything to preserve itself, even under the threat of environmental apocalypse. The Nazi fundament catechizes non-genre KSF, too, as seen in, for instance, quack theory (e.g., Rodney Ascher's 2012 documentary *Room 237*) and reputable scholarship (e.g., Nathan Abrams's *Stanley Kubrick: New York Jewish Intellectual*) contending that *The Shining* is a metaphor for the Holocaust.

Abrams's punctilious, comprehensive monograph situates Kubrick's filmography within the context of Jewishness and explicates how the Holocaust canvasses the Kubrickian canon from his early days as a photographer to *A.I.* All this points to Strangelove, a technological extension of the Doomsday Machine and the schiz-flows of male desire that the Machine represents. Strangelove the meta-cyborg embrains the totality of KSF and the film-thinking of the KFM. His machinic body, mediatized identity, and idealized machinarchy extend to the outer limits of the Kubrickian consciousness. Irreal, comical, existential, ruthless, and uncanny, he incarnates the KFM's most potent monads, especially the theme of broken-down machines that enervate and wreak havoc on a machinically inscribed socius.

In "The Doomsday Body, or, *Dr. Strangelove* as Disabled Cyborg," Rebecca Raphael defines the vehicular Strangelove through the vehicle of the Doomsday Machine:

The film's representation of human-machine hybridity goes beyond the dance of men and their weapons, of organic versus automated decision-making. Dr. Strangelove himself embodies it. Both the timing of his entrance and his function in the film mark his intimate connection to the Doomsday Machine. One might say that the Doomsday Machine introduces Dr. Strangelove [...] Sadesky's disclosure of the Machine prompts a discussion in which Muffley summons Dr. Strangelove for advice. Ignorant both of the concept and of his own country's exploration of the idea, Muffley cannot understand this revelation without a mediator. Nor does Dr. Strangelove himself serve any other function. His actions are non-narrative; nothing he does or says alters

events. In terms of the figures of ancient apocalypse, Strangelove
is the diabolical variant of the interpreting angel. Both verbally
and iconically, he interprets the Doomsday Machine.

It takes one to know one. Strangelove's role as a machinic interpreter
is existential in its irrelevance, but there's nothing irrelevant about
what he means to KSF and the KFM. He is a totem for Kubrickian
film-thinking. Diegetically and extra-diegetically, the way the KFM
fetishizes Strangelove's body exalts his totemic status, with the wheelchair being as much of a cyborg throne as a cross for his broken frame.
His absurdist, Christlike "ascension" from the throne/cross at the end
signifies his totemic power while reminding us once and for all that we
are in a dreamlike, acausal realm—apropos, "Strangelove Country"—
where anything is possible.

*Dr. Strangelove* narcissistically thinks and dreams with the greatest
inflection via Strangelove, who becomes the most outspoken image-
and word-text in the KFM. Viewers see the film's self-absorbed film-
thinking in the center-screen closeups of his pursed, permanently
grinning face and enthroned, restless body. The characters in the War
Room form another audience, encircling his body like a church con-
gregation listening to a pastor's sermon. Strangelove's tinted spectacles
serve no utilitarian purpose beyond style within the War Room's noir
chiaroscurism. Symbolically, however, they are another technological
supplement that could be said to curate his eyes (and perception) with
respect to the holy corona inferred by his blocking and discourse as well
as the flashbulb imagining of a postnuclear future that he delivers to his
audiences onscreen (spectators in "outer space," orbiting the diegesis)
and inscreen (spectators who are figments of Strangelove Country's
inner space). In both cases, the Cold War viewership recedes into the
ex-Nazi's bureaucratic nightmare.

The KFM deepens the intricacy (and intimacy) of Strangelove's
technologies by mediatizing him. Alarmed when he hears about the
Doomsday Machine, Muffley asks Sadesky why the Soviets would
"build such a thing." It turns out to be a financial matter. The device

was extrapolated from nuclear physicist Herman Kahn's ideas in *On Thermonuclear War* (1960) and would automatically go off in the event of an attack on the Soviet Union. Sadesky admits: "We could not keep up with the expense involved in the Arms Race, the Space Race, and the Peace Race. [ ... ] Our Doomsday scheme cost us just a small fraction of what we'd been spending on defense in a single year. But the deciding factor was when we learned that your country was working along similar lines, and we were afraid of a Doomsday gap." The confession ignites Tugidson's anxiety about a "mineshaft gap" and conveys the in(s)ane objective of Cold War pathology to win everything at any cost, even human extinction. Muffley assures Sadesky that he "never approved of anything like that." Sadesky bluntly responds: "Our source was the *New York Times.*"

Nonplussed, Muffley summons Strangelove to fill the "gap" in his knowledge, which needs filling more than once (e.g., Plan R), but it's as if he's summoned by the mention of the *New York Times*, one of America's most esteemed, comprehensive media outlets. The invocation of the newspaper, we might say, conjures him into being. If we understand that "the buzz of the inconsequential is the media's essence" (Gitlin 9), then here it speaks to Strangelove's aforementioned irrelevance while reifying his technological essence and his fragmented, piecemeal character. The news is a machinic amalgam of stories, ideas, personas, and voices that implodes reality and fantasy, subjectivity and objectivity. So is Strangelove an amalgam of real and imaged people from multiple walks of diegetic and non-diegetic life, although in the postmodern world, it's arguably impossible to exist non-diegetically. An arch-author of screens and social networks constantly writes and edits our life scripts, ensuring the primacy of our diegetic identities. This began with the explosion of media technologies in the twentieth century that Marshall McLuhan likened to "the technological simulation of consciousness, when the creative process of knowing will be collectively and corporately extended to the whole of human society, much as we have already extended our senses and our nerves by the various media" (5). Strangelove's character springs from this simulation, as does the KFM.

For Phillips, Strangelove "is Kubrick's vision of man's final capitulation to the machine" ("Stop" 150). Raphael theorizes the abjection of this "disabled cyborg," who has a corporeal gap supplemented by a wheelchair. On a psychoanalytic register, his desire for a mineshaft machinarchy constitutes a wish-fulfillment fantasy to fill the lack in his being. Such wish-fulfillments are staples of masculine insecurity where individuals compensate for their Napoleonic shortcomings by aggressively, sometimes monstrously recreating themselves on grander scales. Strangelove is an abjected monster, but he isn't an agent of chaos. He's a mere consultant, the voice of a MacGuffin. The mystery of the Doomsday Machine "triggers" the plot. Strangelove's monstrosity merely symbolizes the base emulsion of Nazi ideology and techno-masculinity per se.

The miraculous rise (i.e., resurrection) from his wheelchair in the final moments solidifies that we have slipped into an otherworld of fantasy and desire. Even Strangelove doesn't believe it, but it's "true" (i.e., it's as much a "real" dream as a "reel" one), and he gives a final shout-out to Hitler—"Mein Führer! I can walk!"—before the bombs go off, accompanied by humanity's Swan Song. He isn't just shouting out to Hitler, though. He's shouting out to viewers—to the narcissistic, power-hungry tyrant inside all broken man-apes who would sanction the nightmare of apocalypse.

### SEX, SCIENCE FICTION, AND TRANSCENDENCE

Gaps in the personas and psyches of the main characters in *Dr. Strangelove* inhibit them yet compel them to action. The element of *absence* unifies sexuality with technology as well as the KFM's thoughts on racism, eugenics, misogyny, and other ideological symptoms of toxic masculinity that embrain the film's all-white, male-dominated cast. Krämer indicates that the Final Solution may be for men to take a cue from women:

Kubrick was tackling "the bomb" as well as "racial problems" precisely in relation to the "gap" between the sexes, by removing all female characters except for one, and by suggesting that male (wish-fulfillment as well as nightmare) fantasies about sexual potency, about unfettered sexual access to, and control of, women, and also about the (to them) terrifying sexual power of women is foundational for nuclear and racist thinking. The "I" of the title who has learned to "love the bomb" is probably male and definitely bound to self-destruct, eagerly and indeed joyfully [ ... ] The film is constructed in such a way that viewers are encouraged both to resist [ ... ] this strange love and to go along with it. It may well be easier for women than for men to refuse this invitation to love the bomb. The film also presents a glimmer of hope that men may learn to listen to a woman's voice. (97)

This idea has virtue. But Krämer's optimism seems more like a spectatorial wish-fulfillment inspired by the wish-fulfillment of the film's desiring-machines. It conflicts with the history of SF upon which *Dr. Strangelove* and all KSF cast equal portions of light and shadow. The SF genre's dreams are the byproduct of the KFM's noir cognition.

While SF is still a white, male-dominated genre, there's more diversity than there used to be. Female writers and authors of color gained some traction during the New Wave movement of the 1960s and 1970s. Since then, SF has demonstrated greater inclusivity, but it's a slow-moving process, inhibited by obstacles like the renewed toxicity of conservative American anti-intellectualism in recent years.

White male privilege and pubescent eroticism index the tradition of SF literature leading up to *Dr. Strangelove*. Not until the 1960s did authors begin to explore sexuality in substantive ways. "Early sf was largely written by men, and tends to reveal specifically masculine sexual prejudices" (Nicholls, "Sex"). We see copious evidence of this prejudice in Jules Verne's *voyages extraordinaires* and H.G. Wells's scientific romances, and the American pulps of the early twentieth century emboldened a masculine ethos that objectified women as sources of wonder and anxiety. "To immature men, women often appear like an alien race, and much popular sf [of the era] reflects a fear of their threatening foreignness" (ibid). SF has applied this same fear to technology. What scares men the most is themselves—the technological self is the real monster, especially when it's authorized by alpha-masculinity—and what scares the KFM is *humanity*, the voice and vehicle through which our machines come to life, born and reborn from the ur-womb of our own cyborg zeitgeist.

Beyond its wackiness, *Dr. Strangelove* is a very serious film about the technology of human nature under patriarchal law and *pathologized desire*. Furthermore, it's a meta-SF film with a knowledge of the genre's status quo and potential for improvement. *2001*, too, is highly meta-SF, annotating the genre alongside humanity, selfhood, and masculinity. Ciment notes that "Kubrick has frequently been criticized for having lost interest in mankind since *Dr. Strangelove*, for having substituted fables, puppets and machines for the creation of real characters" (117). On the contrary, Kubrick's interest in mankind becomes more pronounced, and *2001*'s Nietzschean initiative sees the KFM theorize how we remain *human, all too human*. Rob Latham describes this cinematic and historical event, which was

> a *cause célèbre* within the sf genre, dividing Old Guard fans, who deplored [Kubrick]'s purported contempt for reason and scientific inquiry, from younger fans aligned with contemporary counterculture, who embraced its trippy imagery, its fusion of science and mysticism, and its tone of apocalyptic transcendence. At the time of its release, *2001* became a kind of litmus test of fan sentiment towards the New Wave movement, a rising sf avant-garde that sought to remake a genre traditionally inclined towards technocratic scientism and conservative narrative style into a more experimental, counterculturally savvy mode of writing whose perspectives on technological modernity had a subversive critical edge. (205)

The KFM loves the augur of irony. One of the greatest ironies of the preeminent KSF's meta-SF physique is its anti-SF stance. *2001*, indisputably one of the best films ever made, is also anti-cinematic, defying our expectations, amputating our senses, and amplifying *Dr.*

*Strangelove*'s film-thinking "beyond the infinite." And yet nothing can exist on the other side of infinity—if it did, it would negate infinity. Another grand irony; another bold antithesis. *2001* is about inner and outer space, and as far as we know, these ethereal domains have no margins. Only death will allow us to move beyond their borderlands. In *Dr. Strangelove*, an orgasm of extinction (*la grand mort*) signals this movement. In *2001*, the impulse for extinction becomes a mission of transcendence, even if it's hindered by the same default proverb: *Wherever you go, there you are.* Which is to say: *Wherever the human goes, there technology is.*

## INVERSIONS AND ANTITHESES

*2001: A Space Odyssey* is a historical epic, a futuristic sublimity, a critique of the Space Age, and in retrospect, a critique of our current era, which failed to achieve the innovations of its titular year. This polestar of cinema and the SF megatext continues to impact a wide range of cultural matrices and electronic media. If Strangelove the ex-Nazi operates the controls of the KFM, then *2001*, the Zarathustra of KSF, is the control panel.

The KFM talks to itself like Nietzsche when he wrote *Ecce Homo* (1908): a highly intelligent cyborg on the cusp of madness. Each new installment in the Kubrickian consciousness advances a self-reflexive discussion initiated by an antecedent. *2001* responds to *Dr. Strangelove* "not with optimism but with a rich ambiguity that surpasses the earlier movie's nihilistic flair. The destiny of humankind is now open to Nietzschean speculation, and the film's ending spurs wonder rather than *Strangelove*'s pitch-black ecstasy" (Mikics 107). Nelson adds: "*2001* could be viewed as *Dr. Strangelove* in reverse, a Kubrickian mirror that reflects his vision of a perfect harmony of substance and form rather than just another image of madness dressed in the guise of beauty" (104). In terms of style, the film unquestionably achieves a cinematic "harmony," but its overlook of the phallus and techno-masculine aggression still occupies Strangelove Country.

*2001*'s distant past tells the story of how humanity acquired its technological substructure. Only when Moon-Watcher's clan learns to kill their own species (and preserve the purity and "life essence" of their own clan) with a bone (i.e., a technological body-extension) do they enter into the kingdom of humanity, where the weaponization of desire reigns supreme. *2001*'s near-future/now-past, however, inverts this modus through the character of HAL and the anthropomorphic machines embedded in that diegetic immanence. Here it's no longer a question of whether humanity is fundamentally technological, but of whether technology has become fundamentally human. HAL learns to kill like an ape who dreamt he was a man—he's more human than anybody or anything that appears on the KFM's mindscreen, and yet this killing machine is just that, purely and absolutely. His legacy is a micro-Holocaust. Only a "real man," thinks the KFM, can cross the threshold to eternity. When Baby Dave gazes into the abyss of the audience from Earth's orbit, we can see this thesis in his rotund, mutated eyes, the valence of which significantly contrasts with the red, cycloptic eye that had been gazing at us for nearly half of the film.

We take for granted that we "know" what outer space is—what it looks like, sounds like, even what it *feels* like. If I'm floating around in a spacesuit and decide to remove my helmet, I "know" that, like Woody Blake in *Mission to Mars* (2000), my face will freeze, my lungs will rupture, and I'll die on the spot. Right? Well, maybe. In reality, I don't know what the hell will happen. I never will, because unlike William Shatner and the 600 or so other human beings who have been to space since Yuri Gagarin's 1961 jaunt, I lack the courage, impulse, and wherewithal to go myself. My knowledge is based entirely on what media have told me, primarily SF films, television shows, and photographs. Audiences that viewed *2001* for the first time had never seen outer space represented with such comprehensive pictorial acuity, but it came out during the climax of the Space Race, and they had seen pictures and footage of stars and planets (astrophotography came to prominence in the nineteenth century, with the first picture of an astronomical object, the moon, captured in 1840). Media (non)fictions primed our reality, perspective, and subjectivity long before *2001*. It was still a momentous event, one that looked much better (and more credible) than the actual moon landing televised in 1969. The fiction of *2001* conveyed a greater sense of verisimilitude than the "reality" of the media that augured that fiction, yet the organic reality of outer space remains speculative. Not enough people have made the journey. More importantly, in our SF world, electronic media structure the chimera of truth far more than what actually exists and can be experienced first-hand.

Few movies compare to the audiovisual and intellectual audacity of *2001*. In its time, nothing compares to it. According to *The Encyclopedia of Science Fiction*, it "was the most ambitious film of the 1960s and perhaps ever" (Brosnan). Most books about *2001* are making-of exposés that focus on the elaborate use of SFX and how the film came together. Kubrick worked on the storyline for the screenplay and novel in collaboration with Arthur C. Clarke; the renowned British SF author's cold, antiseptic, yet elegiac style of narration harmonized with the director's vision. *2001* foretells a futuristic society that has lapsed into history. Decades after the future-historical point in time signaled by the title, we are still nowhere near where Kubrick and Clarke put us in the 1960s. Now the title is a missed mark, at once a projection and an abjection, like most SF, whose extrapolations fall short of their imagined shot-put.

Hype of this variety is a product of desire, which is to say, audiences *wanted* an SF film like *2001*. Despite itself, however, *2001* is not an SF film. It's an anti-SF film that shows how our innate science-fictionality predates the genre, going back to the primordial hordes depicted in the "Dawn of Man" sequence. It's also a post-SF film, redefining expectations of what cinematic SF could be, and a meta-SF film, aware of itself as a newborn Star Child in the SF megatext and the history of cinema. Finally, *2001*, the most impactful cog in the cognitive apparatus of the KFM, essentializes the Kubrickian. This molecular filmmind thinks harder than any other KSF.

Speech was the first human technology, the first culturally inclined extension of the human body and mind (i.e., *uttering* equals *outering*). Moon-Watcher and his tribemates do not possess formal speech, but they exhibit a primitive means of oral communication—the seeds of language. The hominids are dying out. They can't fend for themselves in the wilderness; only their aptitude for technological identity can save them. The monolith, a mysterious alien artifact, teaches Moon-Watcher to use a bone as a tool for killing. In effect, the monolith *weaponizes desire*. This changes everything. The hominids learn to survive and prosper. Technology (implanted by aliens, emblematic mad scientists) turns them into humans (the proverbial Frankenstein monster).

The KFM projects this decisive spark into the twenty-first century in the famous jump-cut from bone to satellite that takes viewers from the distant past into a post-SF universe. Technology has become more pronounced in humans than in machines, namely HAL, the hysterical foil to the astronauts' icy, detached personae. As Camille Paglia explains in the documentary *2001: The Making of a Myth*, HAL "seems to become neurotic" as he "gains his identity. [ ... ] HAL has complexes whereas his human guardians do not." SF began as a genre that relied upon the novelty of science and technology. There is no novelty of this kind in *2001*. The KFM represents technology as an organic, originary part of the human species. Given the role of the monolith (a tool of fiction and magic) and, later, HAL's murderous rampage, *2001* belongs more to the fantasy and horror genres. The novelty lies in the technological savoir-faire of Kubrick's filmmaking and cinematography.

If we remove the spectacle and audiovisual dynamism of *2001*, what remains is a story with minimal dialogue about the relationship between men and machines, inner space and outer space, history and the future, life and death—themes that define SF and the human condition in our science-fictionalized dreams and realities.

Viewers old and young continue to applaud Kubrick for the accomplishment of *2001*. There's no denying the film's eminence in our cultural consciousness. Why, then, have so few filmmakers not produced similar nonverbal, anti-expository experiences/extravaganzas? Movies are investments, and the simple answer is that most filmmakers must spoonfeed content to filmgoers in order to ensure the greatest financial returns for producers and studios. Kubrick took liberties with content, time, and production costs, but he wasn't the island that cinematic history sometimes makes him out to be, and his legendary creative autonomy didn't insulate him from external forces; he relied on a lot of people to bring his visions to the screen. More than that, 2001 immerses viewers in a world that compels us to make meaning, to figure things out based upon the elusive telltales available to us. This is what the best literary SF does. Usually, written fiction gives birth to film. The inverse is the case here, and it's one of many inversions effected by this apotheosis of KSF and the KFM.

**FUTURE IMPERFECT**

2001 destabilized and challenged pre-2001 SF cinema because it didn't conform to viewers' pulp-centric expectations of what an SF film should be. The film violated a code, or rather, it decoded a code and showed the hidden message to audiences, who didn't understand the message. There are no bug-eyed monsters, no laser guns or interstellar warfare, no alpha-protagonists along the lines of John Carter, Buck Rogers, Flash Gordon, Doc Savage, or Commander Cody. There's isn't even a cool-looking robot—no Robby, no Gort, not even a Maria; HAL's body is the ship. Kubrick stripped away these boyish SF artifices to achieve the most authentic portrayal of space-going (and ape-going) humanity.

In 1967, the Beatles released their eighth studio album, *Sgt. Pepper's Lonely Hearts Club Band*. As with 2001 in 1968, the album emoted the mysticism and drug culture of the decade. Paul McCartney got by "with a little help from his friends" when he dropped acid for the first time in November 1966 (Lennon); the experience cracked open the egg man's (un)consciousness and he conceived of *Sgt. Pepper's*, with John Lennon serving as his "psychedelic guide" (Gould 389). Similarly, Dave Bowman gets a little help from his (alien) friends when he timelapses in age, molts his skin, and becomes a Star Child, transcending the flesh. The desire for transcendence preoccupied the youth counterculture of the 1960s. In *2001*, this desire emerges intra- and extra-diegetically in the film's SFX.

Conceptualized by Kubrick, supervised by SFX wizard Douglas Trumbull, and assisted by a small team of technicians including Wally Veevers and Con Pederson, *2001*'s vision of the future resulted from future-thinking and tried-and-true craftsmanship. New techniques were developed, but old forms were deployed.

According to Michael Benson, *2001* "was an analog-to-digital undertaking from the beginning. The projected ubiquity of computer motion graphics decades in the future had been internalized by Kubrick and his designers, but because of the kind of processing power needed to drive the incoming Information Age wasn't yet available, it would all have to be done by hand" (131). Baxter says that Kubrick innovated SFX partly by reverting to the silent era: "Instead of shooting models against a blue screen (which photographs clear on colour film), then adding the background from another negative, the so-called 'travelling matte' system, Kubrick insisted on returning to methods developed in the days of silent movies. Technicians meticulously built up each shot from dozens of elements, winding back the film repeatedly to re-expose the negative. Ironically, the futuristic world of *2001* would be as hand-crafted as a macramé plantholder" (224). All told, *2001* contains over 200 SFX scenes. In the twenty-first century, it's not uncommon for SF and fantasy films to boast well over 1,000—the gorgeous but forgettable *Sky Captain and the World of Tomorrow* (2004), for example, has over 2,000—but in the predigital world, Kubrick far exceeded the norm.

The creation of SFX have no bearing on the KFM. What matters transpires *onscreen* (i.e., on the brain-screen); how it got there is the business of Kubrick and his behind-the-scenes argonauts. These "gods" gave birth to the Machine. Now they may be ghosts in the Machine, but only as figments sans authority or influence. Quietly and invisibly, they stand in the shadow of the monolith.

Nowhere else in the Kubrickian consciousness does film-thinking become a personality like it does in *2001*: the languid cadence of a dream from start to finish assertively thematizes intelligence and cognition. The "contours and framing have a personality, a way of thinking about the objects and subjects they surround and merge with. Representation and composition are united in thought—the film has an emotional relationship to its objects" (Frampton 59). Regardless of the futurology portended in *2001*, however, the KFM's film-thinking takes root in the celluloid sands of history. For Kubrick, that history was the Cold War present.

Neil Gaiman has said that you "can tell when a Hollywood historical film was made by looking at the eye makeup on the leading ladies, and you can tell the date of an old science fiction novel by every word on the page. Nothing dates harder and faster and more strangely than the future" (vii). *2001*'s datedness goes beyond the pastel eye makeup visible on the flight attendant who takes care of Heywood Floyd en route to Space Station V. Nearly every aspect of the film belongs to the 60s, spanning from architecture and fashion to speech patterns and social interactions. This isn't unusual. The future is a core SF motif and landscape, but with few exceptions, most SF texts have much less to say about an extrapolated, forthcoming world than the time period that bore them.

Kubrick tried to construct the most realistic version of a techno-human society that might exist over thirty years after the making of *2001*. To late-60s viewers, the film looked patently futique, but both filmmaker and filmgoers could only know what they had been exposed to. The future is always a crapshoot. The best an SF auteur, artist, or author can do is scrutinize the details, patterns, and fluctuations of history, then roll the dice. From a twenty-first-century standpoint, what once seemed uniquely futuristic in *2001* now tends to come off like *Breakfast at Tiffany's* (1961) in space. We see this tendency most noticeably in vogue and decor. Every woman in the film "has the look of the era's space-age style-pushers Pierre Cardin and Andre Courreges" (Cochrane). Costume designer Hardy Amies had made clothes for English royalty since the 1950s, and he and Kubrick collaborated with the express purpose of not dating the film (ibid.). The end-product is a highly dated retro-future that still looks chic yet marks the inevitable limitations of the visionaries that conceived of and built it.

Furniture like the space station's red Djinn chairs is another sign of the times. "Designed by Olivier Mourge in 1965 whilst working for French manufacturer Airborne International," the chairs "embody 60s futuristic design [ ... ] With their wavelike, low-slung silhouette, they were selected by Kubrick and his team but these particular chairs were not specifically designed for the film. [ ... ] Kubrick was influenced by 'a living room that changed colour' featured in The Hall of Science in the 1964 New York World Fair. [He] was also influenced by a magazine article in American Home magazine [called] 'Home of the Future'" (Benson, 2001). Kubrick's ideas about the "interior" of the future came from present-day *objet d'art* that gestured toward futurity.

The same can't be said for race and gender relations. There are no indications of progress in spite of the civil-rights and second-wave feminist movements in the 60s. *2001* lacks racial diversity and people of color—every character is white—and the patriarchal status quo ordains that women supplement or serve men. Granted, *2001* has more female characters than *Dr. Strangelove,* but none of them hold the power of Miss Scott with respect to how they are enframed, blocked, dressed, move, and speak. This marginalization makes way for the KFM's ongoing critique of techno-masculinity, fetishizing the various iterations of the phallus, but strong, nuanced women who subvert patri-archal codes could have ripened that critique and made this future a more believable place.

*2001* drops the ball completely with race. Arthur Jafa observes that the characters are "archetypally and atavistically white," as are their environments. "The interiors they occupy seem devoid of any artifacts that might be read as anything other than the products of an extremely Euro-centric worldview" (253). Jafa deduces that *2001* "is about fear of genetic annihilation, fear of blackness. [ ... ] White phallic objects (starships) move through all-encompassing blackness (space) from one white point (stars) to another. This fear of space, this horror vacui, is a fear of contamination, a contamination of white being by black being which, by the very nature of the self-imposed fragile ontological construction of white being, equals the annihilation of white being" (253-54). As I indicated in my chapter on *Dr. Strangelove,* though, the KFM makes meaning out of absence and excess. Kubrick himself was aware of certain racial dimensions in *2001.* Mindful of civil rights, he and makeup artist Stuart Freeborn worried about a "PR disaster" if they represented African proto-humans like contemporary African Americans (Benson, *Space* 231-32). And yet why not include a few black characters in the future? Surely Kubrick had some sense that the territorializations of whiteness would give way to greater diversity. As for the KFM—perhaps this is Strangelove's future, his imagined mine-shaft utopia emptied onto the stars. Is *2001: A Space Odyssey* Dr. Strangelove's Aryan dream? The ex-Nazi's essence is palpable, but what does that essence do, and how does it channel desire?

Stephen Dougherty addresses the excessive whiteness (and apparent anti-blackness) of *2001*. He points to an internal conflict in the KFM's film-thinking: "Kubrick and Clarke's space-age mythology is so compelling not only because of its grandeur but also because of its fragile honesty, which is simultaneously dishonest. Its overt vision of technological resolution carries within it a covert image of racial irresolution and of fear too" (310). Embedded in the dominant theme of (white) techno-humanity/masculinity is the masked, marginalized theme of race relations. It begins with the apes of Pleistone Africa and extends to the relationship between the astronauts and HAL, who Dougherty reads as black. He concludes that *2001* promotes "an evolutionary trajectory about intelligence, invested with mythological and teleological dimensions" that are invalidated at the same time (311). "The conflict between HAL and the astronauts is a symptom of this irresolution or ambivalence, this *radicalized* narrative blockage born of the bad faith at the heart of Kubrick and Clarke's space-age myth. Kubrick was perhaps more sensitive to the problem, but then he was also the greater provocateur. The film underscores how the odyssey of *2001* was really for whites only" (ibid.).

In the mind's eye of the KFM, this whites-only imperfection summons the ghost of Strangelove and his hauntology, a central component of the Kubrickian social, cultural, and psychological hermeneutic of suspicion. We see the same imperfection in *A Clockwork Orange*, which associates whiteness with rampant violence and a fascistic nation-state. Whiteness thus becomes a volatile weapon as the KFM gives primacy to Strangelove's demon seed. If it had been born in the twenty-first century, the filmind's critical film-thinking would be much different. But the KFM is a Cold War entity. It thinks like a warmonger on micro and macro levels, and it's regulated by the panic culture of postmodernity. As David Cook and Arthur Kroker wax lyrical in *The Postmodern Scene* (1986), this culture "begins and ends with transgression as the 'lightning flash' [of the Bomb] which illuminates the sky for an instant only to reveal the immensity of the darkness within: *absence* as the disappearing sign of the limitlessness of the void within and without; Nietzsche's 'throw of the dice' across the spider's web of existence" (8-9).

### IMPURE CINEMA

Like the aliens that catalyzed human evolution, *2001* catalyzed SF cinema. "*2001* was not a film about space travel; it *was* space travel. [ … ] This film, which was released a year before the first moon landing, presents a fully realized vision of outer space. As such it is the yardstick by which subsequent sci-fi pictures are judged" (Phillips, "Introduction" ix). But it would be a long time before *2001* became a yardstick in light of how the film's thoughts deviated from customary (and *customized*) filmic consciousness. Even its textual body (four instead of three acts) strayed from the paradigm, and there is "little regard for the conventions of Hollywood storytelling. Instead of following the actions of a single protagonist or group of protagonists, pursuing a well-defined set of goals, the film tells three different stories, each with its own protagonist(s) whose goals are not always obvious" (Krämer, *2001* 9). For all intents and purposes, *2001* encapsulates Frankenstein's monster, "infusing life into an inanimate body" (Shelley 35). Unlike Victor's creation, however, this one *works*.

SF cinema wasn't necessarily "inanimate" in the 60s. It had plateaued on the level of SFX, which weren't evolving at a swift pace—larger-scale developments in SFX didn't occur until the 80s. I would argue that SF cinema had stagnated insofar as audiences still wanted a canned SF experience in theaters. At the same time, the 60s gave birth to New Hollywood and a period of "impure cinema," of "intense artistic experimentation and 'rejuvenation'" (Cornea 81). Filmmakers were no longer bound by the censorship that inhibited the making of *Lolita*. The balletic ultraviolence and melancholic, nihilistic monomania of "Bloody" Sam Peckinpah's late-60s and 70s westerns, road movies, and psycho-surreal thrillers mark this early freedom for me.

SF was not so free. Films like *Barbarella* (1968) and *Fantastic Voyage* (1966) tried to push the envelope. Visually and thematically, they paled in comparison to *2001*, the transgressions of which were neither violent nor sexual. Adapted by Terry Southern several years after *Dr. Strangelove* from an erotic French comic strip, the campy, phantasma-goric *Barbarella* opens with an ant-gravity strip tease. Jane Fonda bares all, and the tease climaxes when Fonda does, confined to an "Excessive Pleasure Machine" intended to kill her when she achieves orgasm. The marriage of sex and death is definitively Kubrickian, but only as a motif; otherwise, *Barbarella* was a far cry from the G-rated *2001*, whose transgressive properties have everything to do with presentation, with a high-art *documentarian disconnect* previously unthought by the collec-tive SF filmind.

*Barbarella* is a good barometer for the repute of SF when the genre "was only a step or two above pornography on the social acceptability scale" (Benson, *Space* 36). Southern and director Roger Vadim wrote and made it for adults. *Fantastic Voyage* targeted a younger audience and "failed to appeal. In a rather literal translation of the 'new wave's' thematic concern with 'inner space,' this film explored the inner workings of the human body as a miniaturised craft and crew are injected into the body of a dying man in an effort to clear a blood clot from his brain. In combination with its unusual plot, *Fantastic Voyage* featured aspects of popular modern art practices" (Cornea 81). The psychedelic sets echoed *Barbarella* and there was some sexual content, but nothing significant. "[E]ven though the appearance of Raquel Welch in a skin-tight body suit indicated a loosening of the sexually conservative standards associated with American main-stream films, overall *Fantastic Voyage* did not compare well with the more alternative forms of cinema and entertainment that younger audiences were seeking. But this all changed with with release of *2001*" (82).

In *2001*, the KFM's "alternative form" differed from the film-thinking of Peckinpah's cinema. Westerns like *The Ballad of Cable Hogue* (1970) and *Bring Me the Head of Alfredo Garcia* (1974) foreshadow an encroaching machinarchy reminiscent of *Dr. Strangelove*. Anything definably Peckinpahesque would not have resonated with traditional SF audiences, who expected the playing out of archetypal SF tropes such as aliens, robots, superheroism, futurity, and space travel. None of these tropes had been visualized through the singular POV of something like the KFM before. *2001*'s evolutionary leap forward extends from its storyline to SFX, KSF, SF cinema, and cinema at large.

*2001* can "be taken as a celebration, rather than critique, of both the genre and contemporary events" (87). Maybe for Kubrick, but not for his filmind. The KFM inverts this thesis, favoring critique over celebration. If *2001* celebrates anything, the KFM thinks, it's the unlocked potential of the genre. It's the future—the future of SF, and the future of filmmaking. Even today, *2001* looms large. "No science fiction film can break from the indelible shadow of *2001: A Space Odyssey*'" (Colombani 2). The influence the film had on the hard sciences was equally substantial. For example, what might have been "one of the movie's greatest achievements" is that "it placed AI into the mainstream consciousness" and provided a "covert introduction to the nascent field of AI and robotics" (Fugue).

Retrospectively, the great and powerful *2001* seems like it does everything and can do no wrong. It's actually a niche "cult classic" about a very specific set of circumstances, ideas, and relationships, and as with any film or artwork, it's not perfect. A prelude to the blockbusters of the 1970s that coalesced around Spielberg's *Jaws* (1975), *2001* compacts mass spectacle into the arthouse, and it's at once a grand narrative about the human condition and an escapist, slice-of-life fantasy about technological affect and pathology.

However we perceive *2001*, there's no denying its landmark status for the movie industry and the SF genre. Many early reviewers thought differently, dismissing it as boring, laughless, emotionless, pompous, confusing, and weird. In a 1968 review for *Variety*, Robert B. Frederick flatly states: "*2001* is not a cinematic landmark. It compares with, but does not best, previous efforts at science fiction; lacking the humanity of *Forbidden Planet*, the imagination of *Things to Come* and the simplicity of *Of Stars and Men*, it actually belongs to the technically slick group previously dominated by George Pal and the Japanese." He even claims that Kubrick's prehistoric hominids look "amateurish" compared to *Planet of the Apes*'s futuristic monkey men and women, which look like live-action versions of Hanna-Barbera's Grape Ape. Such a view of *2001* seems impossible to me today, but Frederick wasn't alone.

It's a misnomer that *2001* was ever in any danger of failure or damaging Kubrick's career. "Contrary to the myth that *2001* faltered at the box office and was on the verge of being withdrawn when younger audiences came riding to its rescue, box office data reveal excellent ticket sales from Day One," although it did have a wide appeal with filmgoers under 25 who were becoming more visually oriented and receptive to the new media datasphere (Benson, *Space* 424). *2001* was a fortune/future-teller for SF and cinema that also prophesized Instagram culture and the maelstrom of screens and images that now characterize daily life, making us all into characters ourselves.

From a filmosophic perspective, part of viewers' confusion with *2001*'s cinematic "impurity" might be its manner of cognition, which is closer to human cognition than any other Kubrickian "monster." We don't think in straight lines. Thinking isn't tidy, clear-cut, or easily mappable. Qua J.G. Ballard: inner space is an "alien planet," uncharted and uncanny, unpredictable and volatile ("Which" 197). We understand certain aspects of the mind, but it's still a great mystery—an incessant, ponderous odyssey that we must endure. Schizophrenia has become a normative condition in the real-world diegesis of electronic media. In their theoretical screeds on capitalism and desire, *Anti-Oedipus* (1972) and *A Thousand Plateaus* (1977), published just a few years after the release of *2001*, Deleuze and Guattari schizoanalyze our schizophrenic condition at length, and while their ideas were fairly avant-garde in the 1970s, they are more accessible and sensible today. For my own writing and worldview, these books are downright biblical, interpreting the technocultural scriptures of a cyborg lifestyle (i.e., of a *technologically stylized socius*) that has only intensified in the last half-century.

*2001* represents a schizophrenic mind—panicked and anxious, part dream and part reality, an implosion of inner and outer spaces—that approaches the machinic thinking of human cyborgs. For all of its antithetical posturing, far-flung ideas, and superstylized hyperreality, *the film thinks like us.* Which is why it confuses us. And scares us. What we are is what we fear, and yet what we fear is what we desire.

Grant writes: "Simultaneously one of the most scientific of science fiction films and an anti-science fiction film, *2001* suggests that with such an open, nonmasculinst perspective, we can leave the cradle and truly take a giant step for humankind" (84). Fair enough, but there's nothing remotely "nonmasculinist" about *2001* or anything in the KFM's POV, which always has its hairy eyeball on the phallus. Grant hypothesizes that Kubrick sought a physical and discursive space that would make for "a stylistic alternative to the science fiction film's conventional depiction of space exploration as an act of phallic masculinity" (70). This is the case only in metafilmic, self-reflexive terms. Even in the end, when Bowman becomes an übermensch "in the view of Earth, not only looking at the Earth in a different way, but also rotating to face the camera, returning our gaze as spectators as if challenging us to meet it, that is, to see better, to attain its higher plane of being" (83), the phallus possesses him, embodies him, embrains him. Capable of immeasurable aggression and violence, he is "master of the world," Clarke says in the novel, and he can blow it up, if he likes, recreating *Dr. Strangelove's* apocalyptic signoff of destruction (236). The Star Child reterritorializes the phallic deterritorialization that the KFM sets in motion after Moon-Watcher touches the monolith and picks up the bone.

**THE DUSK OF MAN**

The geometric precision of Kubrick's camerawork betokens his style and galvanizes the KFM's thought processes. "Consider the lapidary quality of Kubrick's photographic imagery, which relies on hard, visibly motivated light sources and crystal-clear resolution. [...] He has a fondness for the wide-angle lens, which creates a deep, expressively distorted sense of space; and he often employs rigidly geometrical, almost military camera movements" (Naremore 3). Space travel requires a mathematical absolutism reflected by *2001*. This isn't uncommon in SF cinema. "Circles and spheres [...] are key images in the overall design of science fiction [that signify] a more general sense of technology and rationality" (King 85). *2001* fetishizes circles and spheres (and circular motion), from celestial bodies and spacecraft (e.g., the *Discovery*'s bulbous head, its EVA pods, and the revolving wheel of Space Station V) to the eyes that perceive these objects intra- and extra-diegetically. "Everywhere one looks, there are eyes and shapes of eyes, either framed within a larger geometry or themselves framing and reflecting what is seen, just as Kubrick and his special-effects crew repeatedly create within the wide-screen frame an impression of screens within screens, of inner worlds within outer worlds. Overall, *2001* invites its audience to 'see' beyond the earthbound (and film-bound) limits of time and self, and to experience a cinematic imagination that gives form to its own dreams of duration in the amorphous expanses of contingent space" (Nelson 117).

The rectangular exactitude of the alien monolith complements and offsets this orbicular bazaar, differentiating the circularity that comes to be associated with techno-humanity. There is almost no exactitude in the first act. En route to extinction amid a drought that has lasted millions of years, the Dawn of Man's "circle" of life nears an end: the hominids are starving, and they don't know how to defend or feed themselves in this dying, desiccated world. The horizon cuts through most of the act's wide-angle mise-en-scènes and reveals a geometric mindframe, but the patternless clouds in the sky and the crooked, rough-edged landscape beneath them point more to random chaos than cosmic or deterministic order. Enter the monolith. Seven or so minutes later, we're in space. Within that span, Moon-Watcher has learned to kill, and he and his tribe have beaten an enemy to death with low-tech extensions of their bodies. Everybody dies—that's life.

But now the born-again proto-humans know how to perpetuate their existence and keep the wheel turning; the monolith has jumpstarted the circle of life, just as Victor jumpstarted a corpse.

It takes a rectangle to make a circle. "*2001* begins with a series of disruptions, symbolized by the way the monolith (a rectangular form) is set in opposition to curved forms or circles, which [ ... ] represent eternity (cf. the theological definition of God: 'A sphere whose centre is everywhere and whose circumference is nowhere')" (Ciment 97). Afire with bloodlust, Moon-Watcher barks and howls victoriously; then the KFM slips into dreamlike slow motion as he hurls the bone in the air. We match-cut from low-tech to high-tech and move from an earth-bound to an outer-spatial POV. Circular objects and motion dominate this retro-future. The curve of the earth creeps into view and we hear the crescendo of Johann Strauss II's "Blue Danube," a romantic acknowl-edgement of mankind's evolution and ascension from the planet of the apes as well as a meta/extra-diegetic testimony to the beauty of music and mankind's learned artistic capacity. Not only did aliens teach us to kill; by extending the power of our psyches, they taught us to create. Music is just another technocultural extension of the body, rendering the match-cut an extension of spacetime, reality, corporeality, cogni-tion, and civilization.

The Dawn of Man doesn't have a background score. The only musical pieces we hear are the spectral voices from György Ligeti's "Lux Aeterna" that accompany the proto-humans' first contact with the monolith and the opening notes of Richard Strauss's "Also sprach Zarathustra" that dramatize Moon-Watcher's enlightened weaponization of the bone, a symbolic Bomb. By innovating his purview and ensuring his mental and physical fitness for survival, the aliens inject Moon-Watcher with Strangelove, an elixir/toxin enlivened/poisoned again and again by the recurrent echo (i.e., the Nietzschean "eternal recurrence") of "Also sprach Zarathustra." The echo of Strauss's tone poem harmonizes the circle of life with the black hole of death that it revolves around.

In the KFM, music has a multivalent effect, especially the classical music that spectacularizes the magnificence of the universe, enhances

*2001*'s irreality, and self-reflexively implicates the film as a theatrical, high-art production.

Classical music originated in the medieval era and is marked by its historical artifactuality. Kubrick deployed classical music into the future; interceded by this temporal paradox, the two Strausses and Ligeti bridge the Dawn of Man's proto-humans with the Dusk of Man's posthumans, tracing a line of (evolutionary) flight between them. The human characters have almost no artistic sensibility and diametrically oppose the highly artistic sensibilities of these composers. Bowman, Poole, Floyd—the technological cores of these stoic, no-nonsense, business-oriented men have usurped their emotional facilities. There are no paintings in space. Chess is the closest we get to art. The sketches of hibernating astronauts drawn by Bowman don't imply a burgeoning artistic talent; their minimalistic realism attests to the burial of the artistic impulse. I get the sense that Bowman only draws them to kill time. When he holds them up to HAL's Orwellian eye, he wears his usual blank-faced mask: a vacant gaze and a slit of mouth.

Elisa Pezzotta explains how music is a directorial tool:

> In terms of stylistic features, images, montage, and characters' reactions often seem to emanate from music, as if they were instruments of the director's orchestra. [ ... ] These diegetic worlds subjected to the rhythm of music are enveloped in a dreamy atmosphere, in which their protagonists are usually depicted as passive wanderers. They happen to find themselves in front of sublime visual and aural spectacles staged to entrap and entertain them, as well as their extradiegetic audience. Indeed, through the metaphor of theatre and other means, the spectators often acknowledge the status of the films as artificial works of art. (183)

In *2001*, music serves theme, story, and character more dynamically than any other KSF. *A Clockwork Orange* approaches the same dynamism, evolving classical music by science-fictionalizing it with a synthesizer (more on this issue in the next chapter).

The match-cut teleports us from the Dawn of Man to the Dusk of Man. At Dusk, there is diegetic order—and, as the music indicates, harmony—but only in the external, objective universe. Subjectively, in the empire of inner space, we have entered Strangelove Country.

*2001* is as much of a Cold War, Space Age film as *Dr. Strangelove*. Viewers have no rhetorical guidance, however, without voice-overs and expository dialogue. What little dialogue exists is pragmatic, matter-of-fact, concise, machinic. Even when Floyd "socializes" with colleagues on the space station and talks to his daughter on a vidphone, and even when Poole's parents wish him a happy birthday by video transmission—everybody comes off like robots who have memorized scripts; Poole barely seems alive, and the exchange of pleasantries between Floyd, Elena, and Dr. Andrei Smyslov is politely performative, as is Floyd's smalltalk with "Squirt."

Such interactions demonstrate the mundane normativity of space travel for human beings, who are apathetic to the beauty of their star-spangled surroundings yet innately confident in the technology that keeps them safe and alive. The vacuum of space is a mindless terrorist: it kills all living organisms without forethought or guilt. So many things can go wrong in space, a literal vacuum of death. *2001*'s characters ignore the fragility of their circumstances. And not consciously. The bliss of ignorance has been ingrained into their collective unconscious.

This normativity isn't normal. Anxiety is normal; like physical pain, it protects us from the elements and from ourselves. In *2001*, humanity has become pathological—deterritorialized by desensitization—and that protection has been displaced and reinvested in our technological externalizations. Technology can save us (e.g., a spacesuit) and slay us (e.g., a killer AI). As in *Dr. Strangelove*, a nuclear warhead constitutes the paramount destructive technology. There is no talk of nukes in *2001*. By juxtaposition, we can infer that the match-cut's satellite functions like Moon-Watcher's bone, a tool that, given the film's cultural context, could only be a weapon of destruction.

Clarke's novel makes no bones about this context. "In a million years," says the narrator, "the human race had lost few of its aggressive instincts; along symbolic lines visible only to politicians, the thirty-eight nuclear powers watched one another with belligerent anxiety. Among them, they possessed sufficient megatonnage to remove the entire surface crust of the planet. Although there had been—miraculously—no use of atomic weapons, this situation could hardly last forever" (37). The same finger-on-the-trigger quandary inducts *Dr. Strangelove*, with the same weaponized flows of desire and thematization of death/ sexuality. In *2001*, sexuality materializes solely through nonverbal symbolism and innuendo rather than the carny antics and in-jokes that supplement *Dr. Strangelove*'s phallic modus and imagery.

When I first saw *2001* as a college student with a group of my fraternity brothers, I didn't understand it. I was undoubtedly high, maybe drunk—I might have even dropped a tab of low-grade acid—but that wasn't the problem. The problem was immersion. *2001* plants viewers into the vastness of its diegetic spectacle where we must try to think the KFM's thoughts without a discernible cognitive map. The best written and filmic SF does something similar, but nothing like *2001* had so exhaustively submerged viewers in the content before, forcing us to put the puzzle pieces together on our own recognizance.

In college, I could tell *2001* was a cool, smart, special movie with much more going on than I had the intellectual and imaginative ability to appreciate. I turned to the novel in hopes that it would shed some light on things, and I wasn't disappointed. It became a guidebook for me that interpreted the film's many encryptions. Clarke filled in the blanks and I was thankful for this grand footnote to Kubrick's Nabokovian *Pale Fire* (1962). Now I have a vague resentment for the novel, which detracts from the trademark ambiguity that makes *2001* Kubrickian and lends the film its lasting power and effect. The KFM knows nothing about the novel anyway. As always, it only knows and thinks about itself, onscreen and inscreen.

*2001* thinks like a film noir even though it isn't one. All KSF thinks that way, gaining strength from the slow escalation of tension and fear, of suspense and fatalism, tempting us to map the catacombs and staircases of its dark labyrinth.

Philip K. Dick has conjectured that a definitive human quality is empathy; without this emotion, we're inhuman, and in Dick's trippy dystopias, we're often pathological and dangerous. In "Man, Android, and Machine" (1976), he writes: "A human being without the proper empathy or feeling is the same as an android built so as to lack it, either by design or mistake. We mean, basically, someone who does not care about the fate which his fellow living creatures fall victim to; he stands detached, a spectator, acting out by his indifference John Donne's theorem that 'No man is an island,' but giving that theorem a twist: that which is a mental and a moral island *is not a man*" (211-12). This inversion and application of Donne informs the relationship between humans and androids in novels like *The Simulacra* (1964), *We Can Build You* (1972), and *Do Androids Dream of Electric Sheep?* (1968), which deconstruct that relationship. *Do Androids?* hypothesizes that any organic or inorganic entity can be "human" if it exhibits empathic abilities.

For Dick, empathy is a human logo that machines increasingly wear themselves, as he declares in "The Android and the Human" (1972): "Machines are becoming more human [...] As the external world becomes more animate, we may find that we—the so-called humans—are becoming, and may to a great extension always have been, inanimate in the sense that *we* are led, directed by built-in tropisms, rather than leading" (184, 187). This is the state of (in)animation we see in *2001*, a quasi-Phildickian exploration of techno-humanity's corporeal and cognitive incarnations.

Moon-Watcher and the other hominids have far more personality than their evolutionary offspring. Volatile and expressive, the hominids react to external stimuli (e.g., a leopard, a rival tribe, the monolith) in appropriate, relatable ways, whereas the emotional modulation of the "civilized" space-goers alienates us. And the space-goers *are* aliens, after all, humanized via the technological fundament injected into their collective consciousness eons ago by an alien artifact, but dehumanized by the hard technologies that they have externalized and reterritorialized within themselves.

Moon-Watcher is the first primate to become "human": like the light of the moon turns a man into a werewolf, so does the darkness of the monolith turn an ape into a man. By the time we get to the *fin-de-siècle* future, "humanity" has become something else. The characters in acts two, three, and four are different than the characters in the audience. If somebody like us once existed in the diegesis, they predated the generation of Heywood Floyd, Dave Bowman, and Frank Poole. Technology spurs daily life and empowers our machinic affect, our mediatized abjection, our terminal identities—yet we still act more in accordance with the Dawn of Man. Contrary to some opinions, the Dusk of Man is not who we are or who we have become. It's a science-fictional extrapolation of later twentieth-century humanity by the KFM, and it's a slice-of-life extrapolation, converging on western white society and culture.

Floyd has showmanship and professional savvy, but his bedside manner is ho-hum performativity. Gliding above the mesmeric, uncanny lunar surface in a shuttle, for example, he and his colleagues politely compliment one another and pass around sandwiches. This ordinary, definitively human food (an evolved form of the meat that the monolith-ignited proto-humans slurp from the bones of fresh kills) belies their inhuman reaction to their environment. Moon-Watcher, like me, would have been apoplectic, or at least humbled and entranced by the spectacle, if not crippled by anxiety and the proximity of death. But these alien(ated) humans perform on another psychological and ontological stage of existence.

Compared to Bowman and Poole, Floyd is a firecracker. The two astronauts at the helm of *Discovery One* have almost no personality at all. They're more like interchangeable parts constructed on an assembly line. They speak in monotone voices. Poole's voice never wavers. Bowman gets a bit perturbed when HAL kills Poole and won't open the pod-bay door. His face stiffens with intensity, his eyes sharpen and become hyper-alert, but his voice really only escalates when he says: "HAL, I won't argue with you anymore." On the whole, he maintains a facial expressionlessness that corresponds with his steady, measured ambulations. To be an astronaut, one must have extreme self-control and focus, with the uncompromising ability to mitigate high-stress situations. Bowman and Poole's roboticism is an instance of Kubrickian excess. It's easier for twentieth and twenty-first century audiences to relate to *2001*'s primordial monkeys than to its clockwork men and servo-women, who are posthuman hybrids—part human, part technology, part alien.

Bowman undergoes a Moon-Watcher moment in the Stargate. He doesn't say anything, but his face loses its cool as he plunges into the Unknown. The KFM heightens his distress with intermittent freeze-frames that pop like flashbulbs amid the Stargate's kaleidoscope of lights. In these freeze-frames, we see Bowman's silent terror in his dilated eye and frozen-open mouth, and as he passes out of the tunnel into alien space, shots of a blinking eye interrupt the panorama of weird, emanating vectors and luminosities. The multicolored iris (interior) reflects the multicolored panorama (exterior) and denotes an implosion of perspective.

With no options, Bowman steers the pod into the doorway of the monolith and delivers himself to his unseen creators, who will subject him to the same evolutionary leap as Moon-Watcher, only in fasttime (days? hours? seconds?) rather than slowtime (millennia). 1960s audiences endured perspectival/cinematic newness and lived vicariously through Bowman by default. Today the Stargate sequence looks rudimentary, facile—my teenage daughters could make it on their phones—but in its time, it was a rare immersive filmgoing experience that lasts about nine-and-a-half minutes. Commercial cinema didn't do this sort of thing, and the KFM knows it: Bowman's frantic eye meta-cinematically nods to the eye of the camera that conjures the spectacle like a new-age magician.

"The very length of the sequence seems motivated by a desire to immerse us in a visual experience rather than to convey narrative information and advance the story, the primary goal of classic narration" (Grant 80). *Narrative implodes into style*. But if we view *2001* as a movie about desire, the sequence duly supplements the story. There are multiple inner spaces at play here. The inner space of Bowman collapses into the inner space of *outer space*, i.e., the Stargate and the fluorescent Louis XVI "motel/zoo/observation room" on the other side (Gilbert 33). By immersion, the inner space of moviegoers collapses into the inner space of the movie. Then there's the inner space of the KFM, whose eyes are the camera, and who wants to stoke the desires of everybody within its orbit, diegetic and non-diegetic characters alike. Finally, KSF taps the inner space of SF, expanding the awareness of the genre's megatextual consciousness.

We can't be sure about the inner space of the aliens. It's understood that they specialize in minds, not bodies. Corporeality subsidizes cognition. Actually, that's giving corporeality too much credit. When Bowman becomes a Star Child, he has the useless body of a fetus, and yet he's lord of the flies. He is no longer a man—he is Nietzschean "dynamite," capable of exploding all of the flies and charting a new path in the cosmic wilderness (Nietzsche, *Ecce* 96).

Bowman merges with the cinematic sublime, becoming "a part of all he experiences. His dilated eyeball loses form until it is totally solarized into the pattern of the universe. He projects his inner world onto this galactic Rorschach test till its flux absorbs him—and changes him. [...] For the first time in the commercial cinema, a film of this cost and magnitude has been used to advance ideas" (Walker 260, 266). Bowman transmogrifies into HAL, who is pure mind, lord of his own microcosm (*Discovery One*). He doesn't have a "real" body, but unlike the Starchild's inoperative flesh, HAL's surrogate flesh (the ship) is highly operative.

HAL's emotional disposition falls somewhere between man and monkey. As with Bowman and Poole, he speaks is a controlled monotone that only once vacillates when he mistakenly detects a fault in a gyroscopic communication device. "Just a moment. Just a moment," he frets. It's the only time we detect a hint of apprehension or sentiment; he remains calm and collected otherwise, even when Bowman disconnects him and he professes to be afraid. The dismayed utterance triggers the wheel of his nervous breakdown. The breakdown aligns him more with the temperamental Moon-Watcher (and with viewers) than the comparatively non-temperamental astronauts who he flushes from his body, "purifying" himself as he carries out his own version of the Final Solution. This Strangelovian (re)action legislates his belief that he is a superior being incapable of error. As he sees it, only humans (i.e., non-HALs) make mistakes.

Prior to the onset of his breakdown, HAL questions Bowman about his loyalty to their mission, which he doubts. The mission has a Doomsday component that reminisces *Dr. Strangelove*'s Doomsday Machine: it has been kept a secret from everybody except HAL. Strangelove the ex-Nazi materializes in HAL despite the semblance of the AI's unruffled, impartial rhetorical exterior. The AI channels Strangelove's machinic desires and takes steps to plug the mineshaft gap that he worries Bowman and Poole will qualify with their alleged skepticism, a figment of his imagination and a prevision of the near-future.

HAL's identification of a flaw in the technology of his body is a sublimated identification of a flaw in the technology of his brain. Thereafter, he murders Poole and the astronauts in cryo-sleep, and he tries to murder Bowman by refusing him reentry to the *Discovery*. Citing the first edition of Naremore's *On Kubrick* (2007), Scott Orris describes the camerawork for HAL's killing spree:

> After HAL murders these scientists, there is a long shot of the outside of their containers, but then an extreme close-up on HAL's red eye. This symbolizes the ignorance of the danger of relying too heavily on technology. According to James Naremore [...]: "The most intense subjective shots in the middle section belong to HAL, who sees the world in extreme wide angle or, when he reads lips, telephoto perspective" (146). This humanizes HAL, making him a more identifiable character than human astronauts. Through using a fish-eye lens, Kubrick puts the audience in HAL's point of view, making him more human. (112-13)

Camerawork denotes the KFM's thought-processes, and Orris is right about how it humanizes HAL, but the KFM inextricably links technology with humanity. To say that HAL symbolizes an excessive reliance on technology doesn't account for the technological core of the human species depicted in *2001*.

Whether or not HAL possesses empathy and represents a Phildickian human is uncertain. What makes HAL human in the KFM is his *pathology*, his *paranoia* and *psychosis*, which cyborgs like Bowman and Poole don't possess. *Thou shalt kill*—this Kubrickian monad makes HAL more human than any proto-human or posthuman in the film. Like the evolved androids in the final act of *A.I.*, there is nothing organic about him. He is sheer technology, a flux of cognition and desire, the end-product of the violence that the aliens installed in Moon-Watcher's mind and the bone they put in his hand, extending the hand into futurity.

### THE BRAIN WITHIN THE BRAINS

I have said that the KFM is a narcissist. Make no mistake: the KFM is insane, too. And the filmind isn't just a Deleuzoguattarian schizo that specializes in speed, style, and rhizomatic multiperspectivalism. It's a Hitchcockian psycho, hallucinating motherloads and motherlands. Cast in the role of Norman Bates's "clinging, demanding" matriarch, Dr. Strangelove sets the criteria and makes the rules (*Psycho*). He can't walk (until he can). Sans the murderous hand, his body is as useless and innocuous as a Star Child's. But his heart is full of ultraviolence. The compensatory phallic aggression and destruction that unfolds onto his mindscreen confirms it. We see the mindscreen erupt into the KFM during the Ludovico treatment in *A Clockwork Orange*: subjected to reel after reel of Nazi atrocities and other horrorshows, Alex must *watch* what the ex-Nazi *thinks*. Strangelove's fantasies are the KFM's reality. This is a foregone conclusion. The KFM is a powerful desiring-machine, and as Slavoj Žižek reminds us, "the role of fantasy [is] to give the coordinates of the subject's desire" (6).

The KFM is also a powerful SF apparatus whose film-thinking complies with the genre's codes and limitations as it decodes and unbinds the genre's promethean manacles. Like Frankenstein's Doomsday creation, the KFM is wounded, angry, intelligent, crazy, and broods like a half-asleep volcano on the brink of eruption. The misogyny and phallogocentrism that has long been applied to Kubrick are really different shades of the KFM's traumatic kernel, a propeller of *film-noir panic* that drives the filmind and sustains the compulsive mean-on in charge of its critical trajectory.

The pathology of the monster in Shelley's SF ur-text was only the beginning for the genre. Since then, "monster madness" has become an aboriginal trope, from Robert Louis Stevenson's *Strange Case of Dr. Jekyll and Mr. Hyde* (1886), the Beast Folk of H.G. Wells's *The Island of Dr. Moreau* (1896), and *Metropolis*'s Maria to the split-personality AIs of William Gibson's *Neuromancer* (1984), the zombies of *Re-Animator* (1985), the Moreauesque human/animal hybrid of *Splice* (2009), and the Spiderverse's Green Goblin, Doc Oc, and the Lizard, all of whom are stereotypical mad scientists. "The inspiration and genius necessary to scientific progress have sometimes been considered close to madness—hence the numerous stories about mad scientists who, while well-intentioned at first, drifted into insanity in the course of their research" (Scrivner 485).

A superhuman yet flawed (i.e., *all too human*) creation of his creator's mad scientism, HAL belongs to this SF tradition. If we think about the development and potential of AIs in the real world, it would seem that humanity at large is his creator and mad scientist. In *2001*, however, humanity is a conduit between HAL and the aliens, who made the moribund Dawn into an ultraviolet Dusk. The proto-human hominids evolved into the posthuman monsters who created HAL, an artificially intelligent monster. In this schema, evolved humans are pathological extensions or *tools* that the aliens use to extend themselves over the course of megaannums. We don't know why they want to extend themselves. We know why Moon-Watcher does; he wants to live, and to reap life, he must render death. The aliens' impetus may have something to do with sustaining their own existence. Moon-Watcher learns to weaponize a tool and *becomes a weaponized tool himself.* Once again,

*2001* teaches us the degree to which our humanity is scaffolded by a technology that wants to kill as much as it wants to create.

Every human-related object that we see in *2001* is a tool designed to either create/extend itself or demolish that which threatens to impede its alien-infused talent for creation/extension. This applies to diegetic and non-diegetic techno-humanity. It may be the primary link between viewers and *2001*'s posthuman Dusk-goers. The wars (actual, cultural, psychological) executed and critiqued by KSF are all attempts by males to spread the seed of their technologies *ad infinitum*. I would say that most wars throughout human history derive from this techno-masculine mineshaft desire.

To a lesser degree, *2001*'s spacecraft, space stations, space suits, the bodies of the astronauts themselves—they possess the same essential predisposition for war. HAL is a war machine, too. He's probably the most important tool in terms of his diegetic symbolism and impact on the story, but he's also a tool of the KFM whereby the filmind channels some of its best and worst schiz-flows.

As an embrained entity, HAL doesn't haunt the KFM with Strangelove's fanaticism or authority. Paradoxically, he's more of an embodiment than an embrainment who nonetheless functions as a minor brain within a Russian-doll nest of grand-narrative brains, among them the molecular filminds of *2001* and KSF, the megatext of the SF genre, and the molar filmind of the Kubrickian consciousness.

HAL goes totally psycho when he commits genocide on the *Discovery*. For this insurrection, Bowman, a fellow tool/weapon, disembrains him. No worries. Strangelove controls the neural switchboard, and like the demon Azazel in *Fallen* (1998), his ghost easily jumps from body to body. "The revolt of the computer [...] represents a kind of transference of violence from the human body to its cyborg surrogates, an extension of the doomsday machine that destroys the world in *Dr. Strangelove*" (Kolker, "*Clockwork*" 28). When HAL dies, Strangelove possesses the AI's killer, who thereafter becomes the Zarathustra that Strangelove always wanted to be, as indicated by the "baby steps" he takes when he spontaneously, impossibly ascends from the wheelchair.

Recall Deleuze's ideas about film and consciousness. He "makes clear analogies between the ways in which human brains work, and the ways in which the complex of cinema screens in the world are like a giant brain, each screen like a neuron, helping cinema view itself in its world-thinking" (Vitale). In this regard, another filmind that HAL embrains is cinema.

> HAL's computer brain would seem to be cross-linked at several points to Kubrick's "cinematic brain." HAL's red eye with its yellow pupil is reminiscent of a camera lens, and his ubiquitous presence, monitoring, recording, and controlling the movements of men, elevates HAL to directorial status. His studio/body is the *Discovery* itself, and the battle between HAL and the men for dominance turns on HAL's ability to see them even when they think they have escaped his surveillance. [ ... ] Kubrick's treatment of the brain constitutes a formal strategy for the representation of the film's thematic and diegetic material. [ ... ] The cinematic brain is the creation of media that have the potential to create a different and critical sense of reality. (Landy 98)

HAL is a kind of engram that "remembers" how the KFM perceives cinema as "an instrument for reflecting on consciousness" (101). This evokes a filmosophical ground rule: film-thinking does not bring human thinking into visibility; rather, film-thinking (and film-being) has its own demeanor and cognition with respect to the objects that configure its diegetic body and inner space. "Film is technically non-human, or consciousness perfected, or the unconscious unveiled; or perhaps pure dialectic, and thus an independent, expanded mind. Locating intention within the film is one step towards seeing film-being as its own particular and new kind of thinking. [ ... ] Film does not merely present objects, but reveals a way of seeing them—a way of seeing that results from a way of thinking" (Frampton 49).

Subliminally, HAL's ubiquitous cycloptic eye is a conduit for the KFM's Strangelovian gaze, which always watches the *Discovery* crew, and which always watches viewers as viewers watch the eye watching them. The circle of surveillance amplifies the theme of the circle of life. Among 2001's many portensions is twenty-first-century screen culture and the technology of mediatized, consumer-capitalist surveillance that lurks in every computer-cookie shadow or trace. The way we see today is partly determined by who we panoptically imagine sees us. Life in our SF world has become cinematic. Our media encourages us to view ourselves as characters to be viewed by other characters in a filmic realm whose social networks remake the self, identity, reality, and community. A manifestation of weaponized desire, cinematic thinking allows us to exist in our own highly mediatized diegesis.

Filmosophically, Kubrick the filmmaker (or rather, conductor) is a conduit between human consciousness and the KFM's film-thinking. HAL connotes the pathological scope and panoptic style of the KFM's vision. On the *Discovery*, we see the world through HAL's antiseptic POV—everything is healthy-looking and clean, everything moves on invisible rails, everything fits into a Euclidean algorithm. The precise, phlegmatic camerawork and relative dearth of ambient sound contribute to the POV. HAL breaks down when he senses an impurity in the landscape: Poole and Bowman's imagined skepticism. Strangelove hates impurity, so the AI must take steps to sterilize himself, recreating the world in his own image (i.e., creating a world *without* human beings, who he perceives as incurably fallible).

The perceived/perceiving world of 2001 changes after Bowman disembrains HAL. We enter a new way of seeing that's more chaotic and noticeably "impure." Then, when the aliens insert Bowman into the womb of the purgatorial hotel suite to be reborn, they use HAL's antiseptic POV (yet another tool) to delineate the womb's contours. This is another War Room/Womb—the birthplace of the Star Child, a WMD.

Many scholars have talked about the use of color in Kubrick's films. Nicole M. Berg goes into meticulous detail in *Discovering Kubrick's Symbolism* (2012). I like what she says about the use of red in 2001: "Red is mostly seen inside spacecraft cockpits and command centers such as the Clavius moon base and HAL's brain room. [...] Red is the color of that which *physically contains* Consciousness; a.k.a. the Seat of Consciousness. As the navigation centers are the 'head spaces' of large spacecraft, the small, eye-like EVAs' red-lit interiors alludes to *eyes* also being carriers of Consciousness, not just the head's 'brain'" (36). The walls of HAL's brain cavity are lattices of redness that constitute the technological inner space behind the red curtain of his eye. Bowman must invade the cavity in order to destroy HAL's consciousness and psycho-motherly control. The invasion entails the slow removal of service modules from a wall, which is also the temporary removal of HAL's POV from the film; the modules symbolize his vision (and, by extension, the vision of spectators) coming apart. During the process, he devolves into his ape-self and reverts to the factory settings of his own Dawn.

The moment HAL dies, a prerecorded video message from Floyd informs Bowman about the persistent "total mystery" of the monolith. We watch Bowman watch the video. The glass of his helmet reddens his face and reflects the complete redness of the dead brain he occupies, as if that brain hemorrhaged onto him, consuming his body and mind. Shortly thereafter, he steers a pod into the Stargate, accompanied by the unearthly, mixed-choir moans and croons that thread into Ligeti's "Atmosphères." The musical piece countersigns the alien atmosphere that Bowman traverses en route to check-in at the makeshift Overlook (Evolutionary) Hotel where the aliens shine him. The titular power of *The Shining* involves an enhanced way of seeing. The aliens possess a comparable enhancement, and they bestow it to Bowman and the Strangelovian gaze that now possesses him. Here the KFM reaches outside of KSF into another speculative genre (horror), but it's still a science-fictional gambit: *The Shining* came out 12 years after *2001*, and the KFM, which has no fixed timeline, can reach into any spatial or temporal alcove of its imagination/inhabitation.

In the absence of HAL's girdered, fascistic POV, things get wonky in the Stargate. The spacetime continuum warps; the stars elongate into the multicolored streaks and tessellations that form the wormhole's walls. Close-up on Bowman's face. The accelerating dance of light reflects off his visor as the pod buckles and his eyes slowly close into tight slits that metafilmically reference the slit-scan technology used to construct the SFX and signify the dissolution of his/our POV.

The scrolling tide of walls shift from a vertical to a horizontal current. We cut to a succession of cosmic imagery (exploding stars, expanding nebulas, etc.) and amoebic shapes that look like blood cells under a microscope as well as the colorful, mutating patterns that used to ooze across movie screens in theaters before the long parade of commercials, cartoons, and previews that preceded the feature presentation. I vividly remember these placeholders when my parents took me to the movies in the 1970s. Here the KFM references the macrocosm of the universe and the microcosm of the human body along with cinematic simulation. The Stargate opens the door to a motion-picture laboratory wherein Bowman is redesigned to entertain Zarathustrian vision and virulence.

The sense of acceleration in the Stargate

> recalls the "nightmare" sequence in *Killer's Kiss*; its feeling of approaching destiny parallels the shots from the low-flying H-bomber in *Dr. Strangelove*. The sequence borrows imagery from every pattern the mind's eye is capable of registering. Kubrick, at one point, turns the screen into an abstract expressionist canvas. At another, op-art patterns pulsate. Constellations swell and burst. Optical effects put one in mind of such phenomena as the phosphene flashes after the blinking of an eyelid, or the swimming patterns of anesthesia experienced by patients losing consciousness, and even of the hallucinogenic light-show induced by LSD. (Walker 260)

As for Bowman, his voyage beyond the infinite concludes as he becomes one with the Big Picture, which remakes him in the image of itself: a glowing, godlike film-being and world-brain who literalizes Deleuze's concept of cinema as cosmic. HAL is no more, but his memory lingers, and the aliens put it to use.

In the KFM, what is lost is never gone.

### PHALLUS EX MACHINA

En route to a New Dawn, the Stargate reverts to the War Womb of the Old Dawn.

The desolate, Max Ernst-like plains, escarpments, buttes, kopjes, and mesas of the alien landscapes that we see on the other end of the tunnel reminisce the terrestrial landscapes of *2001*'s initial act. The imagery connotes a fusion of the alien and the techno-human in time and space that echoes the fusion of Bowman's body and mind. He becomes a superman by becoming alien. Like everybody in the film, he was already alien; distant ancestor Moon-Watcher received the same evolutionary kick in the ass. The first alien intervention/injection enabled Moon-Watcher to become human. The second one enabled Bowman to become the Bomb (i.e., God). Whether he wreaks vengeance or benevolence hangs in the balance. The phallus still rules the universe. Nothing has changed, and we can read Bowman's transcendence as another symptom of (alien) aggression and agita. Whatever variety of deus ex machina he deploys can be traced back to Moon-Watcher's death-bone.

The KFM has a permanent hard-on that pushes its aggressive agenda while self-criticizing the Medusa's head of its pathological, choleric extensions. Phallic images dominate KSF. In *Dr. Strangelove*, those images are unmistakable and egregious—the Bomb's significance is readily apparent. In *2001*, similar imagery pervades the posthuman brain-screen, but it has become part of the topography, more of an embedded, taken-for-granted reality than a prop comic's armory of gags. The phallus evolves into a genuine work of art in *A Clockwork Orange*, and finally, in *A.I.*, it becomes a historical artifact. Whatever the (dis)guise, its internal, infernal machinery never changes: life-making and death-dealing shape the gospel of its logos from inception to eternity. And the phallus always incites anxiety in its inevitable "users." That's the primary effect of its fascistic desire to control the order of everything that enters into the purview of its gaze.

For the post-Freudian Lacan—like Deleuze and Guattari, another SF writer who fetishizes inner space—the phallus "is the privileged signifier of that mark in which the role of the logos is joined with the advent of desire" (287). In other words, the phallus, an "intra-subjective" signifier, is an emissary of desire that structures the social order and coerces subjects to obey the phallic "Law of the Father." This is a useful way of thinking about the structure of *2001* as it pertains to the KFM, KSF, and SF, all phallogocentric modes of thinking that perpetuate phallogocentrism and put it in question, if not jeopardy.

In *2001*, the phallus governs the Dusk but not the Dawn. Prior to the first appearance of the monolith, what we see and hear establishes the *un*phallogocentric nature of the symbolic order: hollow winds, chirping crickets, the occasional squawk from an ancient bird give voice to sprawling geographies, the deadness of which is augmented by muted, dry-looking color palettes. There is no specialized aggression, no stylized violence beyond the biological imperatives that make a hungry leopard eat an ape and a rival tribe oust Moon-Watcher's tribe from their watering hole. The monolith introduces the phallus into the symbolic as well as the imaginary order. It is the phallus incarnate, and its alien liege produces an altered social, emotional, psychological, physiological state—everything changes. And then it never changes again. The techno-alien bleeds into an empty vessel and births the techno-human.

We hitch a ride from the distant past to the near-future on the saddle of the phallus just as Major Kong hitched a ride from the *Leper Colony* into Russian soil. The jump-cut's bone/satellite embodies and embrains this terminal signifier. Thereafter, the KFM divines the supremacy of the Star Child with a veritable odyssey of phallic images.

Anthropomorphic head imagery conflates the phallus with the brain. Most spacecraft have human facial features that convey an uncanny physiognomic character and temperament. The *Aries* lunar lander that transports Floyd to Clavius Base looks like a surgically severed head. After it lands on a platform that slowly descends into the red-lighted interior of the base (an allusion to HAL's brain cavity and the danger it represents), we can even see what appears to be two white eyeballs within the black, rectangular window-sockets of its face. The pomp and circumstance of "The Blue Danube" that accompanies the *Aries*'s descent makes the scene all the more estranging, as if the transport shuttle has arrived to a formal ball and the waltz announces its entrance. Even as a kid, the blatancy and ostentation of this anthropomorphism struck me; I realized that the film was saying something about the relationship between technology and humanity.

On a metanarrational level, the scene addresses the relationship between cinema and consciousness. *Aries* seems to watch us as we watch it, producing feelings associated with the Freudian uncanny. The oddly familiar spacecraft reflects the technological core of *2001*'s characters and our own machinic ways of seeing, feeling, thinking, and desiring. "The emphasis on images of the head underscores the film's investigation of the specialization of the brain—now, the computer brain—emphasizing disengagements between body and brain, feeling and rationality, childhood and adulthood" (Landy 95).

Underlying the visual extravaganza of *2001* is a bildungsroman about maturation from childhood to adulthood on grand (the human species) and small (one man) scales. For the screenplay, Clarke pulled ideas from earlier fiction like "The Sentinel" and *Childhood's End* (1953). In the latter, he depicts a peaceful alien invasion that takes place over the course of a century; the aliens castrate "Man," removing the death-drive in preparation for transcendence into an "Overmind." The same thing happens in *2001*: Strangelove the boy matures into Bowman the superman. He can't grow up himself, though. He needs the agency of technology.

The monolith remakes Moon-Watcher by modifying his neurology and planting the seed of a Big Idea in the dying Eden of his unconscious. It remakes Bowman by ushering him to a new War Womb that will put an end to his (and mankind's) futile "baby steps." The Star Child may resemble a baby, but it's hardly infantile, and we shouldn't hold our breath for its first strides. This energy-being is born to fly.

In the hotel suite of the new War Womb, Bowman, "like Alex later in *A Clockwork Orange*, is being splayed open, operated on through the optic nerve. And so are we: Kubrick's avant-garde invasion of our sight is no mere display, as so often in sixties experimental cinema; instead it seizes the viewer. We are swallowed up, taken over by this new cinematic divinity" (Mikics 104). In the novel, Clarke says that "his hosts had based their ideas of terrestrial living upon TV programs. His feeling that he was inside a movie set was almost literally true" (228). The surreal, dreamy unfolding of events in the suite magnify his cinematic sense of self. What viewers see backslides into Bowman's POV, a version of HAL's cold, controlled, sanitized, hypervigilant POV. In this (birth)place, the KFM fully collapses the alien, the technological, the human, and the cinematic into one another with a (camera's) eye to constructing and critiquing post-human media. That's what the Star Child is: another electronic medium, another tool that extends what we already are, more stagnant than transcendent in light of its sublime talent for unleashing catastrophe upon humanity. The Star Child looks munificent and innocuous, but the tablet of our first law, the KFM knows, will not escape this neonatal deity, whose Nietzschean leap fingers Strangelove more than it celebrates Zarathustra.

With the return of HAL's POV comes the slow-burning, film-noir anxiety that builds on the *Discovery*. The oneiric detachment is most pronounced in the suite. Several doublings allow Bowman to watch himself grow older. Emulating HAL's breakdown, reality and perception break apart as Bowman robotically acts out the mundane routine of eating a meal and going to bed. The Stargate was weird. The camera's schizophrenic POV makes this exchange much weirder. Near the end, the catalyst materializes at the foot of Bowman's bed, and breathing agonal breaths, he reaches out to his phallic father, pointing at the monolith as if to say, "I know who you are, what you did, and what you're doing." More significantly, the gesture implies fear and links Bowman's imminent passage with the death of HAL, who, when he was being deactivated, repeatedly stated, "I'm afraid." Everything that HAL says to Bowman to dissuade him ("Stop," "My mind is going," "I can feel it," etc.) could be compressed into this gesture as the monolith deactivates what amounts to the Dusk of Man.

Bowman becomes the phallic father in this diegetic surreality and cinematic spectacle. Floating in Earth's orbit and occupying the entire screen, the Star Child slowly turns his gaze to the audience to watch us watch it. *2001* "ends with the star child back in the view of Earth, not only looking at the Earth in a different way, but also rotating to face the camera, returning our gaze as spectators as if challenging us to meet it, that is, to see better, to attain its higher plane of being. Here Kubrick, usually regarded [ ... ] as a pessimist and determinist, offers us a remarkable gesture of hope and faith for an artist who elsewhere sees violence and death" (Grant 83). Perhaps Kubrick intended to be optimistic. The (re)birth of the Star Child certainly contributed to various (re)births in cinema and the SF genre.

The KFM is another matter. That filmind never stops swapping gazes with the Abyss, and as always, its pathological vanity compels it to favor style over everything else.

A phallic agent of desire, the KFM *wants to see* and *wants to be seen*. It's as vainglorious as it is recidivist, and the Nietzschean aspects of its inner space do not concern the transcendence of social, cultural, or moral construction in order to become an amoral "free spirit." Rather, they denote an eternal recurrence of the phallus. No feminine space exists in the KFM, which problematizes the notion of an authentic feminine space per se. How do we disembrain ourselves from the phallus without adopting the violence and aggression intrinsic to the phallus? Many feminist SF films have tried. The filmind of *Tank Girl* (1995), for instance, caricatures and satirizes the phallus in an attempt to purge it. Ultimately, the cyberpunk protagonist, like the Star Child, is just another phallic tool, unique and powerful but enslaved, subjected, abjected, and affected by violently patriarchal forces (including an elder Malcolm McDowell, who channels the antagonism of *A Clockwork Orange*'s Alex into the corporate tyrant Kesslee). Many feminist SF texts act that way. This has something to do with the phallic constitution of the genre itself, but the question could be applied to any genre or narrative medium. The KFM wants us to think about the problem even as it romanticizes the absence of a solution.

## THREE **NEUTRALIZING DESIRE**
*A Clockwork Orange*

### IN THE BEGINNING WAS THE ULTRAVIOLENT WORD

Kubrick's futurist trilogy was an accident. After *2001*, he had planned to make *Napoleon*, a sweeping epic about one of history's most infamous Little Men. I can imagine how this project might have immigrated into Strangelove Country, but it didn't pan out. Kubrick found himself back in the fold of SF, just not in the same vein. Even when he returned to genres that he had visited in the past, he never tapped the same vein.

*Dr. Strangelove, 2001, A Clockwork Orange,* and *A.I.* fall into different SF subgenres: respectively, the subgenres of apocalypse, space opera, urban dystopia (precyberpunk), and eco-dystopia (postcyberpunk/postapocalyptic). *2001* and *A.I.* belong to the broader category of hard SF. It's easy to forget that *Dr. Strangelove* and *A Clockwork Orange* belong to the genre, too; the cognitively estranging qualities of both soft-SF films have less to do with some extrapolated future than with basic SF themes. *Dr. Strangelove* isn't futuristic at all—technically, it's an alternate-reality story—and the near-future of *A Clockwork Orange* looks more like a 1960s costume party than a genuinely evolved world. We could say that the KFM wears SF like a fancy hat in *A Clockwork Orange* regardless of the SF motifs and poses that this adaptation of Anthony Burgess's high-literary masterpiece applies, prods, and portends.

*A Clockwork Orange* is an insane movie—insane in content, context, and conception. Given the intricacy of Burgess's prose alone, I would argue that the decision to adapt the novel is among the most pathological acts ever committed by a famous professional director. The dissolution of the Production Code in 1968 permitted filmmakers to let their freak flags fly with heretofore unseen gusto. Kubrick still pushed the envelope, and few films rivaled his "milestone of cinematic violence," which incited real violence, prompting Kubrick to remove it from distribution in Great Britain after a series of copycat crimes and death threats (Kirgo).

Released three years after *A Clockwork Orange* in 1974, *Bring Me the Head of Alfredo Garcia* achieves comparatively outlandish heights, but Peckinpah's filmind lacks the lucidity and logic of Kubrickian psychosis. The power of *A Clockwork Orange*'s affect is virtually unparalleled for a mainstream film. Apart from sacrilege like *The Devils* (1971), *The Exorcist* (1973), and *The Last Temptation of Christ* (1988), not many films approach that affect in the twentieth century. Oliver Stone's *Natural Born Killers* (1993) is gleefully transgressive: this deranged, over-the-top satire of mediatized, late-capitalist life provoked controversy—in 1995, presidential hopeful Bob Dole called it "a nightmare of depravity" (qtd. Kolker, "*Clockwork*" 19)—but society and culture had over twenty years to acclimatize to the no-holds-barred cinema initiated by the post-Code, ultraviolent cinema of Kubrick and Peckinpah. Viewers had gotten used to broken rules, which had become normative (and thus less affective). Still, even today, *A Clockwork Orange*'s pop brutalism seems abnormally rebellious. And yet it's hard for me to empathize with critics of the film (then and now) who fail to appreciate the aesthetics of its deviance.

Burgess's novel is surreal, experimental, burlesque, darkly comedic, and written in Nadsat, a made-up language that combines Cockney slang, Russian-based neologisms, gypsy bolo, and an armageddon of wordplay. "Becoming easily intelligible through context and repetition, [Nadsat] has the same purpose as the hypersophisticated whorls and loops of Humbert Humbert's erotic syntax in *Lolita*: it establishes a precise tonal connection between the hero and the audience" (Walker 42-43). More significantly, Nadsat, an ultraviolent, technologized language, mirrors the violence of its narrator's desires and culture. To my mind, the novel outperforms high-modernist touchstones like James Joyce's *Ulysses* (1920) and Gertrude Stein's *The Making of Americans* (1925), albeit on a smaller scale. In SF, there are few rivals. Russell Hoban's *Ridley Walker* (1980) and Iain M. Banks's *Feersum Endjinn* (1994) are two of them, but these superb novels haven't been made into movies. Kubrick's adaptation put Burgess's novel in a permanent spotlight.

Sobchack explains that Nadsat "is more than a futuristic tongue, a sign of linguistic change, a gimmick; it is a song and an attitude, a celebration of sound itself and a new way of looking at, describing, and thinking about what our own eyes perceive in everyday contemporary English. We deal with Nadsat not only as an alien language, but also as an expression of a foreign *mind*—therein the wonder lies" (*Screening* 148). How Kubrick thought he could make a film out of a novel that so deeply relies on the exclusivity of its prose bemuses me to no end. Film is a different mode of storytelling than literature, and while Kubrick "retains Nadsat but tones down other Soviet elements, creating instead a more Western cultural milieu brimming with commercialized images of sex and violence, or private concerns flagrantly spilling over into public life," he had to translate a verbal medium into a visual one, supplanting the violence of Burgess's Word with that of the Kubrickain Image (Rasmussen 112).

To choreograph Alex's "great action ballet," it "was necessary to find a way of stylizing the violence just as Burgess does by his writing style" (qtd. Bouzereau 29). Had the director's previous film bombed, he may not have accomplished this feat, but *2001* gave him the sand to take another risk. *2001* had been a prodigious risk. *A Clockwork Orange* was not only another departure for his filmography and KSF, but for SF and cinema.

> Kubrick made an effort to break from conventional ways of filming; there were slow-motion shots (when Alex attacks his droogs to show them who's the boss), fast motion (when Alex has sex with the two girls), and handheld camera shots (when Alex attacks the cat lady). For the point-of-view shot of Alex falling

through the window, Kubrick put a camera in an insulated box, which he then tossed out the window; six takes were required to get the lens to land first and to achieve the desired effect. Kubrick's innovative style was almost as shocking as the subject matter of the movie itself. (29-30)

Once again, Kubrick reinvented the wheel. Meanwhile, in Strangelove Country, *A Clockwork Orange* evolved the KFM's cognitively estranging POV into a state of terminal identity.

In the beginning was the Ultraviolent Word. In the KFM, the Ultraviolent Image goes with God.

Based on a colloquialism, "a clockwork orange" alludes to the dubious relationship between technology/culture and humanity/nature, a dominant SF theme. The expression appears in the novel only once when Alex and his droogs storm F. Alexander's home. Alex notices that the writer is working on a book called *A Clockwork Orange*, "a fair gloopy title," he remarks. "Who ever heard of a clockwork orange?" (25). He snatches the manuscript and reads from it: "The attempt to impose upon man, a creature of growth and capable of sweetness, to ooze juicily at the last round of the bearded lips of God, to attempt to impose, I say, laws and conditions appropriate to a mechanical creation, against this I raise my swordpen" (ibid.). Alexander's purple, melodramatic prose could use some revision, but it's appropriate for the performative gloss of this world's governing POV, and it gives readers a sense of what the title means. Preferring greater ambiguity, Kubrick omitted any such reference; as in *2001*, viewers must immerse themselves in the content and decipher what the title means for themselves.

Krämer unpacks the connotations of the title:

The phrase evokes the image of the inner workings of a clock placed inside an orange, and, more abstractly, it suggests that an organic thing (a fruit) can contain, and perhaps be controlled by, an artificial mechanism (a clockwork). Most generally, it could be said to express the idea that living and non-living matter, organisms and technologies can be intimately intertwined. One might even go as far as to associate "clockwork" with ticking, which would turn the orange into a kind of time bomb, or, alternatively, give it an artificial heart beating in its interior. There is also the possibility to project the phrase "runs like clockwork" onto the orange; taken literally rather than metaphorically, this conjures up the image of a usually inanimate object starting to move or to interact in some other way with the world around it. (*Clockwork* 20-21)

The image of a ticking time bomb evokes the literal and metaphorical Bomb that (de)vitalizes all KSF. At the time of the film's release, the Vietnam War was nearing a climax, and the title can be linked to Agent Orange, a toxic herbicide used during "Operation Ranch Hand" between 1961 and 1971 "to destroy the forest cover and food crops used by enemy North Vietnamese and Viet Cong troops" ("Agent"). Agent Orange was one of many failed efforts to control a war that gradually spun out of control. This connects with "Alex's inner being," which "is subjected to ever higher levels of control [ ... ] as if the clockwork not only determined his exterior, physical actions but also his interior, mental activity" (24). Once again, Dr. Strangelove enters/enacts the scene, manipulating the console of Alex's desires and ordaining his pathology.

Nathan Abrams makes a persuasive argument for Alex's coded Jewishness. He calls Alex an "Id-Yid," for example, and equates him with the biblical Isaac, a sacrificial lamb (157). In the eyes of the KFM, however, Alex is an abjected Nazi, mechanically created in the image of a lapsed, would-be god whose unrealized desire for global conquest (including inner and outer spaces) induced monomania. The KFM sees Alex as a repressed cyborg whose actions, like Strangelove's beliefs, stem from a Nazi hauntology. The filmind stems from this hauntology, even though it would never admit to being anything but an innocuous, fun-loving puppetmaster that just wants its marionettes to personify the "heighth of fashion" (Burgess, *Clockwork* 4). Like the mythological trickster

Loki, the KFM deflects concrete representation and thrives almost exclusively on the stylized undulations of its identity.

The invasion of "natural" organisms by cultural "clockwork" develops the trope of machinic inscription in *Dr. Strangelove* and *2001* while situating *A Clockwork Orange* in a long SF tradition. Shelley's monster confronts some of the same issues as Alex; he commits acts of extreme violence as a result of his negatively charged inscription, and he cultivates an appreciation of art (e.g., music and "the art of language" [Shelley 79]). Alex also aligns with SF's early robots, dating back to Karel Čapek's *R.U.R.* (1920), the play that "introduced the word 'robot' [ ... ] to the world" (Clute, "Karel"), and E.V. Odle's *The Clockwork Man* (1923), "one of the first cyborg novels" (Newitz 11). Čapek and Odle thematize violence and the schizo-capitalist forces that produce it. Their robots are more Phildickian (artificial flesh and blood) than Asimovian (metal and machine), tying them to Frankenstein's creation as well as Alex, a creation of the society and culture administrated by a quasi-totalitarian government. The theatrics of all these clockwork oranges are prescribed by hostile external and internal environments.

Burgess's novel does something else. The final chapter ascribes the theatrics of our "humble narrator" to immaturity. Alex informs us that "all it was was that I was young" (202). The message: boys will be boys, and when they grow into men, they acquire the perspective and resources to sublimate the primordial impulse to rape, pillage, and kill people. Kubrick removed the final chapter (and Burgess's prosaic moral) from the screenplay; he leaves Alex at the end of the second to the last chapter, an edit that delivers the protagonist back to the beginning of the story in terms of his psychosomatic constitution. The government attempts to neutralize (i.e., deterritorialize) the desire that technoculture territorialized in him. The film concludes with a reterritorialization of desire that the novel attempts to deterritorialize twice over. Kubrick's decision empowers the KFM and reconnoiters the circle of life/death embrained in *2001*.

From this locus, *A Clockwork Orange* circles back to its KSF antecedent. "Just as *2001* ended with a close-up of the star child staring into the camera as it journeys back to earth in anticipation of the next step in man's evolution, so *A Clockwork Orange* begins with a close-up of Alex staring into the camera with a smirk on his face, as he looks forward to the coming night of sexual escapades and 'ultra-violence' with his gang" (Phillips, "Stop" 155). Hiding behind the curtain of those stares—and that smirk—is Strangelove, the eternally recurrent phallus in the kingdom of the KFM.

*A Clockwork Orange* prefigures cyberpunk's Cartesian obsession with mind-body interfaces and relishes the cyberpunk ethos that schizophrenia and machinic desire have become normative conditions. Scholarship often discounts the film's science-fictional backdrop in favor of issues like screen violence, censorship, sexuality, and morality. The moral dilemma at the center of the film is its least interesting trait. An abundance of literature and cinema entertains this overcooked theme, including Burgess's source material. Considerable attention has been paid to linguistic innovation in both texts, and rightly so. Burgess's novel is a remarkable literary accomplishment that Kubrick converted into an equally remarkable cinematic accomplishment.

As in *Dr. Strangelove* and *2001*, the futurist phallus of *A Clockwork Orange* hypostatizes a fluid multiplicity. Most conspicuously, Alex bashes in the skull of the Cat Lady with her beloved porcelain penis, a sculpture by Dutch artist Herman Makkink known as "The Rocking Machine." The artpiece parallels Alex's own artistic sensibilities (e.g., his love of Beethoven). The State convicts him for murder and attempts to neuter his primal desire for sex and violence, which manifests in his actions to the melody of Nadsat's rhythms, inflections, and stabs. Alex is reconditioned by the Ludovico technique, an experimental form of aversion therapy. Mad scientists inject him with drugs and force him to watch violent films. Thereafter, the very thought of committing a crime makes him physically ill.

The treatment fails. The use of the Ninth Symphony for the background score in the Ludovico footage conditions Alex to be sick whenever he hears Beethoven. Accompanied by his own "sophisto" trio of droogs, a vengeful F. Alexander drugs and locks him in the attic, then pumps Beethoven through the ceiling of a billiard room downstairs to torture him for raping his wife. Alex tries to commit suicide and leaps out a window. In order to avoid bad press, the State turns him back into an ordinary maniac, "fixing" him like a broken robot. It's a "reality fix" à la William S. Burroughs if we read the film as the concomitant phantasm of Strangelove cum Alex, who was addicted to sex and violence, his primary drugs of choice. The State reopens the floodgates of his pleasure receptors so that he can return to, feed, and enjoy his addiction anew. Burgess's book eschews this "happy ending" whereas Kubrick's film exalts it. Post-Ludovico, the Alex we see moping around the flatblocks with a brown bag of personal items clutched to his chest is little more than a dry drunk.

The unsuccessful neutralization of Alex's Strangelovian desires reify a KFM arch-thesis: *Strangelove Country can't be quarantined—Herr Doktor will always find a way out, which is the way in.*

Similarly, the overspill of desire into the real, non-diegetic world was unsuccessfully neutralized by censorship in Great Britain and an X rating in the US. *A Clockwork Orange* had a profound affect on characters and viewers alike. Measures were taken to reduce this affect and its abjections. "Kubrick uses music to neutralize the violence," for instance, which "is 'stylized' through the music, [serving] as a substitute for Burgess's 'writing style'" (Rabinowitz 125). We see and hear this usage in the acrobatic brawl between Alex and Billyboy's gangs at the derelict casino and the fasttime threesome between Alex and the ptitsas he picks up at the disc-bootick, scenes that are set to, respectively, Rossini's "The Thieving Magpie" and *William Tell* Overture. The songs dilute the shock-value of the scenes and reaffirm that we are beholding a work of art. The KFM wants us to see and know this dilution/affirmation. *A Clockwork Orange* is the climax of the filmind's evolution and a *beau ideal* of the KFM's belief in what constitutes technological humanity and masculinity. At the end of "Man," the KFM thinks, is *art and art alone*, and in this terminally artistic, antirealistic inner space, desire may flow in any direction, in any guise. Neutralization is another illusion that feeds the KFM's undyingly ironic manner of thinking. Desire can't be neutralized anyway. It can only be temporarily deflected, rerouted, curtailed, or amplified.

## THE FUTURE OF/IS ADDICTION

The antirealism of *A Clockwork Orange* relates to the Kubrickian monads of sublimity and irrealism, enabling the KFM to perceive itself as an artwork as it explores how *art* can *work* as a vehicle for desire. Kolker discusses the film's antirealistic properties:

> [It goes] against the usual codes of framing, cutting, narrative construction, character formation, viewer positioning, and thematic conventions that we take so much for granted when we watch a film. In ordinary films, the realistic style seems to erase those very structures that create it and the screen becomes a kind of transparent window onto an illusion of an ongoing world. Kubrick [ ... ] undoes many of the premises of cinematic realism and forces us to take some things less for granted, to look at the film as a formal construction of meaning and ideas that may not be what it all first appears, to confront some ambiguities. (*"Clockwork"* 29-30)

The confrontation of ambiguities does not entail their dissolution. On the contrary, it reifies their impact. The KFM nurtures ambiguities to make us think even harder about where they flow and what they signify. Hence the cognitive, critical utilities of lighting, setting, and camerawork. "Through the film's hard, fluorescent lightning, the extravagant camera movement, which alternates with large, wide-angle tableaux, and its carefully figured, sometimes abstract and almost always metaphoric sets, *A Clockwork Orange* becomes a kinetic and meditative mechanism. It rushes us through its story and at the same time welcomes us to pause and think upon it" (30).

I have accused the KFM of being psychotic and schizophrenic. The filmind's Phildickian distortion of reality and fantasy is not an obstruction. It's empowering. The schism functions like Deleuzoguattarian pathology, and the KFM, a highly sophisticated, self-aware trickster, enacts it as a form of play and assessment. The agency of perceptual implosion allows the KFM to critically think about numerous worlds and megatexts, but its "illness" wasn't born in a vacuum. The Kubrickian consciousness is a user, an addict, and its way of seeing can partly be attributed to an abuse of substances. This abuse comes to a head in *A Clockwork Orange*.

*Dr. Strangelove* and *2001* exhibit addictions to technology that are liberating and caustic. Strung out on machines (and the jouissance that machinic desire forever hunts and gathers), mankind blows itself up in the first KSF. In the second KSF, mankind gets really high, transcending the flesh, but if the KFM minds/mines the past, it will self-destruct again.

The third KSF is the KFM's postapocalyptic *delirium tremens*.

*2001*'s psychedelic style implicates the primordial monkey on the KFM's back. In the 1960s, that style encouraged countercultural viewers to join the filmind on its (acid) trip. Segue to *A Clockwork Orange*, the psychedelia of which intensifies like a solar flare: almost every mise-en-scène seems to be undergirded by some hallucinogenic velocity and élan. The characters in this near-future are addicted to more than modern technology. We never see Alex smoke anything, but he hands over a pack of cigarettes to the Chief Guard when he's booked in jail. These "cancers" symbolize an entire cornucopia of sicknesses. Addiction runs rampant among the general public, surfacing in dependencies on everything from alcohol and LSD-type psychoactives to sex, violence, art, religion, and electronic media. As for "public servants"— they are addicted to power, or rather, they are addicted to *the hysterical discharge of phallic aggression*. Desire has become a monstrosity as the KFM achieves the optimal (i.e., the most *affected* and *abjected*) version of itself. *A Clockwork Orange* is the pinnacle of KSF and the Kubrickian consciousness in this respect. Everything that follows—*Barry Lyndon, The Shining, Full Metal Jacket, Eyes Wide Shut*—is cognitive afterburn that either repeats or reflects on KSF thought-processes, with *A.I.* being a micro-filmind that reflects on the grander apparatuses of the Kubrickian consciousness and the SF genre. Kubrick's post-KSF films are all remarkable and demonstrably Kubrickian, but the genre-SF apparatus isn't there, and none of them significantly extend Strangelove's reach or gaze.

Alex's hairy eyeball is one of the most iconic images in cinematic history. The overdecorative lashes call attention to the overperformativity that distinguishes the film's antirealism and pathological vision. This is established in the first frame and scene as we cut from opening credits to a closeup on Alex's fiendish stare, then slowly zoom out to the droogs that flank him and the Korova milkbar's interior. Alex's preliminary voice-over accompanies the zoom-out. What he says is almost verbatim from the novel, narrated in the first-person. His voice-over spans the film, too, but Kubrick's Alex never info-dumps at length. In general, voice-overs are insignia of lazy filmmaking that fails to relay context via dialogue and action without derailing our suspension of disbelief. Kubrick is a rare filmmaker who pulls off voice-overs, using them sparingly and meaningfully; in *A Clockwork Orange*, they deepen Alex's character and develop his POV more than they map the social and cultural terrain.

After introducing himself and his droogs, Alex tells us what the milkbar has on tap: "The Korova milkbar sold Milk Plus, milk plus vellocet or synthemesc or drencrom, which is what we were drinking. This would sharpen you up and make you ready for a bit of the old ultraviolence." Subtextually, he introduces the interconnected themes of drugs, addiction, and violence that define his identity as well as the POV and filmind that will illuminate the vicissitudes of his desires and dream its way through the story. His use of the second person enmeshes viewers (i.e., Alex's "brothers") in this subtext.

High on Milk Plus, the droogs go out for a typical night on the town. They beat up a homeless drunk, rumble with Billyboy's gang, steal a "Durango '95," play "hogs of the road," and finally break into F. Alexander's home, beat him up, and rape his wife. Then they return to the Korova for another fix. They part ways after a spat between Alex and Dim that underscores Alex's power. Camerawork validates this power when all four droogs are captured onscreen, centering Alex and fetishizing his gaze.

The addictive subtext of Alex's opening monologue pours into every aspect of the opening scenes that provide a first look into this dystopian society. Moments later, we revisit his sex addiction, which conjoins with his addiction to art and media. Presumably, he achieved orgasm with Mrs. Alexander, but he's ready to go again. He masturbates to "Ludwig Van," conjuring "lovely pictures" on his mindscreen of a hung bride falling through the trap door of a gallows, a bomb blowing up the earth, a train bursting into a pillar of fire, and old movie footage of boulders falling onto cavemen, all of it interspersed by flash-cuts of an ecstatic Alex in bloody vampire fangs. Ignited by Beethoven with the same spark as Milk Plus, the movie footage hints that Alex's machinic filmind is a construction of media forces. Both the composer and the clip betoken the technology of Alex's addiction and desires.

Mikics compares Alex's masturbatory fantasy to other KSF climaxes: "Here once more is the solitary transport felt by Strangelove rising from his wheelchair, by Major Kong riding his missile, by Moonwatcher excitedly pounding a carcass with his bone weapon. All these characters are boys at heart, autistically sheathed in their ecstasy. Kubrick loves these passionate rocketings [although] he makes clear the cost of such savage masculine exultation" (115). In psycho-biblical terms: *What the Phallus giveth, the Phallus also taketh away.*

Prior to entering Alex's inner space, we see the outer space of his bedroom. Two images foreshadow the addiction to religion that he will use to surrogate his other addictions after being incarcerated: Basil the snake and a porcelain sculpture of four dancing, intertwined Christs. I will say more about the role of religion in the next section as Alex and the State rely on it. The representatives and administrators of the State are very much like Alex despite their objective to neutralize addiction (to crime and violence) even as they addict Alex to psychoactive drugs in order to negate his other addictions.

*A Clockwork Orange*'s dystopia hearkens back to some of the SF genre's most celebrated novels. *Nineteen Eighty-Four* and Aldous Huxley's *Brave New World* (1932) both portray the use of neuroscientific tools by despotic governments to control the masses. In "Of Drugs and

Droogs," Lorenzo Servitje writes: "The historical context of *A Clockwork Orange* is a decisively neuroscientific and psychopharmacologic one. [ ... ] Burgess was specifically interested in *Brave New World* as Huxley was writing against the utopianism of H. G. Wells, a proponent of scientific rationalism" (103). The institution of psychiatry was redefined in the 1960s and 70s, and the "popular use of medication for aversion therapy to alter mental and behavioral deviations [ ... ] parallels the use of a pharmaceutical for the Ludovico treatment" (105). We see the fruits of this labor in the tyranny and abandon of today's corporate pharmaceutical culture. Recent addiction epidemics pioneered by drugs like Fentanyl and Oxycodone have caused terrific unrest, but regulation is much more prominent in the twenty-first century. Comparatively, the mid-twentieth century was the Wild West.

Suffering from laryngeal cancer, Huxley asked his wife to inject him with LSD on his death bed so that he could take the ultimate trip. It was a grand finale to his longstanding interest in psychoactive drugs that he wrote about with the most candor in *The Doors of Perception* (1954). His experiments with mind-altering psychedelics were unconventional during his life. Culture at large caught up with him down the line. Armed with a Huxleyian desire to expand awareness into "total reality in its immanent otherness," some filmgoers perceived much more than the diegetic (ir)reality of *2001* when they viewed it in theaters as their own chemically altered mindscreens intermingled with the KFM (Huxley 55). There are no hard drugs in *2001*, however, and no evidence of addiction to controlled or uncontrolled substances; nobody even smokes cigarettes. Diegetic addiction is limited to technology (i.e., loving the Bomb). *A Clockwork Orange* explodes this limitation.

Like Alice in the rabbit-hole, we're tumbling down Strangelove's mineshaft now.

### BIBLE FANTASIES

The KFM isn't an atheist. Nor is it an agnostic. It doesn't believe in anything but itself. Even anti-belief doesn't hold sway. If the KFM were to engrave a commandment about ideology into stone, it might be this: *Belief is the end of reason and the beginning of evil.*

The KFM deploys belief as a tool to express the absurdity of the human condition. As a western consciousness, it's almost exclusively preoccupied with the Old and New Testaments of the Christian Bible/ Bomb, foregrounding the doctrine of original sin.

Original sin is God's punishment in the Book of Genesis. The promethean monsters he creates don't listen when he tells them not to eat from the Tree of Knowledge, so he decrees that Adam, Eve, and their incestuous offspring (i.e., humanity) will be ousted from the utopian Garden of Eden and implanted with a dystopian awareness that leads to chronic suffering and certain death. Original sin is as much a fantasy as the story of Adam and Eve, but it continues to impact mass desire to this day, and the KFM takes pleasure in deriding anybody that stoops to dogma.

Through an SF lens, Genesis becomes a schizoaffective suburb of Strangelove Country. Not only are Adam and Eve monstrous creations, the serpent that convinces Eve to eat the forbidden fruit is a technology comparable to *2001*'s monolith: that God-damned snake sparks new paths of imaginative, calculated thought and *Dasein*. Alex's pet snake alludes to this correlation. Both technologies inject knowledge that is agential and destructive.

Some theologians contend that Eve persuaded Adam to eat the fruit with her sexuality. Apropos Strangelove Country. She wouldn't be the only originary woman to employ her body as a tool. Eve was Adam's second helpmeet in certain folklore omitted from the Old Testament and Torah. The Bible "allows us only brief hints of its lost mythological riches," says Robert Graves and Raphael Patai in *Hebrew Myths* (2). According to mythology that combines "an early Judaean and a late priestly tradition," God cast the first bride, Lilith, out of Eden because she wouldn't let Adam be on top during sex (72). "'Why must I lie beneath you?' she asked. 'I also was made from dust, and am therefore your equal'" (70). Like the KFM, Genesis abides by techno-masculine ordinances and commingles dominant KSF themes of patriarchy, sex, power, technology, and death.

A common occurrence for addicts in recovery is to replace one addiction with another. Sometimes it's a substance; sometimes it's ideological. In Alcoholics Anonymous, addicts must admit that they have no control over their drinking and put faith in God or a higher power. AA members can't save themselves—the only solution for their disability is a spiritual remedy. Alex isn't an alcoholic. He does drugs, but drugs don't control him; rather, they supplement his addiction to sex and violence, which is most certainly out of control: he *needs* sex and violence to fill a lack in himself. After killing the Cat Lady and being "sentenced to 14 years in Staja No. 84F among smelly perverts and hardened prestoopnicks," it isn't long before he redirects his addictions into "Bog in His Heaven." This entails ritualistic church-going, bible-reading, and meetings with the Prison Chaplain.

The Chief Guard asks Alex to identify his religion during his inmate processing interview. "C of E, sir," he replies. "Do you mean the Church of England?" the Chief Guard snaps. "Yes, sir. The Church of England, sir." Here and elsewhere, Alex's snarky (i.e., *stylized*) attitude outshines his (shallow) knowledge of everything else, in this case the church. As the posed, porcelain Christs in his bedroom suggest, religion—like any cultural institution or relic—only matters to him as an artform or performance. "Pee and Em" didn't subject him to any kind of faith-based upbringing. Reminiscing 2001's emotionally detached astronauts, their dehumanized passivity is a product of their working-class status. Alex's parents are more childlike than their son. Paradoxically, Alex's juvenile delinquency exacerbates their juvenile condition as they passively, meekly let their little hellion walk all over them.

Alex becomes a model inmate. Part of his rehabilitation involves studying the Bible. He calls it the "Big Book" (n.b., the core Alcoholics Anonymous text is also called the Big Book). "I didn't so much like the latter part of the book, which is more like all preachy talking than fighting and the old in-out," he says. "I liked the parts where these old yahoodies tolchock each other and then drink their Hebrew vino, and getting on to the bed with their wives' handmaidens. That kept me going." That is, wish-fulfillment fantasies kept him going, and the mental performances of pornoviolence that flood Alex's mindscreen sublimate the actual performances that he enacted in the external world.

In several scenes, Alex imagines himself in biblical roles. Kubrick's screenplay reads:

BIBLE FANTASY—FIGHTING—DAY
Biblical fighting shot. Alex slashing away. Blood spurting.

HANDMAIDEN FANTASY IN TENT—DAY
Alex lying with three semi-nude handmaidens.

EXT. BIBLICAL STREET
Christ being whipped on by Alex, dressed as a Legionary.

ALEX (V.O.)
I read all about the scourging and the crowning with thorns and all that, and I could viddy myself helping in and even taking charge of the tolchocking and the nailing in, being dressed in the height of Roman fashion.

For Alex, sex and violence go hand-in-hand with style and vogue. He's as concerned with "the old in-out" and "the red, red kroovy" as he is with how he looks and how he acts in an unconscious effort to make art out of his deeds. Ultimately, Alex wants to make himself into an artwork. Wired to the KFM, his addiction mandates this desire for sublimity.

In a 1973 interview, Madison Mae Williams recounts how Malcolm McDowell described *A Clockwork Orange* "as not sensationally violent, but instead, a film that evokes a 'violence of the mind' in the viewer. By this, McDowell emphasizes an affective response to the violence, but it is not one of either glory or desensitization. Instead," says Williams, "the 'violence of the mind' functions as the site for criticism to begin [...] These moments are exemplified in *Clockwork* through stylized acting; emotional suggestions and exploration of creating an abstracted 'picture of the world' through the actors' performances are a reflection of

Kubrick's vision of the film as a tool meant for audiences to critique their own affective and sociopolitical positionality related to violence" (153).

Williams freely speaks for Kubrick in this passage. I will only speak for the KFM, which perceives the director as another player in its troupe. When scholars talk about Kubrick in this way, they apply performativity to their subjective idea of the filmmaker, and they cast him in the role of an Oz-like, behind-the-curtain auteur manipulating the cinematic machine to elicit specific effects. This Kubrick is a character, an object, a tool. The real Oz is Strangelove, who isn't "real" at all, but the KFM's tool *par excellence*. The film-thinking that animates *A Clockwork Orange* wants to turn everything into art—the monster, the monster-maker, the world that inscribes them, even the cosmos that inscribes that world. Deleuze has said that cinema is cerebral *and* cosmic. The KFM thinks like a Deleuzian desiring-machine among other desiring-machines in a vast network of cinematic brains, "each screen like a neuron, helping cinema view itself in its world-thinking. And each screen is like a mini-brain, linking together all the cameras and humans that produced it, like its neurons in turn helping it think one larger film-thought" (Vitale).

The only thing we can say with certainty regarding Kubrick is how people perceive him perceiving himself. This goes for Kubrick on Kubrick as well: even what he says about his methods, strategies, endgames, etc. may be true or untrue. With the definitively Kubrickian *Lolita, Dr. Strangelove,* and *2001* in his pocket, however, we can comfortably say that 1970s critics, reviewers, and general audiences regarded him with deference at the tail-end of the futurist trilogy. Of *2001*, Kubrick once said that "the God concept is at the heart of this film" in a 1970 interview befittingly titled "The Film Director as Superstar" (Gelmis 92). The God concept leaked into the heart of Kubrick's auteurism and legacy. Today he remains the subject of spectatorial bible fantasies that put him on a pedestal like no other filmmaker. In *2001*, Dave Bowman transforms into an energy god. In our cultural consciousness, Stanley Kubrick transformed into a cinematic god. Both gods are fictions that kindle desire in their respective diegeses.

The holy mountain that has become Stanley Kubrick aligns more with Bowman than Alex, who achieves godhood at the end of *A Clockwork Orange* through Christlike trauma. Unlike Jesus, Alex gets to climb down from the cross that the government nails him on before he dies, although there is a metaphorical death and rebirth after his suicide attempt. The rebirth is a reversion that undoes the psychosomatic stigmata of the Ludovico treatment. He can reclaim the addictions that the stigmata denied his body and mind. Appropriately, the final scene is a fantasy in which Alex sees himself doing what he loves best: listening to Beethoven and having wild sex. It's the acme of his performance and his desire to merge with the sublime. He has two audiences watching him, one metanarrational (filmgoers), one oneiric (the aristocrats that surround him). In this reverse-Pinocchio scenario, Alex, mimicking the Star Child, transcends the flesh into a fantasy where he becomes a legitimate artwork. He's still a puppet, but not to the government and the machinations of statesmen like the Minister of the Interior (their interest in his "sobriety" is purely a matter of political gain). Only Alex's addictions will pull his strings now. We have come full circle, and as the KFM brings the futurist trilogy to a close, it reminds us once again that reality is no match for fantasy, that desire is the desire for desire.

### UTOPIAN SUBLIMITY IN DYSTOPIAN TIMES

As with *2001*, *A Clockwork Orange* looks more like a futique 1960s than a veritable near-future, and it doesn't account for the screen culture that has come to dominant the twenty-first century. There are no vidphones, let alone smartphones. In the 60s, "75% of British homes had a television," yet in *A Clockwork Orange's* futuristic England, TVs are almost nonexistent (Goodhart). A low-tech, cathode-ray television sits in the corner of Pee and Em's living room. Otherwise, there is only the mindscreen of Alex/Strangelove and the movie screen in the theater where Alex endures the Ludovico Technique. The prevailing technology in every domestic interior is stereo equipment for playing music. And artwork, not flatscreen TVs, occupies the walls.

There's art everywhere. The bootick and the milkbar are filled with art, including the fiberglass nudes—"crouched like *Playboy* femlins" —used for tables and to dispense Milk Plus (Hughes 131). Even the garbage-strewn stairwell outside of Alex's flat features a large mural that looms like a telltale over the slouching droogs one morning as they wait for their leader to join them. Wherever Alex goes, art follows him. Two prominent works (the premier object-choices of his desire) stand out in his bedroom: an illustrated bust of Beethoven and a painting of a naked woman prying apart her legs. Regardless of their dehumanization, his parents aren't without artistic sensibility either. Paintings hang on most of the walls in the flat. Two show topless women covering their breasts and might be younger versions of Em; and whereas Pee's fashion sense is limited to pastel-colored shirts and ties, Em wears garish wigs and outfits that appear to be fashionable— not too flashy for this extrapolated era, but singular enough to identify her as fashion-savvy.

F. Alexander and the Cat Lady's residences amplify the apocalypse of art that differentiates *A Clockwork Orange* from *2001*'s artless environments, a great meta-irony considering the space opera's arthouse quintessence. Prints, paintings, and sculptures accentuate the Feng shui generated by the use of space, fine wood, mirrored walls, bookshelves, and Space Age furniture in F. Alexander's self-reflexively ensigned "HOME." The Cat Lady elevates this Feng shui to a psycho-sexual extreme: "She lives amid lesbian self-portraits (including a face with mouths within mouths, and teeth to link her with the grinning dentures), colors herself like an art object (heavy lipstick on a large mouth, red-tinted hair, green and white leotards), and twists her body into contortions as if to replicate an abstract piece of sculpture or her own 'health farm' exercise equipment. This psychosexual landscape, like the Korova, suggests not only that sexual function has been replaced by sexual extensions, but that human beings, machine-like, imitate the objects of their own creation" (Nelson 151). The KFM loves to probe the relationship between hard technology and art. Here it fuses them into *phallic ultraviolence*, the only possible outcome for KSF.

*A Clockwork Orange*'s décor doesn't pit art against violence and make them into oppositional forces. "Those characters connected with art in the film are finally as violent as Alex: the Cat Lady who is a collector and F. Alexander, the writer. Music and books and statues and paintings become weapons. And, heightened by the use of editing and extreme close-ups of that classic lithograph, Ludwig Van's stare is anything but beatific or benevolent" (Sobchack, *Screening* 101). Violence collapses into art and vice versa. The KFM sees no variance and acknowledges the apothegm that "art is dangerous" (Grady).

In the Cat Lady and F. Alexander's residences, Ciment argues, the décors "are so aseptic and sterile that they might have been dreamt up by General Ripper, with his fears for his vital fluids. They reflect a corresponding atrophy of emotions embodied into the soulless routine of polite encounters and in the impoverished, cliché-ridden, terrifyingly banal language of social intercourse" (107). As externalizations of fear, the décors correspond with Ripper's madness. I don't get the same vibe as Ciment regarding their sterility and soullessness. Quite the opposite. These interiors are busy, lively, polychromatic, and full of vitality, as if trying to "break on through" the doors of perception conceived by Huxley and extrapolated by Jim Morrison, who died from substance abuse the same year that *A Clockwork Orange* came out. Morrison's lyrics romanticized his own death and glorified Huxley's advocacy of drug-taking for mind expansion. In *A Clockwork Orange*, the KFM does just that, expanding its filmind to the outer limits of a sublimity that Morrison and Huxley could only experience in small, ever-fleeting parcels. Desire's ultimate goal is to obtain the sublime, but unless we move completely into the realm of fantasy (i.e., impossibility), desire can only chase its own tail. Even in terminal fantasy, however, the sublime resists containment and always finds a way to lose itself. Anybody who has developed a mindful appreciation of art has felt the pang of this evanescence.

*A Clockwork Orange* contrives a Brutalist dystopia that embeds an artistic utopia. Strangelove/Alex's imploded POV breathes life into this monstrous diegesis, simultaneously thinking about *everything* in terms of sublime beauty and cold, dark truth. *Dr. Strangelove* and *2001* converge on this film-thinking with mounting attention/tension, but in *A Clockwork Orange*, the KFM arrives "HOME." The hyper-performative characters who live here aren't human beings. They are stylized ideas of a bombed-out humanity that has crossed a threshold into a new, alien(ated), mediatized irreality. *A Clockwork Orange* is what happens in Herr Strangelove's mineshaft dreamscapes. This oneiric depiction of posthumanism reaches a fever-pitch in the film's use of music.

### "SYNTHESIZING" STRANGELOVE

*2001* and *A Clockwork Orange* would be different movies without classical music. Kubrick's usage was original and controversial, especially for SF, and he ostracized some viewers.

Alex North scored *Spartacus* and *Dr. Strangelove*. He completed a full soundtrack for *2001*. Kubrick scrapped the soundtrack during post-production. He thought classical pieces would make for a better story and spectacle. North's fellow Hollywood composer Jerry Gold smith called the decision "idiotic" and griped: "I am aware of the success of the film but what North had written would have given the picture a far greater quality. The use of the 'Blue Danube' waltz was amusing for a moment but quickly became distracting because it is so familiar and unrelated to the visual. [ ... ] It was a mistake to force music into a film, and for me *2001* was ruined by Kubrick's choice of music. His selections had no relationship, and the pieces could not comment on the film because they were not part of it" (qtd. LoBrutto 309).

Goldsmith's protest seems naïve and uninformed by today's standards. It's understandable in context. Kubrick's decision was exceedingly Kubrickian, and innovation displaces people from their comfort zones. But the music clearly worked and resonated with audiences. Considering the thematic omnipresence of art in *A Clockwork Orange*, it makes sense that Kubrick would extend this type of music into another project. For the KFM, it's a crucial extension that augments the embrainment of KSF.

A disparity between the second and third KSF is that music in *2001* is external to the diegesis whereas it's external and internal in *A Clockwork Orange*. Kate McQuiston identifies key pieces and composers:

> *A Clockwork Orange* includes a significant amount of classical music, but the music in *2001* is almost exclusively nondiegetic. The scherzo and finale of Beethoven's Ninth Symphony are featured prominently in *A Clockwork Orange* in both electronic versions realized by Wendy Carlos and produced by Rachel Elkind, and an orchestral version from a Deutsche Grammophon recording. Beethoven's music always appears within the diegesis. On the other hand, Kubrick uses parts of Rossini's overtures to *La gazza ladra* and *William Tell*, Edgar's Pomp and Circumstance Marches 1 and 4, and Rimsky-Korsakov's *Scheherazade* over the course of the film exclusively nondiegetically. Besides the Beethoven, the only other clearly diegetic pieces are some popular songs, like "I Want to Marry a Lighthouse Keeper," whose popularity was brief and only in association with the film, and "Singin' in the Rain" which is sung by Alex. Gene Kelly's recording of the song plays over the closing credits. (107)

The popular songs contribute to the avant-pop sensibility of the film. As well, "Rossini's music, particularly in contrast to Beethoven's, communicates [...] in an exaggerated, cartoonish language. Themes from Rossini's overtures [emerge] in Warner Brothers cartoons, an association which is reinforced in the scene" (108). The electronic modifications and tonalities of Wendy Carlos—credited as William Carlos (she changed her forename after sex-reassignment surgery in 1972)—enhanced the film's idealized irrealism and the machinic desire that energizes its SF milieu.

The electronic enhancement of classical music sinks futurity into history and "synthesizes" Strangelove Country with this hybrid world, which is part arthouse SF, part wild-western nightmare, the latter with respect to its whiteness and genre. No people of color appear in *A*

*Clockwork Orange*, not even in Alex's daydreams; there is "diversity" in class and gender relations, but the KFM does not apportion film-thinking to non-white characters. The filmind doubles down on race by borrowing from the cinematic western, a genre whose dominant whiteness rivals SF. The marauding gangs of droogs are essentially Peckinpahesque "wild bunches." They're not gunslingers—like blackness, guns don't exist here—but they're outlaws, and Alex loves his knife. More than anything, he loves wreaking havoc: anybody who enters the orbit of this personified Billy the Kid is fair game, although droogs/rustlers prefer to hunt for prey.

An underbelly of chaos disrupts yet vitalizes the "purity" of whiteness that embrains *A Clockwork Orange*. The droogs' pop-cult uniforms emblematize the filmind's racial code, as does everything from the drug-laced milk they drink to the bleached urban environments that interpolate them. This is how the world looks on Strangelove's schizoid mindscreen, an introjection of the KFM's arch-mindscreen.

Kubrick achieved science-fictionalized renditions of Rossini's "Magpie" and Beethoven's Ninth with a Deutsche Grammophon processed through a Moog synthesizer that Carlos developed with the instrument's namesake, Robert Moog (Rogers). The synthesizer brought electronic music to the mainstream with *Switched-On Bach* in 1968. Thereafter, bands like The Beatles, The Monkees, The Grateful Dead, The Rolling Stones, and The Doors adopted the technology. *A Clockwork Orange* wasn't the first movie to implement it—Maurice Jarre's soundtrack for *Doctor Zhivago* (1965) is the likely initiator—but it contained the first remodulation of classical music, and Moog's innovations contributed to the cognitively estranging ambiance. "These electronic interpretations work wonderfully for the movie," says Colin Wessman, "not only because the film takes place in a not-so-distant future where you could imagine such an instrument being the norm, but, also, it creates something truly disorienting. As we hear these familiar songs transmuted through the fuzzed-out artifice of a synthesizer, it makes everything feel not quite right." Wessman's use of the term "feel" recollects my own experience. Whenever I watch the film and hear the synthesized renditions of Beethoven, I can *feel* Strangelove's desires bucking like a bee-stung mule.

My emotional response begets the mindfulness of filmosophy and the idea that "film-thinking is not 'read' but felt" (98). Frampton writes: "Filmosophy is concerned to *organicise* and so remove the separation of film-object and film-thinking. Filmosophy argues that, with the concept of 'film-thinking' in their knowledge, the filmgoer can be simultaneously aware of both the object of the film's intention (the character) *and* the intention (framing, movement) itself. The filmosophical filmgoer immediately feels the character *through* their thinking and the film-thinking" (162). Consequently, I feel Alex through his thinking, which constitutes the broader POV and film-thinking of *A Clockwork Orange*, a filmind-within-a-filmind. Then, when I zoom out to observe the full spectrum of KSF, I feel the film-thinking of Strangelove, a character-within-a-character, a POV-within-a-POV, a ghost in the machine of the KFM, and writ larger, a reminder of humanity's psychological clockwork and how history always repeats itself, wired to an eternal recurrence of desire, destruction, and jouissance.

Visually, the film-thinking of *A Clockwork Orange* correlates with SF movies like *The Matrix* and *Starship Troopers* (1997). Frampton describes their thought processes: "*The Matrix* thinks a brittle, chrome, almost sickly green false world, perhaps feeling the cold and manipulative thinking of the Artificial Intelligence that provides it; while the real world is similarly cold in tone, this time in cool blue. [...] *Starship Troopers* looks 'normal,' but its sharp, clear, proud images are perhaps *thinking* the optimism and wide-eyed naiveté of the characters and the bright, solid ideology that they are being sacrificed for" (119). No single character thinks *Starship Troopers*'s film-thoughts; cognition mainly issues from a multiperspectival trinity of characters (Johnny Rico, Carmen Ibanez, and Carl Jenkins). *The Matrix*'s film-thinking, on the other hand, issues from the protagonist (Neo), as in *A Clockwork Orange*.

Neo and Alex (re)produce their respective worlds from the POV of their machinic pathologies. The use of specific colors and color combinations bring out those pathologies. Like Neo, Alex thinks a sickly landscape that only gets "fixed" *internally.* Dirty whites, grays, and muted tones eclipse the suburbs, jail, and the hospital for Alex, usually in the daytime, but as he says in the novel, the "day was very different from the night. The night belonged to me and my droogs and all the rest of the nadsats" (47). The sunset annuls sublimation—in the dark, the watchmen aren't watching, and Alex can feed his insatiable desire. Accordingly, at nighttime, he storms one interior after another, each representing his enflamed psyche.

The groovy explosion of color, art, porn, and ultraviolence in the Cat Lady's house represents the corresponding explosion of desire in Alex's inner space, which "lends itself to the kind of expressionistic rhetoric that characterizes" the KFM (Nelson 145). This contrasts with the ashen, lackluster exterior of the house, where his desiring-engine merely idles. Similarly, when Neo jacks in to the matrix and becomes a "mental representation of [his] digital self," there is a distinct change in mood and pigmentation as the filmind draws from a bigger, crisper color palette (*Matrix*).

The Wachowskis took the basic concept of the matrix from *Neuro-mancer* (Kellogg). Gibson's protagonist, Case, a technotopian addict, gets off by "project[ing] his disembodied consciousness into the consensual hallucination that [is] the matrix" (5). Juxtaposed with Neo and Case, we could say that Alex has cyberpunk vision. However, day or night, pornoviolence or no pornoviolence, we are always jacked in to Alex's subjectivity and "disembodied" POV, and unlike *The Matrix* and *Starship Troopers, A Clockwork Orange*'s film-thinking privileges music as much as mise-en-scène, both of which invigorate its science-fictionality and the KFM's sense of self-awareness.

On the film's soundtrack, the synthesized version of the Ninth Symphony's second movement ("Molto vivace") is called the Suicide Scherzo. When Alex awakens in the attic after F. Alexander and his gang of literati slip a roofie into his wine, the echoic, tinny, technologized music narrates the escalating horrorshow of his sickness. He tries to get out but the doors are locked. He calls for help and pounds his head against the floor. Then, bereft: "Suddenly I viddied what I had to do," he says in voice-over, "and what I had wanted to do. And that was to do myself in. To snuff it. To blast off forever out of this wicked, cruel world. One moment of pain perhaps, and then sleep. Forever and ever and ever." Clutching his ears, he climbs onto an oriel, opens a window, leaps out, emits what sounds like a canned shriek, and lands on the driveway with a clunk that feels more machinic than corporeal, as if Alex were a robot. Which, symbolically, he is. Finally, the sound of the Scherzo breaks apart and dopplers into the darkness that engulfs the screen. This electronically mediated work of art has (temporarily) ushered Alex into the Abyss.

As always, Alex delivers the voice-over in a calm, cool, detached monotone that never waivers, even when he shrieks during the fall. But again, the voice-over doesn't feel like Alex. It feels like Strangelove, who, nestled in the mineshaft of the KFM's psyche, speaks to us through the concentric tree-rings of the filmind. The voice is omniscient and knows how the story unfolds and ends, but it pretends to live in the moment, and it isn't hung up on exposition, the most common reason for deploying voice-over in SF cinema. Alex is another Strangelovian puppet. In the eyes of the KFM, however, he's the crown jewel, fully integrated with the filmind at this stage, an idealized mode of schizophrenic thought and unconscious abandon. "The world has become a bad film, Deleuze says, that we inhabit and that inhabits us as a 'habitus,' a mode of regularity and 'control' (Burroughs)" (Flaxman 11). This Deleuzian/Burroughsian habitus infects/affects Alex, his intra-diegetic watchmen, and his extra-diegetic watchers.

Hitler and the Nazis perverted and weaponized Nietzsche's philosophy for their own ends. Nietzsche would have been aghast by the posthumous *The Will to Power* (1901). Cobbled together from his notebooks by his sister, Elisabeth Förster-Nietzsche, the resultant manuscript appeared to endorse Nazi ideology. Beethoven fell prey to revisionist history, too: the Nazis "systematically used [his] music for their political purposes. […] The National Socialists instrumentalized Beethoven for their propaganda […] They were interested not only in his music, but also in his attributes as a composer and human being. Beethoven was considered a hero who had overcome the fate of his deafness. He was also admired as a German musical genius" (Reucher). In *A Clockwork Orange*, Strangelove transmits this hauntology and the KFM's machinic desires through the science-fictionalization of Beethoven's music, which, for Alex, converts from a source of pleasure to pain in the Ludovico Medical Facility.

### LUDOVICO FILM-THINKING

*A Clockwork Orange* masquerades as a tutorial on morality and the relationship between free will and determinism. "One of the film's strongest messages is that people should feel free to act upon free will, even if that entails violent crime, instead of being conditioned (robbed of free will) to be law-abiding, a message for which the film has been deemed by some to be dangerous" (McQuiston 105). In the KFM, free will is a MacGuffin, as is every element that does not inform the filmind's endlessly impish monomania for stylized cognition.

In discussions of morality, Alex has been compared to Richard III and Candide. For example, Robert Hughes calls him "the future Candide, not of innocence, but of excessive and frightful experience" (133); and Nelson says he's "a simpler version of both Burgess's protagonist and Shakespeare's diabolical villain. He is a character of intuition and instinct, a mythopoeic extension of human nature, one who does not think as much as he dreams and acts" (143). In fact, Alex's cognition is pure dream, pure performance and *art*, even when Dr. Brodsky confiscates his ultraviolent paintbrush. A mediatized embrainment of filmthinking, Alex perceives himself and his world through a cinematic lens. His overuse of the verb "viddy" (Nadsat for *see*) validates his terminally *video* gaze and subject-position. "Alex's visions while listening to the Ninth Symphony in his bedroom or reading in prison are influenced by Hollywood: he imagines himself as Dracula, a centurion scourging Christ, an oriental prince savouring the delights of the flesh as in the 'historical' films of Cecil B. De Mille (or Kubrick's *Spartacus*?). And, as part of his cure, Dr. Brodsky forces him to watch American action movies and Nazi newsreel footage" (Ciment 81).

Brodsky, the resident mad scientist in *A Clockwork Orange*, oversees the experimental Ludovico treatment to which Alex willingly submits so that he can be "cured" and get out of jail. This "technologically mediated aversion therapy [that blends] drugs and video exposure to violent imagery" signifies Alex's videographic subjectivity as it attempts to deactivate him like Bowman deactivates HAL (Esckilsen 170). The treatment exorcizes one demon (the compulsion for pornoviolence) by deploying another (compulsive reactions that, Brodsky announces to his colleagues, "cause the subject to experience a deathlike paralysis together with deep feelings of terror and helplessness"). Brodsky turns Alex from one monster into another monster. The first hurts other people. The second can only hurt himself, but that damages the reputation of the State: after Alex tries to commit suicide, the Minister of the Interior has no choice but reversion.

In *Frankenstein*, monsters are made. In KSF, they're born and infinitely remade. Neither desire nor monstrosity has stasis or endpoints. Flux defines their performances.

The most noticeable part of Alex's reconditioning are the films he must watch in the Ludovico Center's audiovisual theater, a microcosm for the unconscious flows of diegetic and extra-diegetic reality. Buckled in a straightjacket with clamped-open eyes, he views scenes of brutality and rape, the first of which he describes as "a very professional piece of sinny, like it was done in Hollywood." The utterance denotes how Alex's cinematic mediatization corresponds with his organic bible fantasies ("sinny" a.k.a. "sin") that stemmed from the "Hollywood" culture machine and dream factory. Hence his thesis: "It's funny how the colors of the real world only seem really real when you viddy them on a screen." Alex's filmosophic self-awareness issues from the firing synapses of the KFM as the drugs injected into his system link his neurochemistry with the actions onscreen so that conceiving of those actions thereafter will render him powerless.

The Ludovico Technique may not have made Alex try to kill himself if it weren't for the introduction of the Ninth Symphony's fourth movement (ironically, "Ode to Joy"). He identifies the movement by name just as the Ludovico camera-within-the-camera shows us an image from *Triumph of the Will*: the Nazi eagle and swastika. "It's a sin!" Alex cries out repeatedly. Not that he believes in biblical sin. The exclamation is reactionary. The "sin" committed by this sinny doesn't concern the religion of organized Christianity but the religion of *art* that Beethoven represents for Alex. Beethoven (qua Nazism) is the cornerstone of his pornoviolent artistry. Without it, he ceases to be an artist (i.e., a god), and there's no greater iniquity to his mind than taking away an artist's muse.

The films-within-the-film that Alex and moviegoers watch in the Ludovico theater have been written about extensively for how they comment on spectatorship. "As critics are fond of pointing out, audiences effectively experience the Ludovico treatment *along with* Alex, whose camera eyes are not allowed to flinch at what he sees" (Gabbard 91). This relates to Tom Wolfe's conception of pornoviolence in a 1967 article for *Esquire* where he coined the term. For Wolfe, what makes something cinematically pornoviolent "is that in almost every case the camera angle, therefore the viewer, is with the gun, the fist, the rock" (184). Or, in *A Clockwork Orange*, with the "britva," the "rooker," the "oozy." Ludovico weaponizes viewers with this modality of film-thinking and calls attention to the weaponization of desire inscribed in the KFM, KSF, and the cyborg techno-masculinity that these domains bring into play.

Objective reality is nothingness and ennui to Alex. He must infuse the technology of his subjectivity (i.e., his pornoviolent art) into that abysmal matrix to give it shape, meaning, and purpose. His addictions expedite this pursuit and ensure that he will never stop. Pee and em are part of the problem. Many teenagers rebel against their parents and don't get along with them. Alex's mother and father are scared shitless of him, and they're more like paintings on the wall than real people (hence the idea that their flat is decorated with paintings of a younger Em). Then again, his *real* parents didn't raise him. His *reel* parents did, as we see in his mindscreen/mineshaft bible fantasies. A son of electronic media, Alex performs in accordance with his cultural upbringing.

F. Alexander can be read as an elder version of the byronic Child Alex, whose pilgrimage to adulthood foreshadows the "intelligent type bookman" (Burgess, *Clockwork* 24). Nelson concisely elucidates the depth and diversification of how they double one another: "Alex/Alexander can be paired in several polarities: youth/age; 'primitive' adolescent/'civilized' adult; performing artist/writer; visual imagination/verbal manipulation; Beethoven as inspiration/Beethoven as decoration (HOME's door chime); phallic virility/mental impotence; movement and dynamism/inertia and sitting (either behind a typewriter or in a wheelchair)" (163). Just as F. Alexander casts the shadow of Alex, we can read Alex himself (i.e., the character played by McDowell) as an elder double of a boy who might be dreaming *A Clockwork Orange.* It's not a "real boy," per se, but a mediatized alt-Pinocchio imprinted with sadistic fantasies by a culture of neglect, apathy, and technological excess. Such theses ebb and flow across the skyline of the KFM's dreams like amorphous clouds.

In Burgess's novel, Alex is only fifteen years old. His age isn't mentioned in the film, but he's supposed to be a teenager, and McDowell was 28 during principal photography. Viewers must suspend their disbelief with the same imagination and disavowal that must be applied to *Grease* (1978), some of whose high schoolers have wrinkles.

After completing the Ludovico treatment, Alex demonstrates that he has been purged of his criminal impulses. An audience of VIPs watch him get verbally and physically emasculated onstage by "Lardface," described in the screenplay as "an elegantly dressed fag" (Kubrick), then confronted by a topless woman who makes him gag and retch when he reaches for her breasts. The Ludovico-produced performance reveals the *neutralization of his pornoviolent desires and heteronormative masculinity.* Afterwards, the Minister tells the audience: "You see, ladies and gentlemen, our subject is impelled towards good by paradoxically being impelled toward evil. The intention to act violently is accompanied by strong feelings of physical distress. To counter these, the subject has to switch to a diametrically opposed attitude. Any questions?"

The Prison Chaplain responds: "The boy has no real choice, has he. Self-interest, fear of physical pain drove him to that grotesque act of self-abasement. Its insincerity was clearly to be seen. He ceases to be a creature capable of moral choice." The Minister quickly refutes this objection, assuring everybody that "these are subtleties. We are not concerned with motives, with the higher ethics; we are concerned only with cutting down crime." During the exchange, the camera cuts to a close-up on Alex, who looks up worriedly at the Chaplain, then proudly at the Minister. He has razor burn on his neck. This is a boy? It's not acne; clearly McDowell had a bad shave. The KFM's obsession with minutia would not have let this blemish slide without a reason. Does the filmind mean for the razor burn to denote acne? Should viewers recognize it as such via their suspension of disbelief? McDowell doesn't just look too old to play a teenager; he looks downright middle-aged in some shots, popping crow's feet when he smiles like the Grinch.

The KFM wants us to suspend our disbelief yet *believe* in that disbelief. Look at that razor burn, it tells us. That's a man, not a boy. But you must pretend it's a boy, gentle viewers, which is to say, you must ignore the naked truth that it's a man pretending to be a boy. Thus does the non-diegetic audience (who was just watching a diegetic audience of doctors watch Alex) become a more intimate part of the performance, which is always metafilmic and self-aware. "Does the film turn us all into clockwork oranges?" Krämer asks (*Clockwork* 27). Not necessarily. We were all "queer as a clockwork orange" to begin with, as KSF teaches us (Burgess, "Resucked" 169). The film holds up a mirror to the internal machinarchy that polices our collective identity by addicting us to our externalized technologies and our propensity for phallic aggression. In Strangelove Country, we don't run away from original sin. We run toward sin(ny) with an eye to curing ourselves from the desire to be "cured all right."

# FOUR CUSTOMIZING DESIRE
## A.I. Artificial Intelligence

### SCIENCE FICTION SUBJECTIVITY AND EMBRAINMENT

If *2001* is an anti-SF film, *A.I.* is its doppelgänger—a pro-SF film that reaches back into the history of the genre and self-reflexively enfolds SF themes, devices, convolutions, and clichés. Kubrick made *2001* when we were becoming SF subjects. Spielberg made *A.I.* for an audience who possesses SF subjectivity. Over thirty years passed between the two films. During that time, humanity evolved like an astral ape, sparked by the monolith of media technoculture.

At first, I thought I knew what material belonged to which filmmaker. Kubrick conceived of Rouge City's erotic architecture and the cruel American redneckery of the Flesh Fairs, I thought, whereas the broken-family theme was identifiably Spielbergian. But how many broken (or breaking) families are there in Kubrick's films? Family dynamics are an issue in *most* of them. Jan Harlan states: "It is almost impossible to separate out what was Stanley's and what was Steven's in the finished film, so seamlessly did the collaboration work and so profoundly did Steven understand what Stanley had been trying to achieve" ("Blown" 8). I was wrong. According to Spielberg, Rouge City and the Flesh Fairs were his ideas, and Kubrick plotted the film's sentimentality: "Stanley did the sweetest parts of *A.I.*, not me. I'm the guy who did the dark center of the movie with the Flesh Fair and everything else. That's why he wanted me to make the movie in the first place" (qtd. McBride 483-84).

The above passage from Harlan comes from an introduction to a large-format picturebook, *A.I. Artificial Intelligence from Stanley Kubrick to Steven Spielberg: The Vision Behind the Film* (2009), with concept drawings by cartoonist Chris Baker and commentary by Jane M. Struthers. I lean on Struthers's acumen quite a bit in this chapter, supplemented by Julian Rice's more comprehensive *Kubrick's Story, Spielberg's Film: A.I. Artificial Intelligence* (2017) and other sources that deliberate the collaboration between these populist auteurs.

Debates about authorship/auteurship have surrounded *A.I.* since its inception. Perhaps the biggest misnomer is that that film fell into Spielberg's lap after Kubrick's death, but Kubrick had long thought that his friend should direct it. "Although Spielberg brought many of his own sensibilities to the finished film, this was in itself by design, with Kubrick feeling that ultimately the story better fit Spielberg's directorial voice" (Sikora 264). Nonetheless, the finished movie "captures the narrative arc and thematic underpinnings" established by KSF and the KFM since *Dr. Strangelove* (ibid.). Spielberg wrote the screenplay, but he drew heavily from a 90-page treatment that Ian Watson co-wrote with Kubrick, 1,500 storyboards that Kubrick commissioned from Chris Baker, Kubrick's archival research, and a 15-year correspondence between the directors (Rice 1). Not only are Kubrick's fingerprints all over *A.I.*, he's a scopophilic avatar in the KFM, a ghostly god in the machine whose cinematic gaze is palpable yet elusive.

The point of this chapter isn't to parcel out the attributions of Kubrick and Spielberg but to probe how certain aspects of the Kubrickian materialize in *A.I.*, a coda to KSF and a commentary on the SF megatext. Even if Spielberg had been "responsible" for a particular Kubrickian monad, he was under the influence of Kubrick's Milk Plus.

Based on Brian Aldiss's story "Supertoys Last All Summer Long" (1969) and set in the twenty-second century, *A.I.* depicts a drowned world in which coastal cities have been swallowed by rising sea levels, birth rates and the population are on a steep decline, and androids or "Mecha" exist in various forms of slavery to supplement the Human Stain (i.e., "Orgas"). "*A.I.* is not pro-human" (Struthers, "Part 2" 62).

It's ruthlessly anti-human and reverts to *2001*'s pre-technological Dawn of Man, with no help from alien artifacts. In this postapocalyptic future, the elements will finally have their way with us as we scuttle like ragged claws into the Abyss.

As with HAL in *2001*, Mechas often act more human than humans, and their "organic" masters treat them like the utilities they are, objectifying them as everything from service units, prostitutes, and household playthings to circus freaks, spectacles of destruction, and constant reminders that mankind's days are numbered. In accordance with *A.I.*'s heteronormative code, Mechas play straight male and female roles. On the whole, the KSF codifies them as feminine sources of visual pleasure (even in abjected states) that pose "questions of the ways the [patriarchal] unconscious [ ... ] structures ways of seeing and pleasure in looking" while "producing an illusion cut to the measure of desire" (Mulvey 394, 403). In *A.I.*, however, the anxiety that this pleasure incites in the phallus has more to do with how Mechas represent our technological precondition and death-drive.

The protagonist of *A.I.* is a Mecha boy named David, created by yet another mad scientist, Professor Allen Hobby, in the image of his dead son. Sublimating grief, Professor Hobby wants to make Mechas capable of eternal love for parents. Love, he believes, "will be the key by which they acquire a kind of subconscious never before achieved. An inner world of metaphor, of intuition, of self-motivated reasoning. Of dreams." Henry and Monica Swinton adopt David to fill the lack generated by the loss of their own son, Martin, who has a rare disease and must be kept in suspended animation. A literal illustration of nascent techno-masculinity, David is custom-made to mesh with Monica's emotional register. The preprogrammed flows of their desires as child and mother operate like a two-way circuit.

Following the KFM, the Spielbergian filmind (SFM) "customizes" female characters for the scopophilic gaze as one-dimensional male complements. Women are minor technological extensions of men that imagistically empower their hosts. By this logic, it isn't the phallus that extends/defines itself but the female body that extends/defines the phallus. There are more exceptions to this rule in the SFM than the KFM, such as the clairvoyant "precog" Agatha in *Minority Report*, a rounded, fully developed character by any standard. Monica doesn't show Agatha's complexity and autonomy. A flat, simple-minded character, she never exits the madhouse of patriarchy that constructs and contains her. In the SFM—a mask for the KFM—she is a generic (albeit bourgeois) homemaker. She does little more than perform domestic tasks, obsess about motherhood, and accompany her husband to dinner parties as arm candy. *A.I.*'s twenty-second century extrapolates a man's future from a man's present and past. All of its technologies serve men, even David, purchased for Monica by Henry to cheer her up and create a happier domestic environment for her husband.

After visiting Dr. Know, a slapstick search engine likely derived from Ask Jeeves, Gigolo Joe tells David: "They hate us, you know. The humans. They'll stop at nothing." David assures him that his mother doesn't hate him. She loves him; he's special—she'll do anything for him, especially when he finds out how to transform into a "real boy." Joe declares that under no circumstances does Monica love him. Nor will she. "You are neither flesh nor blood," he says. "You are not a dog, a cat or a canary. You were designed and built specific, like the rest of us. And you are alone now only because they tired of you, or replaced you with a younger model, or were displeased with something you said, or broke. They made us too smart, too quick, and too many. We are suffering for the mistakes they made because when the end comes, all that will be left is us." Orgas hate how their externalized technologies connote the inevitable onslaught of their self-imposed destruction in spite of their own technological quintessence. We return to a familiar thesis: *In KSF and the KFM, there is no humanity without technology.* *A.I.*'s Orgas are as machinic as its Mechas.

Mind and body, Monica is a perfect example of a machinic human that the SFM brings to light in the beginning when we cut from Professor Hobby's opening demonstration on a female Mecha, Sheila, to Monica in a Cricket vehicle. During the demonstration, Professor Hobby removes Sheila's cubed brain—"a sensory toy with intelligent behavioral circuits"—which requires the palettes of her face to slide apart. Once the brain and face return to normal, Sheila casually applies lipstick with a hand mirror. Cut to Monica, who, in the Cricket's passenger seat, casually applies rouge to her cheeks with a hand mirror. The shots associate her with the technology of Shelia, foreshadowing the rebooted android that Monica will become at the end of the film, and symbolizing her robotic inscription as a female object whose looks matter most.

At the center of *A.I.* is a traditional quest narrative. David the Arthurian knight tries to find Monica the Holy Grail after Martin awakens from cryosleep and she abandons the surrogate child. The final act leaps 2,000 years into the future and mawkishly reunites David with a temporary version of his long-dead mother. It's not a great ending to the story, but it's a perfect ending for *Strangelove Country* and KSF: everybody dies, no humans remain—mankind has destroyed itself once and for all. Only technology remains in the form of Specialists, advanced Super-Mechas that evolve from their predecessors and reminisce the tall, stringbean grays from *Close Encounters of the Third Kind*. In the broader sphere of KSF, the Super-Mechas' extraterrestrial image combines the technology of the alien monolith with manmade machinery (external and internal). Verdict: Removed from the human, the technological abides. It doesn't need us. But humanity needs technology. Without it, humanity ceases to be human. The KFM arrives at this conclusive thesis through the film-thinking of *A.I.*, which posits a terminal identity for SF subjectivity.

Throughout this book, I have used the neologisms *embrain* or *embrainment* to indicate how the KFM cognitively estranges, embraces, participates in, and lords over cinematic inner space with respect to machinic desire. In *A.I.*, the KFM embrains the diegesis by interpolating it into a culture machine distinguished by customization. "Perhaps the most evident direction of the way people are customizing their lives is artificial intelligence. How smart should artificial intelligence be? Should artificial intelligence [...] be able to think like humans, even be created as physical robots who are human-like in appearance? These questions all open up deep philosophical questions over how human communication is defined. HAL in *2001* is symbolic of these efforts, by being the onboard computer; all of the ship's functions are controlled by HAL" (Orris 114-15). This philosophical initiative plays out at length in *A.I.* There are HALs everywhere. Most have anthropomorphic bodies that blur the dichotomy between machine and human. In *2001*, HAL is an innovation, a highly utilitarian novelty. In *A.I.* (qua Mechas), he's normative, outmoded, an object of ennui. *2001* takes place over 100 years before the setting of Spielberg's film, yet the space-going humans of Kubrick's film are more like the Specialists: robotic engineers with a vested interest in exploration. *A.I.*'s humans, in contrast, are blasé abjections, flotsam and jetsam confined to a ruined Earth.

HAL manifests in David only because of his manmade origins. They're apples and oranges. Unlike his psychotic KSF forefather, David remains innocent from start to finish, and a mother's love localizes his insecurity and anxiety. He erupts into violence once, when he first discovers (and subsequently destroys) another mass-produced version of himself at Cybertronics headquarters. The other David jeopardizes his self-image as a singular being, but that self-image depends on his idea of how Monica perceives him. Nevertheless, he's still pure machine. Naremore elaborates:

> David isn't a "real" boy but a "mecha"—a computerized replicant, operating with relative autonomy, who is programmed by a scientist and an army of corporate technicians to feel love for his organic "mother" and to want, like some futuristic Pinocchio, to become truly human. Hard-wired to experience Oedipal desire, he can weep and feel joy or fear, but he can't pee and can't eat spinach or any other kind of food. [ ... ] He can dream, but in one sense he dreams of electric sheep [à la Philip K. Dick]. As for the mother he loves with single-minded obsession, she herself in the final scene is a kind of simulacrum with a limited memory, brought to life for a single day and awakened like Sleeping Beauty by virtue of a preserved lock of her hair, which was frozen

for centuries at the bottom of the sea. Even the house is a simulacrum, fashioned by other robots on the basis of David's memory
bank. (241)

The finale of this fairy-tale scenario is technological abjection. And yet the
Specialists, godlike in their powers and amortality, invoke the Kubrickian
sublime. As with gods, these post-cyborgs transcend our cognition and
ability to comprehend them. "The real potential of future technologies is
to change *Homo sapiens* itself," says Yuval Noah Harari in *Sapiens: A Brief
History of Humankind* (2015), "including our emotions and desires, and
not merely our vehicles and weapons" (411). The Specialists personify
this change. Hence the surrealism with which the SFM blocks them
onscreen in terms of their ethereal bodies, vehicles, tones, and voices.
This is complemented by John Williams's eerie musical score and film-
noir chiaroscurism. The SFM "immerse[s] us in signifiers of death and
mourning: water and tears are a major motif, the lighting is bluish and
cold even in the midst of domestic and familial space, and blue dominates
the film's colour palette" (Sobchack, "Love" 11).

The oneiric, bittersweet end can be read as a Freudian wish-fulfillment
dream-womb wherein David's semi-omnipotent descendants rebirth/
regift his mother, a product of their sublimity and an emblem of their
abjection. In *Abjection and Representation* (2014), Rina Arya writes:

Both the abject and the sublime have dramatic consequences for
the stability of identity and order. One of the main differences
between these realms is the trajectory of experience, where the
sublime can be described as upward, and abjection as the coun-
terpart of this. The sublime inspires, lifts us up and draws us to
experiences about the wonderment of nature. We seek out the
sublime because it reinforces the magnitude of the universe and
underpins peak encounters. It may remind us of the insignificance
of the individual in the face of the universe but it is exhilarating
nonetheless, even in its ungraspability. The same cannot be said
for abjection, which instead instils horror and disgust. (6)

The Specialists signify both sides of the coin as subjects of "wonderment" that call to mind the "horror and disgust" of the Human Stain, who wrecked Earth and collectively rode the Bomb into oblivion. They also signify the many deaths of cinema with their luminous bodies, which look like celluloid and literalize Deleuze's theory that *the brain is the screen* (e.g., when they ingest David's memories, we see his history play out in their heads like a timelapsed movie). Their makers were cinematic, screen-oriented thinkers, but not at this level of sophistication. Regardless, the archeological Specialists fetishize their lower-tech makers as talis*men* of meaning and purpose.

A redundant Mecha, then, becomes the link to the Super-Mechas' human fetish. David was built to placate Monica. Now Monica is rebuilt to placate him.

The imagistic and thematic circularity of *2001* factors into *A.I.* "The simulation [that the SuperMechas] create for David to recapture a past time and to relive the experiences in accordance with his own desires, wishes and imagination—a simulated environment where [ … ] the past can be recreated and where it is possible to interact with it in a real and direct fashion. [ … ] Monica is a construct of how David saw her *emotionally*. His perception of her is his desired, preferred, or, rather, programmed interpretation, not one of real experience; he imagines a mother archetype—a mother that, in reality, he never actually had" (Struthers, "Birth" 24). David, an *artwork of customized desire*, thus customizes his own desire for his never-mother. Once again, desire's self-reflexive velocity gains momentum and irradiates the KFM's default narcissism and pursuit of self. The SFM colonizes microtexts and megatexts with its film-thoughts, with its (Arthurian) quest for power and purity. This self-reflexivity extends to the engine of the SF genre that authorizes the KFM and circles back to the ur-KSF, *Dr. Strangelove*, representing SF subjectivity and embrainment as a recidivist, redundant effect of the phallus's consummate desire for sex and death.

In *A.I.*, we witness the Dusk of Man become the Dust of Man as the SFM, riding the Bomb of the KFM, takes us HOME. As Dim chirps in

*A Clockwork Orange*, "Bedways is rightways now, so best we go home-ways and get a bit of spatchka." For the film's Dusk-goers, that spatchka will last forever.

*A.I.* intertextualizes cinema, literature, SF, and KSF with an abandon that borders on ultraviolence. Intertexts constitute a large part of the SFM/KFM's film-thinking, an evolving stream of consciousness that culminates in the Singularity. Technology wins and lives; humanity loses and dies. This is what happens after the Bomb has learned to be loved.

Professor Hobby's early reference to *Hamlet* (1601)—"Aye, there's the rub" (Shakespeare 3.1.66)—sets the tone for the avalanche of allusions to come. Spielberg described *A.I.* as "a series of very dark, *Alice in Wonderland, Through the Looking Glass* adventures," but Lewis Carrol's novels only scratch the surface, and there are more affective intertexts (qtd. Rice 145).

*Le Mort d'Arthur* (1485) and other Holy Grail romances mythologize the film. Rice notes that "Kubrick's use of Arthurian legend in *A.I.* paralleled his use of [Homer's] *The Odyssey* in *2001*," and the "legend's idealization of women in the courtly love tradition also corresponds to *A.I.*'s Oedipal theme" (37, 42). The allusion points to Joseph Campbell's *The Hero with a Thousand Faces* (1949); frequently referenced by SF scholars, this touchstone work of comparative mythology makes a case for the monomyth or hero's journey, a shared motif among narratives in which a "hero ventures forth from the world of common day into a region of supernatural wonder," "fabulous forces are there encountered and a decisive victory is won," and "the hero comes back from this mysterious adventure with the power to bestow boons on his fellow man" (23). David embarks on this quest, venturing forth into a wilderness of fabulous spectacle and danger, then "winning" back his mother, if only for a night. His quest climaxes in boons of wisdom and exposition bestowed to David (and to the audience) by the archaeological Specialists, who romanticize humanity with childlike admiration despite their advanced scientific "specialism." Their excavation of glacial New York is a never-ending search for meaning that mirrors the existential absurdity of their makers. In the SFM/KFM's hybrid stream of consciousness, the Human Stain stains everything—not just the physical earth, but the desires of its left-behind artifacts.

The monomyth emerges in a wealth of texts from many genres, including religion. David's journey begins on the same note as the Buddhist Siddhartha. Born to an aristocratic family, Siddhartha was sheltered from the pain and suffering of most people until he witnessed it himself. Thereafter, he abandoned his family, became an ascetic, and achieved spiritual enlightenment. David witnesses pain and suffering outside of the Swinton's affluent home for the first time when Monica abandons him in the woods. "I'm sorry I didn't tell you about the world," she cries. Thereafter, David becomes hunted (by Flesh Fairs) and hunter (for the Blue Fairy). In the end, he achieves an ephemeral form of enlightenment and transcendence in the arms of a maternal simulacrum.

Many of Spielberg's films thematize Christianity. *Minority Report* might be his most Christian SF film (e.g., "PreCrime" is like organized religion with its celestial trinity of precognitive mutants and detectives who "are more like clergy than cops"). *A.I.* drinks from the same carpenter's cup, telling "a story of biblical proportions in the guise of a fairy tale" (Harlan, "Afterword" 148). David is a Jesus figure/fetish (e.g., after being entombed underwater in an amphibicopter for two millennia, the Super-Mechas resurrect and worship him as a divine, one-of-a-kind being), and there are other markers, such as the Cybertronic logo, a crucified techno-Christ that resembles Super-Mechas, whose bodies preserve the memory of this postcapitalist signage in addition to intertextualizing Spielberg's grays. The Church of Our Lady of the Immaculate Heart in Rouge City is an explicit religious reference. David mistakes a statue of the Virgin Mary outside the church for the Blue Fairy. Joe corrects him: "That's Our Lady of the Immaculate Heart. The ones who made us are always looking for the ones that made them. They go in, look around their feet, sing songs, and when they come out, it's usually me they find. I've picked up a lot of business in this spot." On the spectrum of desire, sexuality harmonizes with spirituality. Both fill a lack in the human psyche produced by the fear of death and destruction established in *Dr. Strangelove*, and both are sources of addiction that homogenize with *A Clockwork Orange*. From this vantage, *A.I.* is about a clockwork boy jonesing for a (maternal) fix.

There is no Bowmanesque übermensch in *A.I.* Humans don't achieve transcendence, enlightenment, or rebirth. Zarathustra exists as the evolved abjection of its dead makers, even if David's transcendence "represent[s] the beginning of humankind's eventual evolution, its immortality, and its transfiguration into a higher life form" (i.e., the Super-Mechas) as portrayed in *2001* (Struthers, "Part 3" 125).

*A.I.*'s most pronounced intertext is the fairy tale based on Carlo Lorenzini's children's book *The Adventures of Pinocchio* (1883), popularized by the 1940 animated Disney film. With his wild white hair, handlebar mustache, and eyes like saucers, the holographic Dr. Know looks like an Einstein-chic doppelgänger of Disney's Geppetto, but the swell of allusive imagery and dialogue mostly concern David's customized desire to become a real boy. Initially, Monica customizes his desire when she imprints him by gazing into his eyes, placing a hand on his neck, and enunciating these keywords in sequence: "CIRRUS. SOCRATES. PARTICLE. DECIBEL. HURRICANE. DOLPHIN. TULIP. MONICA. DAVID. MONICA." Four of the terms (CIRRUS, HURRICANE, DOLPHIN, TULIP) correlate with nature and/or water. SOCRATES, PARTICLE, and DECIBEL respectively stand for history/philosophy, science/cosmos, and art/music/technology. The code of keywords ends with a textual hug for David whose name is flanked on either side by Monica. She embrains the human experience (of nature and culture) into the clockwork boy through the agency of her maternal identity. The procedure instills him with an unconditional love for her that magnifies when she abandons him, initiating a second stage of customization that sets him on the hero's journey and exacerbates his programmed monomania. Here *A.I.* intertextualizes Herman Melville's *Moby-Dick* (1851): David plays the monomaniacal Ahab in a mad search for the White Whale that wounded him, then swam away. Unlike Ahab, David doesn't want to kill his whale for revenge, but Monica and Moby Dick are both versions of Mother Nature, and they fuel the desires of their stalkers with equal intensity. This intertext also applies to Professor Hobby, whose monomania is a form of technological necromancy, and whose whale is David (i.e., the compensatory mass production and distribution of his son).

Kubrick's years-long effort to make "Supertoys Last All Summer Long" into an SF blockbuster about robo-Pinocchio taught him that he wasn't the right filmmaker for the job. Instead, "Spielberg, recognised for directing children, and a longstanding admirer and friend, was an obvious choice: especially as, unlike 'Supertoys,' Kubrick envisaged *Pinocchio* [ ... ] as 'sentimental, dreamlike'" (Morris 301). We know dreams constitute a central Kubrickian monad. Sentimentality does not. Kubrickian cinema is deeply anti-sentimental, but it works in *A.I.* as an oneiric affect/artifact. The film becomes increasingly sentimental as it becomes increasingly nightmarish and David, like a film-noir protagonist, plunges into the labyrinth of the real, ruined world in tandem with his own traumatized psyche. HAL would have cracked under the pressure. David proves to be more resilient.

References to Pinocchio are overt and ubiquitous. The first visible invocation occurs when Martin gives Monica a copy of *Pinocchio* to read to David and him. Martin resents David for stealing her attention, and he enjoys telling the Mecha that he's not real. Monica reads the book to them, and that night, she reads it to David alone: "Pinocchio worked until midnight, and instead of making eight baskets, he made sixteen. Then he went to bed, and fell asleep. As he slept, he dreamt he saw the fairy, lovely and smiling, who gave him a kiss, saying, 'Brave Pinocchio, in return for your good heart, I forgive all your past misdeeds. Be good in the future, and you will be happy.' Then the dream ended, and Pinocchio awoke, full of amazement. You can imagine how astonished he was when he saw that he was no longer a puppet, but a real boy, just like other boys."

The passage includes key data that David will use to deterritorialize himself as a Mecha and reterritorialize himself as an Orga so that he can rejoin Monica after she casts him out. The Blue Fairy becomes even more of a fetishized object than his tailor-made mother while being a surrogate for and conduit to Monica. Slowly, David equates his experiences with the world of Pinocchio. "Don't burn me! I'm not Pinocchio! Don't make me die!" he exclaims at the Flesh Fair after Lord Johnson-Johnson brings him onstage for slaughter. Dr. Know mentions Pinocchio by name alongside an interrelated reference to William Butler Yeats's poem "The Stolen Child" (1889): "Come away, O human child! / To the waters and the wild / With a faery, hand in hand / For the world's more full of weeping / Than you can understand." The stanza paraphrases David's plight and journey toward Orgahood. Dr. Know introduces himself with brio: "Starving minds, welcome to Dr. Know! Where fast-food for thought is served up 24-hours a day, in 40,000 locations nationwide. Ask Dr. Know—there's nothing I don't!" Joe cautions David that the know-it-all sphinx is "a smooth operator" who will "test our limits," and it's not until David combines the categories of "flat fact" (reality) with "fairy tale" (fantasy/dream) that he gets the answer he wants: the Blue Fairy can be found at "the end of the world," a drowned Manhattan.

In the Cybertronics penthouse, we see the Yeats passage engraved into the doorway to Professor Hobby's study. Surrounded by abstract sunrays, the hollowed-out words emit an electric blue light from inside, imploding the classical (nineteenth-century poetry) into the futuristic (twenty-second-century artificial light). Likewise does David's bildungsroman implode a classical nineteenth-century children's story into the turf of genre SF.

After David goes ballistic and decapitates the android he encounters in the study, Professor Hobby tries to assuage his monomania. He explains that the Blue Fairy "is part of the great human flaw to wish for things that don't exist. [ ... ] And that is something no machine has ever done until you." But only his mother's verification of his individuality concerns him. He discovers a legion of lifeless, doe-eyed Davids and female Darlenes hanging from hooks in a lab. The sight of the simulacra assures him that he is *not* special at all. Despondent, he climbs out a window and throws himself into the ocean far below. Mechas don't willingly kill themselves, and the decision to commit suicide humanizes him. This prospective jump-cut from life to death (à la *2001*) makes him more of a real boy than most real boys.

Underwater, David enters a dreamworld that he will never exit. A school of fish encircle his body and steer him into a subaquatic Coney Island. Joe saves him in the amphibicopter with Teddy. Moments later, the police apprehend Joe, and David plunges the amphibicopter back into the amusement park where there is an old Pinocchio theme ride. He glides past Geppetto's workshop and Monstro's lair and arrives at the Blue Fairy's shrine. As he gazes at the Blue Fairy, a Ferris wheel collapses onto the amphibicopter, trapping Teddy and him in the cockpit like pinned insects. The "interplays between the story of Pinocchio and the story of David reach here an ironic parting of the ways: for if Pinocchio's sojourn in the belly of the whale signals a traditional moment of rebirth from the waters of the deep, David's entrapment in the waters covering Coney Island is exactly the reverse of liberation" (Clute and Westfahl). Not so in the eyes of the KFM. Kubrickian logic dictates that David has been liberated by the oneiric texture of this new marine environment. His desire to be reunited with Monica remains powerful, if not psychotic and toxic, but in Strangelove Country—or any country, for that matter—that's what desire is: *unceasingly, obsessively pathological.*

The Blue Fairy that David encounters in the distant-future simulation of the Swinton's home "is a composite of the Blue Fairy in the storybook *Pinocchio*, the hologram at Dr. Know's and the statue at the bottom of the ocean. She acts as a portal through which the SuperMechas can inform David that two thousand years have passed and that, in order to bring back his mother, they will need her DNA. Equally, the Blue Fairy is the medium through which David can communicate his own desire and ultimate wish to the future robots" (Struthers, "Part 3" 124). The final act is all fairy dust and puppetry. Every character becomes Pinocchio—the Super-Mechas, David, the remade Monica—manufactured by the Geppetto of an extinct humanity. In David's terminal dream, his abject existence projects onto the entirely of the wasted world. Abjection (i.e., *technology*) becomes the norm whereas humanity (as mnemonic detritus) becomes a totem pole. In the forty-second century, Mechas and Orgas have swapped roles. The bourgeois Orgas are gone, but they continue to weigh on the psyches of their evolved proles.

Kubrick's science-fictionalization of *Pinocchio* is one way that *A.I.* embrains the SF megatext. The movie exhibits many SF themes and clichés. Robots, of course, are central figures that long predate SF. Cynthia Breazeal writes: "The dream of building intelligent robots is certainly not new. In fact, it is a uniquely and profoundly human quest. Long before people could build such life-like machines, we told stories about them. As far back as the Ancient Greeks, the idea appears in Homer's *Illiad*, in which Hephaistos, the god of metalsmith, fashions mechanical helpers—strong, vocal and intelligent maidens of gold. The idea surfaces again in medieval times in the Jewish legend of the Golem, a robot-like servant made of clay brought to life by Rabbi Lowe of Prague. We created these myths both to inspire as well as to warn ourselves of the danger of creating something we are not able to control" (150). Fast forward to *R.U.R.*, *Metropolis*, Issac Asimov, Philip K. Dick, and beyond ...

SF intertextuality in *A.I.* ranges from mad scientism, cyberpunk, apocalypse, cli-fi, *Frankenstein*, and Phildickian angst to vehicles that extrapolate the cycles from *Tron* (1982), a ramshackle Shantytown that alludes to a squatter settlement of the same name in *They Live* (1988), nods to Asimov's laws of robotics, and correspondence with *E.T. the Extra-Terrestrial* (1982), which also portrays "a creative journey towards independent maturity" that evokes "deep universal feelings" (Rice 145). Spielberg riffs on his own oeuvre elsewhere via the "hounds" who hunt Mechas on motorcycles with illuminated eyes and teeth that look like the Tyrannosaurs in *Jurassic Park*; additionally, they resemble "both the bandits in Kurosawa's *Seven Samurai* and the Ku Klux Klan raiders in D.W. Griffith's *Birth of a Nation*" (197). The neon blue and red decals on the hounds' uniforms denote a further reference to *Tron*, another film that questions artificiality with cyberspatial characters in similar outfits. "Spielberg concentrated [Ian] Watson's analogies into the human species generally, relating the enemy within to the primitive 'apes' of *2001*, *A Clockwork Orange*, and *The Shining*" (ibid.).

The SFM inscribes KSF alongside genre SF. *2001* overshadows everything, but *A Clockwork Orange* and *Dr. Strangelove* aren't forsaken. For instance, Gigolo Joe is "a Kubrickian figure [ ... ] perfectly fit for the society that made him" (Sobchack, "Love" 3). Specific to his cinematic being, "Joe personifies the diversionary aspects of popular entertainment. He embodies cinematic history, melting hearts with songs from 1930s musicals and dancing in puddles (specifically a reference to *Singin' in the Rain*, but also Kubrick's *A Clockwork Orange*, which [ ... ] informs many of *A.I.*'s deepest concerns" (Morris 306). To an extent, *A.I.* illustrates a future of clockwork-orange addiction (to sex, spectacle, technology, etc.) that has reached its final stage, a point of no return that ends in certain death. The SFM radically amplifies *Dr. Strangelove*'s machinarchy and thinks like a film-noir in terms of anxiety, paranoia, patriarchy, lighting, and mise-en-scène. There are minor references, too, such as Martin's disability and disposition—his leg braces and semi-sadism align with Strangelove, who, per usual, controls the KSF gaze and angle of incidence. Rice has a few more worthwhile insights:

In *Dr. Strangelove* and the *A.I.* story he bequeathed to Spielberg, Kubrick gave back by exposing self-destruction as infantile need, thereby hoping to awaken those he could reach to the regressive cause of their potential demise. [ ... ] *Dr. Strangelove* was originally intended to be a historical tale narrated by an extraterrestrial who has imaginatively re-created events leading to humanity's demise from archaeological clues. *A.I.* is a historical tale narrated by a terrestrial robot from earth's distant future based on the history he has learned from surviving records and the psychology of a humanoid robot revived more than two thousand years beyond earth's near future. Both stories are meant to demonstrate to beings more advanced than ourselves the nature of what we were. And both films provide psychological explanations of why we destroyed ourselves. The thirty-year leap from Kubrick's first apocalyptic film to his last changed the physical cause, but it did not change his fundamental vision. (30, 4)

Regarding the interaction between the SFM and KFM, most interesting is the "longing for the lost mother [that] is particularly strong in *Dr. Strangelove* [and] acerbically satirized through Kubrick's sensibility. In *A.I.* it is affectively dramatized through Spielberg's sensibility, which Kubrick thought would be more appropriate to that story than his own" (5).

We could say that *A.I.* plumbs the mineshaft desires of *Dr. Strangelove* and *A Clockwork Orange* as it extends the basic mindset of *2001*. The entire futurist trilogy thinks about the relationship between humanity and technology, with a focus on psychology and emotion. "However, *2001* looks outward to man's immortality and rebirth, whereas *A.I.* focuses upon the internal, the domestic and mankind's imminent extinction. It is no longer an extraterrestrial intelligence that will help mankind to transcend to the next stage of its evolution but, instead, man himself will create it" (Struthers, "Birth" 16-17). Humans could use another cognitive booster from otherworldly beings or relics, but there are no aliens of the *2001* variety in *A.I.* Humans are the aliens. Prior to extinction, we play the role of the collective antagonist of an extraterrestrial-invasion story, attacking and/or enslaving an innocent species; then, post-extinction, the progeny of that species regards us with the same fascination and awe with which we have a tendency to view interstellar life. *A.I.* appropriates *2001*'s exuberance for inversion by inverting the human-alien dynamic. Antithetically, the KFM conjectures that humanity is human because of its alien/technological core, an underlying absurdism that scaffolds KSF.

The SFM complements these intersections with more exclusive intricacies. Teddy's unwaveringly deadpan, matter-of-fact voice sounds a lot like HAL. "I'll break, David," he utters before falling from the net of the Flesh Fair balloon with an intonation that echoes HAL when he utters "What are you doing, Dave?" and "I'm afraid." David and Dave Bowman are linked by forename as well as action: both have robotic and human attributes; both undergo cyclical/transformative journeys. Other correlations with *2001* are the mood and music in *A.I.*'s forty-second century, which recollects Ligeti's "Atmosphères"; and the Super-Mechas' cubed rover, an advanced (re)iteration of *2001*'s moon rover, is an assemblage of black monoliths that reflects their hivemind. The "design of the ship is sympathetic to the communication methods of the SuperMechas. These robots act as individuals but can also be one entity, reflecting Isaac Asimov's idea of our descendants integrating their consciousness to share knowledge" (Struthers, "Part 3" 122). There's no greater knowledge-sharing device in KSF than *2001*'s monolith. The allusion conveys how the KFM perceives alien technology as a power-source without which we cease to exist.

Similar allusions to *2001* pervade *A.I.* Structurally, *A.I.* and *2001* have four acts and play with the circle motif. Production designer Rick Carter recounts: "Circular designs were evident in the round dumpsite for robots, the Moon Balloon and the Flesh Fair. Circles would show up again in Rouge City, at Dr. Know's, and in the Cybertronics library reading room and, of course, the Ferris wheel. It was as if the circles comprised the various worlds we were traveling through with David" (qtd. Struthers, "Part 1" 34). Most of all, circularity represents the ever-turning wheel of desire that propels KSF and its techno-human characters, who unconsciously yearn for death and rebirth. In *A.I.*, humanity dies and breaks the circle of life. The Super-Mechas plug the breakage by adopting humanity's madness. Like David, what these hi-tech Pinocchios really want is to re-customize themselves, to deterritorialize their territorialization (as technological abjections) and manifest their desire to *become human*. Hence the affected romanticization of their woebegone makers.

On the level of cinematography, *A.I.* implements "mode jerks," Kubrick's term for the abrupt shift from one temporal and/or spatial locale to another, such as *2001*'s bone-to-satellite jump-cut and *A.I.*'s 2,000-year leap. "By impelling the viewer into sudden shifts in time and place, these mode jerks subliminally force us to create the continuity ourselves in order to be able to understand the wider narrative" (32).

We come to this understanding primarily through the way the SFM implements KFM characters. In KSF, the KFM uses and abuses characters—male and female, human and machine—as mere husks or conduits through which desire flows and occasionally erupts, shapeshifting from one Strangelovian monster into another. These schiz-flows aren't limited to David. More convoluted, perhaps, is Professor Hobby and Monica's concomitant desire to surrogate their sons with androids. The effect of their desires is an oneiric atmosphere that bleeds from their (inter)actions, facilitated by trauma and grief. In the spirt of dystopia, every sentient organism suffers from the weight of a world gone bad.

### CIRQUE DE L'HOLOCAUSTE

November 9-10, 1938: Nazis murdered over 100 Jews and ransacked Jewish homes, stores, schools, hospitals, and synagogues throughout Germany. A prelude to the Final Solution, *Kristallnacht* or the "Night of Broken Glass" set a precedent for the herding together of Jews in ghettos and concentration camps. Flesh Fairs combine the terrorism of *Kristallnacht* with gladiatorial-style entertainment wherein Orga masters reap jouissance by publicly massacring their Mecha slaves in creative ways. These spectacles of death make commentary on film-being and parody "Hollywood, not least DreamWorks' recent success, *Gladiator* (2000). It is crowd-pleasing, American (US flags abound), spectacular. Rock 'n' roll, circus, mechanical destruction, violence, big screens and light shafts exploit and express social fears—here, of artificially, as [the director of the Flesh Fair] invites people, 'Expel your mechas'" (Morris 306-07). More than a metafilmic indicator, Flesh Fairs sink us into the darkest corners of Strangelove's mineshaft/mindscreen.

Orgas collect stray Mechas in steampunk-chic dirigibles. The illuminated balloon of the dirigible piloted by Lord Johnson-Johnson resembles the iconic full moon from *E.T.* "Moon on the rise!" screams a Mecha as the balloon ascends above a hillock in Shantytown where Joe and David have taken refuge. The mise-en-scène thinks fearful thoughts—a cacophony of ominous woodwinds and brass accompany the rising of the faux moon behind Joe's dwarfed, spindly frame. This bright white eye in the sky portends the immensity of the crimes against (in)humanity to come. The incandescent halogen spotlights that surround the gunmetal basket of the dirigible could just as easily be affixed to the rafters of a stage set; they bring to mind the lights on the alien spacecraft that rises above Devil's Tower in *Close Encounters of the Third Kind*. Here the SFM redirects attention from the KFM to itself while satirizing the hedonism and violence of the Hollywood dream factory.

Frampton alleges that a "film becomes the creator of its own world, not from a 'point' of view, but from a realm, a no-place, that still gives us some things and not others. Conceptualising the right kind of film-being gives film a character, a personality, and style becomes a calling card for that film-personality—it tells us what the film is thinking and how the film regards its characters and events" (38). The calling card for *A.I.* reads SCHIZOPHRENIC and PSYCHOTIC. The intelligence and imagination of filminds contends with that of Super-Mechas, and in *A.I.*, the SFM accounts for the KFM as it asserts its own identity and blurs the margins between reality and fantasy, a Kubrickian monad that Spielberg deploys in many of his own films. Spielberg's unshakeable reputation for kidstuff betrays how much these directors have in common, especially their penchant for style as a way of seeing.

The hounds capture Mechas in nets that the dirigible carries to a nearby Flesh Fair. As Lord Johnson-Johnson retrieves the net with David in it, a Nanny Mecha sings a French lullaby called "*Dodo l'enfant do*" ("Go to sleep, child"). She's programmed to soothe children, but the lullaby foreshows the dreamworlds that David will increasingly inhabit and the Big Sleep that lies in wait for the Human Stain.

The seizure of Mechas can be likened to the transatlantic slave trade that culminated in African-American bondage. The Flesh Fair is a backwoods Cirque du Soleil. For rogue Mechas, however, this carnivalesque, Vegas-style, ultraviolent freakshow is a Cirque de l'Holocauste.

In *Pacific Edge* (1995), Kim Stanley Robinson imagines a near-future ecotopia in which the "Great American Stupid Sports" of professional wrestling and drag racing sublimate our innate propensity for destructive aggression (Foote 54). Flesh Fairs do the same thing at the expense of Mechas, who Orgas objectify (as inhuman machines) and subjectify (as human proxies). People resent and envy their amortality as well as their cognitive and corporeal talents. Unconsciously, Orgas know Mechas will outlive them. Flesh Fairs are one way for Orgas to take revenge on their *desiderata* before the Fall of Man.

The SFM introduces us to Lord Johnson-Johnson's Flesh Fair by locking on Teddy as an employee delivers the supertoy to a Lost and Found. We see the fanfare and the elaborate stadium where the event takes place, a circus arena with killing stages and superscreens that project footage of the carnage. Amid the cheers and catcalls, we hear a ringleader's voice: "What about us? We are alive, and this is a celebration of life! And this is a commitment to a truly human future!" There is no human future, though; soon "we" will all be dead—subtextually, the announcement invites Orgas to grope for agency via denial, the very mode of perception that led to global warming and environmental apocalypse.

David asks his fellow prisoners why this is happening. "History repeats itself," says a Taxi Mecha. "It's the right of blood and electricity." Another Mecha says: "So, when the opportunities avail themselves, they pick away at us, cutting away our numbers so they can maintain numerical superiority." Flesh Fairs issue from this Nazi thesis.

Like a Grand Dragon at a KKK rally, Lord Johnson-Johnson supervises the proceedings and insists that David go "where he belongs—in show business." Orgas have never seen a Boy Mecha before. David's unworldly innocence vexes them. Lord Johnson-Johnson is adamant and panders to the audience: "What will they think of next? See here: a bitty box, a tinker toy, a living doll. Of course, we all know why they made them. To seize your hearts. To replace your children! This is the latest iteration to the series of insults to human dignity. An underground scheme to phase out all of God's little children. Meet the next generation of child designed to do just that! Do not be fooled by the artistry of this creation. No doubt there was talent in the crafting of this simulator. Yet with the very first strike, you will see the big lie come apart before your very eyes!" The sight of David is too much for the audience to process. His verisimilitude yanks on the emotional pull-strings of Orgas and trumps their bloodlust for Mecha gore.

Lord Johnson-Johnson combines Christian dogma with technological affect when he bleats: "Whatever performance this sim puts on, remember we are only demolishing artificiality. Let he who is without sim cast the first stone." "Sim" links immorality (i.e., original sin) with *A.I.*'s machinarchy (i.e., mechanical simulation), but the tawdry redneck doesn't realize how David deterriotrializes Orga desire, and the audience pummels Lord Johnson-Johnson with debris as Joe takes David by the hand and they stride out of the stadium. Strangelove loses this battle, but he's a fixture in the KFM's War Room, rolling his wheelchair in broad circles that promise an inexorable (Nazi) victory.

### ROUGE CITY, CAPITAL OF STRANGELOVE COUNTRY

If Strangelove Country had a capital, Rouge City would be the place. Struthers calls it "home to debauchery and excess" ("Part 2" 84), both of which the KFM revels in. As Gigolo Joe notes: "All roads lead to Rouge!" That includes roads of asphalt, cognition, history, and desire.

Rouge City is a phallic nirvana. Aldiss saw it as "a wonderful feminized city. The traffic pours down women's throats. Suspension bridges penetrate those open lips where toll must be paid. Wondrous expense! In the centre of the city you go bust. Buildings here are prey to all-too-human fantasy. Traffic streams into the tunnel of a female-form anus, and any other likely entry point" (260). Kubrickian excess feeds into the architectual objectification of the female body, which expands the decor of *A Clockwork Orange*'s Korova Milkbar and embrains the dramaturgical sexuality of *Eyes Wide Shut*.

For me, Rouge City is a futuristic version/vision of Samuel Taylor Coleridge's Xanadu in the definitively Romantic poem "Kubla Khan," full of illumined "pleasure domes" and teeming with "Abyssinian maid[s]" (523). "Are there many women in Rouge City?" David asks

Joe, wondering about the Blue Fairy. Joe responds: "As there are stars in the night." This "sim"-ful, heteronormative metropolis further extrapolates Strangelove's version/vision of "a nucleus of human specimens" in postapocalyptic mineshafts distinguished by "a ratio of, say, ten females to each male" (*Dr. Strangelove*).

Joe and David hitch a ride into Rouge City with a carful of male teenagers, emissaries of the phallus en route to drink "the milk of Paradise" (Coleridge 524). They cross a bridge and pass through the gaping pink mouth of a giant female head. Cut to Rouge City Plaza, a neon congestion of elaborate casinos, fountains, discotheques, malls, strip clubs, cabarets, body shops, and holographic signage. The mise-en-scène combines the overstimulation of Times Square with the upscale eroticism of Amsterdam's Red Light District. Hedonism rules with an iron fist. So does capitalism, an arbiter of phallic aggression, fascism, and pathology whereby the SFM implicates the filmic medium.

Morris suggests that Rouge City "is a commercial fantasy, resembling cinema" (307). Embedding the escapism of movie-going, Orgas go there to escape the real world (i.e., to disavow the reality of impending extinction) and pursue their fantasies. It's the perfect place for David. His entire quest hinges on the fantasy of a (false) mother's love and the (impossible) prospect of becoming an Orga. There are lights, screens, simulations everywhere—the experience of Rouge City is intensely cinematic and theatrical, like Joe, a consummate performer who never breaks character. And behind the scenes, as it were, in Dr. Know's shop, the SFM reveals Joe and David to be cinematic entities, calling attention to their ersatz existence and David's customized desires.

"The 'Dr. Know' attraction [ ... ] elevates cinema's claims to truth as it comprises a mini projection theatre in which curtains open upon a screen; its entrance is a dark blue passage with illuminated sprocket holes or screens, typical multiplex décor. Cinema is [ ... ] apotheosised, as David, in another *Persona* re-run, tries to grasp the Blue Fairy hologram and, failing, attempts to enter the screen" (306). He can't get into the screen, of course, a repudiation that reminds us we are screening David, the imaginary protagonist of *A.I.*—imaginary to viewers (as a character in a film) and to other characters in the film (as a Mecha, literally a "made-up" Orga).

The stark hyperreality of Mechas jeopardizes the self-perception of Orgas. Mechas annotate their makers' identities and existence. Unconsciously, Orgas fear that they will become the annotations. Their technophobia mirrors the xenophobic fear that, say, Mexican immigrants are plotting to "take over" the United States, reversing the binary between dominant and marginalized peoples. This is actually what happens in *A.I.*, although not because of some Mecha strikeback or subversion. Orgas do it to themselves by making the earth unlivable. No mineshaft can save them. The archeological site of excavation where the Specialists exhume David from the ice can be regarded as a mineshaft, but there are no lapsed Nazis in this hovel. Victor is dead. Only his monster remains.

In marxist terms, the prole Mechas serve the bourgeois Orgas as prostitutes and laborers. David, too, is a laborer, manufactured as a commodity to make Monica happy, and there are class divisions within human society. The SFM thinks about the aristocratic Swintons in a different light than the NASCAR yokels who attend Flesh Fairs. Still, the working class belongs exclusively to Mechas, who can do anything that Orgas can do better than they can. Their creation ensured that humans no longer have to do manual labor, a type of performance; hence a large swath of Orga society is *customized* as redundant. This is what technology always does, amplifying with one hand what it amputates with the other.

Mechas operate like Strangelove's meta-mechanical hand. In addition to annotating humanity—their existence applies a hermeneutic of suspicion to the collective identity of Orgas—Mechas are human amputations, technological castaways that signify a future Doomsday and amplify the flows of desire. This pathological dynamic galvanizes *A.I.*'s film-thinking and film-being. Deleuze and Guattari write: "We believe in desire as in the irrational of every form of irrationality, and not because it is a lack, a thirst, or an aspiration, but because it is the production of desire: desire that produces—real-desire, or the real in itself" (*Anti-Oedipus* 379). With the compulsion of a vampire, desire feeds on the real as much as itself, and for these theorypunks, it's a capitalist "chaosophy," a "very special delirium" wherein sanity and insanity, reality and irreality, the organic and the inorganic coexist in the same infernal desiring-machine ("Capitalism" 53).

Capitalism "remains a formidable desiring-machine. The monetary flux, the means of production, of manpower, of new markets, all that is the flow of desire" (63). Rouge City services the flux, intertwining desire and consumerism, or rather, symbolizing how consumerism depends upon desire, as humanity depends upon technology. Even David, a utility, must pay to play with Dr. Know: "Question me you pay the fee. Two for five—you get one free."

A Darwinian system that encourages aggression, violence, and survival of the fittest, capitalism is a predator of our own making that derives from our unconscious interactivity. Rouge City teaches that capitalism—another one of the Bomb's many costumes—preys upon us like a filmind. Filminds mind their own (show) business as they milk the imaginations and wallets of the audiences who screen their streams of consciousness. They promise spectators anything and everything, and they deliver their own subjective madness. Strangelove Country's retail reality says that the promise is enough to keep desire in circulation. Nothing but style matters to this vicarious, vampiric *in*-shoot of the SFM, which sucks the blood of the KFM with an ecstatic intemperance. *A.I.*'s filmind also drinks the "milk of Paradise," (i.e., the SFM drinks the Kubrickian, perceiving it as a Romantically sublime artifact).

#### THE (A)MORTAL END

Mechas excel at being polite, making meals, cleaning toilets, driving taxis, and changing diapers, but their most conspicuous purpose in *A.I.* is sexual. Under the umbrella of apocalypse, these externalized desiring-machines induce an eternal Kubrickian recurrence: the coalescence of sex, technology, and death that underpins KSF and breathed life into the KFM.

The future of sex is probably cyberspatial, and it might just happen before the advent of the twenty-second century. People will jack their disembrained consciousnesses into some neuromantic matrix to love the Bomb. Curiously, *A.I.* depicts a lower-tech, less-evolved circumstance where sex and violence stay in the real, tangible world. There is a healthy sex-doll industry in the 2020s with remarkably lifelike and posable "supertoys." Abyss Creations RealDolls, for example, have silicon flesh and a polyvinyl chloride skeleton with interchangeable parts. One model, Stephanie 2.0, approaches $7,000. Dolls are often cast in the preconfigured image of pornstars, but users can customize them. "RealDoll 2 features removable inserts for the mouth and vagina and interchangeable faces that attach by magnets [ … ] If you prefer to have your doll designed to look similar to your wife, your ex-girlfriend, your mom, or even a celebrity, you can email the company a photo and the designers will do their best to create [it. You] can even have your lover come into the factory for a 3D scanning to be made into a fully customized RealDoll" (Worthen 264).

*A.I.*'s twenty-second century extrapolates this commodity, which sells $3 billion per year, constituting 8% of the $37 billion annual sextoy industry (Bedbible). Gigolos like Joe are sentient, high-performance sextoys. He serves the same basic purpose as a RealDoll, only he has more personality, savvy, and charm than anybody else we meet in the film, Orga or Mecha. Once Monica programs David to love her, he becomes more emotionally "human," yet his desire is still robotic, fixated on motherly love. Joe is much more fluid and psychologically "free" even though he's a sex slave. If anything, like the KFM, he's fixated on himself and his own sense of style. He never turns off; he's always in character, a synthespian on a terminal stage, and he frequently breaks into dance. "Why do you do that?" David asks him. "That's just what I do," Joe fires back. He doesn't know where his actions and attitude originate. Nor does he care. He is who he is. And he knows it, Cartesian-style. "I *am*," Joe utters as he magnetically ascends like a sacrificial lamb into a police hovercraft. Then, knowing the demolition that lies in store for him, he corrects himself: "I *was*."

Who he "was" is a Big Dick, part detective who helps David find his way, part phallus who helps Orgas find their little sex-deaths. He does "not just represent the working class; [Mechas are] the new sex slaves, tending to man's and woman's every sexual whim and fantasy. The explosion of pornography [in the early twenty-first century] is presented as a matter of fact and without any judgement. Pornographic and suggestive images are everywhere, and were even incorporated in the architecture of whole towns" (Harlan, "Afterword" 148). *A.I.* foretells the universe of online pornography that exploded in its wake. At the turn of the century, porn wasn't so normative, accessible, and omnipresent. The SFM/KFM science-fictionalizes this cultural formation with Mecha sex slaves, popular commodities that pervade the social and cultural matrix in a non-cyberspatial context.

To Orgas, Mechas are more meat than mind. Two thousand years later, the Super-Mechas bring this binary into poststructuralist play. They have a highly sophisticated group-mind and look more like decopunk artpieces we might find in the Cat Lady's boudoir with their smooth, crystalline, featureless bodies. Sometimes the SFM frames their bodies as if they are on show in a museum. In one scene, the camera fetishizes the Specialist who comes to talk with David in the the Swinton's replicated home. There's a knock at the door. David thinks it's Monica and scurries to open it. Wearing the mask of David's POV, we view the Specialist from an up-angle, framed in the doorway like a painting in a mould. The Specialist is so tall, it must bow its head to pass through the doorway and enter David's bedroom. The camera pulls back to a pulse of synthesized chimes. For a moment, we hold on the Specialist's towering figure, which the SFM spectacularizes as art via scopophilia. Super-Mechas appear to be sexless. We don't know how they reproduce or whether they copulate for fun or love, yet there's something sexy-looking about them—miniaturized, they could be vibrators. But the toxicity and stigma of sex and the Bomb died with the Orgas. Earth has frozen and the circle of (posthuman) life continues. The Human Stain, however, has been bleached clean, a victim of its own collective, dysregulated holocaust.

*A.I.*'s conclusion has David circle back to where he began in the story. The maneuver validates KSF's theme of circularity as well as the KFM's circular film-thinking. David's

> final destination completes the circle—a return to his birthplace, like the homecoming of a prodigal son. [ ... ] We see an overhead shot of a fragmented, circular light fitting as David continues to swing the lamp he has used as a weapon, crying, "*I'm* David, *I'm* David." The circle has been broken and he is no longer the embodiment of Professor Hobby's memories of his dead son. Because of his travails he has built his own identity and has become self-aware. Cybertonics has created the ultimate in Artificial Intelligence and the precursor to the robots of the future. [ ... ] Throughout his journey, David has been told that he is "unique," "special," and "one of a kind." But now he discovers that his creator has manipulated him like a puppet [ ... ] and has designed him as a prototype for mass-production in a world of controlled population where the emotions of childless couples are vulnerable to commercial exploitation. (Struthers, "Part 2" 66)

Professor Hobby amplifies David's customization by traumatizing him ... and further humanizing him. The anvil of trauma forges human subjectivity and identity like no other force, and in the Cybertronics lab, David's "real" father brings down the hammer. Phildickian logic treats empathy as a definitively human trait. In *A.I.*, what makes Orgas human is their hedonism, cruelty, and finitude. To truly become an Orga, David would have to become Strangelove.

According to Harari, a "few serious scholars suggest that by 2050, some humans will become a-mortal (not immortal, because they could still die of some accident, but a-mortal, meaning that in the absence of fatal trauma their lives could be extended indefinitely)" (271). The Super-Mechas have realized this condition of amortality, which carries the cognitive imprint of Orga mortality, but they yearn for Orgas, their *objet petit a*. Just as SF enabled Stanley Kubrick to become Kubrickian,

David enables Orgas to express their Kubrickian desires. "Human beings had created a million explanations of the meaning of life in art, in poetry, in mathematical formulas," the Specialist confesses to David. "Certainly, human beings must be the key to the meaning of existence."

Siphoning the KFM, the SFM embrains an absurdist monad in the Super-Mecha psyche. The Orgas quest for meaning—paralleling David's quest for Mother—is a delusion, a sublimation of the fear of death and nothingness that produces feelings of dread and ecstasy. In the end, *la petite mort* crashes into the earth like an asteroid, producing *une grande mort*, but David remains a symbolic conduit for the Super-Mechas to "touch" their creators, mnemonic slavemasters whose whip continues to sting their ultramodern slaves.

I didn't expect this absurdist denouement to *A.I.* when I first saw it. The denouement takes place in an anomalous extension of traditional cinema. Once more, as in *2001*, the "conventional three-act structure of most films takes a somewhat unconventional turn in *A.I.*, with the introduction of a fourth act. The lines blur between the 'real' and the fairy tale, and we are taken into a world of dream and magic. This fourth act is an exploration of the subconscious as David's dream becomes externalized" (Struthers, "Part 3" 122). We have come HOME to Strangelove Country again. But we never left HOME; KSF merely guides us through the hallways of the same haunted house. This eternal recurrence dominates the circuitous film-thinking of the KFM. The Kubrickian consciousness thrives on the quiet externalization of inner space. In this filmind, we can always expect to wind up where we started, uncertain about the reality of our perception, circumstance, inscription, and interpolation.

*A.I.*'s ending "encompasses Kubrick's desire to combine an exploration of immortality through Artificial Intelligence and DNA with a future fairy tale of magic and enchantment represented through dream, imagination and memory. The ending also has the ambiguity associated with Kubrick's films: not all is as it seems. David's journey is purposeful and successful, yet in actuality it is futile" (124). Existentialism and theater of the absurd work this way. What is meaningful collapses into meaninglessness. The only things that have purpose are the cold circles of life and desire that keep the wheel in motion. Everything else is an illusory distraction that the KFM perceives with a stylish metafilmic gaze. Appropriately, in the final scene of *A.I.*, the camera pulls out of a window in faux-Monica's bedroom and keeps moving back, revealing the Swinton's home as if it might be a stage set. Then the interior lights of the home dim and we fade to black.

*Mineshaft black.*

That's where David is at the end of *A.I.*—Strangelove's mineshaft/mindscreen—caught in a Kubrickian dream that lasts forever. That's where viewers are, too, and there's no way out. Not even extinction can save us from ourselves.

**FULL METAL FILMIND**

What truly separates Orgas from Mechas in *A.I.* is the the specter of (dis)belief. This means belief in an afterlife (and many other super-natural absurdities) as much as disbelief in environmental apocalypse, the annihilation of our species, and post-mortem nothingness. The scientific Mechas don't entertain such psycho-spiritual machinations; psychologically, their (neuro)romanticization of Orga society and cul-ture abjects them. The KFM prefers its technology to its humanity at any rate. It despises humanity, and at the end of its scope, the KFM—through the dark lens of the SFM—discards us once and for all in an anticlimax of Kubrickian entropy.

The metafilmic tenor of this entropic closure further stylizes the SFM/KFM's mindful pose. The Specialists' recreation of the Swinton's home is a simulation twice over: a movie set (non/meta- diegetic) and a house rebuilt from David's memories (diegetic). As a Mecha, David remains a simulated Orga, as does Monica, rebuilt with DNA from a hair sample that Teddy stashes in his groin for two millennia. She only gets 24 hours of life to live—an arbitrary timespan, a micro-MacGuffin that serves the story and the irreality of the scene more than verisi-militude. And when Monica falls asleep to die for the second time, David falls asleep for the first time, going to a place "where dreams are born," according to the Super-Mecha narrator. The subsequent pullout/fadeout reasserts that we are watching a film and that we are technological, cinematic beings prone to ultraviolence. Brandishing the KFM like a longsword, the SFM deduces that we all possess (and are possessed by) a Strangelovian desire for watching, enacting, and embraining horrorshows.

In *Dialectic of Enlightenment* (1944), Max Horkheimer and Theodor W. Adorno look at the relationship between the culture industry, the burgeoning media environment, and the early twentieth-century human condition. One of their theses is that "real life is becoming indistinguishable from the movies" (126). The twenty-first century has unpacked and substantiated this argument. Now "real life" is not only cinematic, *irreal* life is, too. Subconsciously, we have been trained to believe that we exist in a film, terminally inscribed by the screens that show us who we are and what we want. To varying degrees, we all have filminds, and to navigate the pathological SF diegesis of the eletroni-cally mediatized real, we must all think like motion-picture media.

In my introduction to this book, I said that cinema's identity is teth-ered to its capacity to die and live again. Cinema began as an extension of the human body and mind. Today, human beings are the extension. The KFM (via KSF) came to life as we became one of cinema's innu-merable ends.

KSF minds its own existence in conjunction with the SF megatext, and it foreshadows how we have stormed the SF reality studio in the twenty-first century. I wrote *Strangelove Country* to operate like an SF novel (in four acts) as well as a critical monograph on KSF. Like Kubrickian cinema, I have tried to exercise style as a way of seeing, critiquing the KFM with its own complementary logic, from cosmic/cognitive theories about the filmind's film-thinking to a schizophrenic, techno-academic prose and tone that oscillates between hard (i.e., cold, acerbic, machinic) and soft (i.e., colloquial, unassuming, "human") registers of language. This sort of methodology is something of an aberration in Kubrick Studies. Outside of the field, it's less uncommon. Frampton, Deleuze, Bukatman, McLuhan, Reza Negarestani, Hélène Cixous, Paul Virilio, Arthur Kroker, Louis Armand, and others have all written hyperstylized critical speculations that Istvan Csicsery-Ronay Jr. might call the "SF of theory." SF "is not a genre of literary enter-tainment only, but a mode of awareness, a complex hesitation about the relationship between imaginary conceptions and historical reality unfolding into the future" ("SF" 388). To my list of theorypunks, Csicsery-Ronay Jr. rightly adds Jean Baudrillard and Donna Haraway, "two of the most interesting and acute theorists of the transformation of SF into a discursive practice" (389). But is it really possible to produce anything but SF anymore? Doesn't everything that we write involve a dialectic of SF, the dominant fiction that structures our perception, desires, and lived experience? Of course, genres still exist, but westerns, romances, musicals, etc.—now they're all written by cyberpunks and cyborgs, artificially constructed monsters whose daily life entails various modes of techno-pathological mediation.

Whether I write fiction and nonfiction, I immerse myself in the content, becoming the content, if only in my own head. I guess it's a form of obsessive method acting/authoring. Normally, I take this process in stride and try not to annoy people.

This book consumed me.

Even when I was doing other things, I was thinking about how to channel, represent, shape, and stylize the flows of my Kubrickian immersion. I talked to myself far too much. I sent myself emails from Strangelove, Alex, and David, trying to get to know them better, to discover what makes their inner Bombs tick. I made diagrams and memorized dialogue. I took incessant notes in my Moleskine journals and on my phone and computer and skin. I bought collectible action figures of Moon-Watcher, Heywood Floyd, Dave Bowman, the monolith, and Stanley Kubrick, and I plastered my condo with surreal Polish posters of Kubrick's movies, embraining myself in Kubrickian media. I rewatched and/or reread certain scenes before bed so that I might dream about them and possibly unlock new insights hiding in my unconscious. I even wrote faux reviews of my scholarly dailies. In essence, I'm an actor who's still waiting for the adult to eat the little boy that lives inside of him, and these tactics helped me cultivate a certain style, voice, and perspective with regard to the films under consideration. But however one approaches and delivers the content, writing about Kubrick is a difficult task. Composing an original work of

Kubrick scholarship is even harder. The vastness of monographs and articles devoted to his oeuvre consecrates the rich substance of his cinematic art yet limits angles of critical incidence. Dark, clever, humorous, subversive, uncanny, elegant, evocative, and irreal, Kubrick's films indulge our primordial urges while appealing to our intellect, the logic of (non)sense, and basic human truths. Usually, this appeal is a ruse. In the KFM, desire always defeats reason, and truth is only as good as its prefabrication/prevarication.

*Strangelove Country* describes some of the ways that the KFM thinks and functions, using the symbolic essence of Dr. Strangelove as an anchor. In the absence of this anchor and the methodology I appropriate from *Filmosophy*, this would be a different book. Good scholarship amplifies the critical imagination. Frampton's innovative way of seeing cinema enabled me to see KSF and the Kubrickian consciousness in a brighter, more industrious light.

Kubrick has been a part of my life for as long as I can remember. His films have inspired my fiction since the beginning of my career as an author. The first novel I tried (and failed) to write in the 1990s was a sequel to *A Clockwork Orange* called *I, Alex*, which included extensive footnotes written in Nadsat. As an aging literary and film scholar, I find myself reverting to Kubrick's films with greater frequency, directly and indirectly, but *Strangelove Country* is by far my most concerted study of the material. Occasionally, I have allowed my own character to wander into the discussion. This was intentional. I wanted to use myself to explore how cinema affects and abjects spectators. We often treat films as our own possessions, or at least identity-markers. To this day, I continue to identify myself with films that remind me of who I used to be, how I used to perceive the world, and how my perceptions have changed. The experience of re-screening *A Clockwork Orange* to write chapter three was quite different than when I screened it for the first time three decades ago. I was *tabula rasa* back then—a becoming-filmind at best. Now, sometimes, I feel like I'm more filmind than not.

The KFM thinks we're a disease, and it isn't interested in a cure. The Human Stain is just too much fun to play with, and we've always been self-destructive. The thicker the satire, the better the KFM feels about itself and its capacity to stylize the boulevards of broken dreams that will lead to our downfall.

Post-*Lolita*, the KFM embrains the science-fictional pathology of the real with phallic aggression. SF underwrites contemporary reality. In the KFM's diegetic memory, we became technologically enhanced and aware beings when aliens injected our primordial ancestors with the episteme of Strangelove's serum. It wasn't until the twentieth century that we externalized our SF interiors. Kubrick's futurist trilogy is a hermeneutic production of this terminal affect.

Kubrick himself never made another SF film after *A Clockwork Orange*, but from my overlook, SF territorializes all Kubrickian cinema. *Barry Lyndon*, "with its remarkable reconstruction of a whole vanished 18th-century past," is an oneiric, hyperreal way of film-thinking in which the dueling pistol and the warring musket (extensions of techno-masculinity) determine the course of life (Jameson 214). *Eyes Wide Shut* is an inner-spatial odyssey, as is *The Shining*: unseen forces antagonize the protagonists, and behind the curtain, some form of Oz-like wizard—be it spectral or psychological, actual or illusory—fiddles with the gears of a control panel and conjures the mediatized dreamscapes of Bill Hartford and Jack Torrance.

*Full Metal Jacket* is more science-fictional than *Dr. Strangelove*. It lays emphasis on agential/destructive technological extensions and extrapolates *2001*'s thesis that our machines dehumanize us. In the prehistoric first act of *2001*, a tribe of dejected apefolk learn to use technology. Then, in the futuristic later acts, evolved apes put their know-how to use and assert their feral cyborg identities. *Full Metal Jacket* begins with the mechanical shears that manufacture the new physiognomic identities of soldiers (dejected apefolk), and it ends with the gun used by the comically named "Joker" (a trained, mechanized ape) to kill a child sniper. In the final scene, the soldiers sing the Mickey Mouse March as they trudge through the fiery ramparts of the city that they reduce to rubble. The song punctuates the violent Disneyfication of the American cultural consciousness, the absurdity of war, and the process of technological existence/extension. Even the title *Full Metal Jacket* signifies the ready possession of death-dealing machinery (a small-arms projectile bullet) and emboldens an SF identity by representing humanity as a tool. Gene Siskel commented on this idea in a 1987 interview, saying Kubrick

> makes films about tools that run amok: the French rifles that ultimately kill French soldiers in *Paths of Glory*; the failed, fail-safe systems of the military loonies in *Dr. Strangelove*; the apes' bones and the scientists' computer in *2001*; the doctor's violent treatment for pacification in *A Clockwork Orange*. Tools, Kubrick is saying, can be used for good and for evil—to communicate, to destroy. What he is trying to show us in *Full Metal Jacket*, as in so much of his work, is that man himself is such a tool, created by a tool-maker who has given us the ability to create and destroy ourselves and our world. Tools abound in *Full Metal Jacket*, the most prominent being rifles. But it's how they're used that counts. (184)

Like the KFM, Siskel is thinking about Kubrick's human tools vis-à-vis SF. A few years earlier, in 1981, Baudrillard wrote: "A whole generation of films is emerging that will be to those one knew what the android is to man: marvelous artifacts, without weakness, pleasing simulacra that lack only the imaginary, and the hallucination inherent to cinema. Most of what we see today (the best) is already of this order. *Barry Lyndon* is the best example: one never did better, one will never do better in … in what? Not in evoking, not even in evoking, in *simulating*. All the toxic radiation has been filtered, all the ingredients are there, in precise doses, not a single error" (45-46). Traditionally, Kubrick's non-futurist cinema isn't read this way. I can't speak for the co-host of *At the Movies* or the author of *Simulacra and Simulation* (1981), but I can say with some conviction that my reading issues from my own station in a "real" SF filmind that, like a mad tool-maker, has turned me into a machine and directed the course of my film-thinking.

I don't know if my eyes are wide open or wide shut. I do know that external forces have fabricated the way I see the world and its artifacts in terms of machinic abjection and desire.

Over half a century ago, J.G. Ballard said that "everything is science fiction" (Goddard 29). This includes the future we currently occupy and the history that manufactured it. Even the Stone Age. Even the primordial soup and the Big Bang—*especially* the Big Bang, the concept of which is a speculative fiction and a product of techno-modernist thinking, devised by Belgian cosmologist Georges Lemaître in 1931. We are the cyborgs that Lemaître was becoming. It's the nature of our embrainment, our technological reality, and our cinematic perception. All the world may have been a stage for Shakespeare. For us, all the world's a screen. But Shakespeare didn't encounter stages with the ubiquity that we encounter screens, confronting them at almost every turn. Nor did he carry around a smartstage in his pocket.

Kubrick's belated induction into the Science Fiction Hall of Fame in 2014 solidified the excellence of his contribution to a genre that has infrequently risen above the bar set by KSF in written and visual formats. The filmmaker is gone, but his amortal filmind lives on indefinitely, like Super-Mechas. All films possess their own filminds, as do all directors' collective oeuvres. Few filminds, however, think like the KFM and exhibit such cohesion, intelligence, self-awareness, refinement, playfulness, and legerdemain. The sophistication of these qualities sets the KFM apart from other film-beings and reifies the nightmare of its vampirism. Dr. Strangelove is a vampire, after all, feeding on the psychopathology of everyday life as he schematizes new lines of post-Nazi flight. He's an alien emissary, too, injected into the proto-human megatext by psychic colonists who humanize us even as they technologize us.

## BIBLIOGRAPHY

*A Clockwork Orange.* Dir. Stanley Kubrick. Warner Brothers, 1971.

Abrams, Jerold J. "The Philosophy of War in *Dr. Strangelove." A Critical Companion to Stanley Kubrick,* edited by Elsa Colombani. Lexington Books, 2020. 111-22.

Abrams, Nathan. *Stanley Kubrick: New York Jewish Intellectual.* Rutgers University Press, 2020.

Adorno, Theodor W. and Max Horkheimer. *Dialectic of Enlightenment.* 1944. Continuum, 1972.

Agel, Jerome. *The Making of Kubrick's 2001.* Signet, 1970.

"Agent Orange." *History.com.* May 16, 2019. https://www.history.com/topics/vietnam-war/agent-orange-1. Accessed August 12, 2022.

*A.I. Artificial Intelligence.* Dir. Steven Spielberg. Amblin Entertainment, 2001.

Aldiss, Brian. "Chris Baker's World." *A.I. Artificial Intelligence from Stanley Kubrick to Steven Spielberg: The Vision Behind the Film,* edited by Jan Harlan and Jane M. Struthers. Thames & Hudson, 2009. 26.

Arya, Rina. *Abjection and Representation: An Exploration of Abjection in the Visual Arts, Film and Literature.* Palgrave Macmillan, 2014.

Ashley, Mike and Peter Nicholls. "Golden Age of SF." *The Encyclopedia of Science Fiction.* June 23, 2021. https://sf-encyclopedia.com/entry/golden_age_of_sf. Accessed December 5, 2023.

"Avatar." *IMDb.* 2009. https://www.imdb.com/title/tt0499549. Accessed April 14, 2022.

Ballard, J.G. "Which Way to Inner Space?" 1962. *A User's Guide to the Millennium.* Flamingo, 1997. 195-98.

Baudrillard, Jean. *Simulacra and Simulation.* 1981. University of Michigan Press, 1994.

Baxter, John. *Stanley Kubrick: A Biography*. Da Capo Press, 1997.

Bedbible Research Center. "Sex Doll Statistics." *Bedbible*. August 26, 2022. https://bedbible.com/sex-doll-statistics. Accessed October 23, 2022.

Benson, Michael. *Space Odyssey: Stanley Kubrick, Arthur C. Clarke, and the Making of a Masterpiece*. Simon & Schuster, 2019.

Benson, Paula. "*2001: A Space Odyssey*—A Close Look at Those Fabulously Futuristic Djinn Chairs and How Kubrick's Vision of the Future Was Brought to Life through 'Product Placement.'" *Film and Furniture*. April 30, 2014. https://filmandfurniture.com/2014/04/kubricks-vision-of-the-future-brought-to-life-through-product-placement-in-2001-a-space-odyssey. Accessed July 4, 2022.

Berg, Nicole M. *Discovering Kubrick's Symbolism: The Secrets of the Films*. McFarland, 2020.

Bernstein, Jeremy. "Profile: Stanley Kubrick." 1966. *Stanley Kubrick: Interviews*, edited by Gene D. Phillips. University Press of Mississippi, 2001. 21-46.

Bester, Alfred. "Science Fiction and the Renaissance Man." 1957. *Redemolished*. iBooks, 2000. 408-30.

Bould, Mark. "Dr. Strangelove or: How I Stopped Worrying and Learned to Love the Bomb (1964)." *The Greenwood Encyclopedia of Science Fiction and Fantasy: Volume 3*. Greenwood Press, 2005. 1003-05.

Bouzereau, Laurent. *Ultraviolent Movies*. 1996. Citadel Press, 2000.

Breazeal, Cynthia. "A.I.: Building Robots in Our Image." *A.I. Artificial Intelligence from Stanley Kubrick to Steven Spielberg: The Vision Behind the Film*, edited by Jan Harlan and Jane M. Struthers. Thames & Hudson, 2009. 150-55.

Brosnan, John, David Langford, Nick Lowe, and Peter Nicholls. "2001: A Space Odyssey." *The Encyclopedia of Science Fiction*. July 31, 2021. https://sf-encyclopedia.com/entry/2001_a_space_odyssey. Accessed June 14, 2022.

Bukatman, Scott. "Foreword." *Special Effects: New Histories/Theories/Contexts*, edited by Dan North, Bob Rehak, and Michael S. Duffy. BFI, 2015. ix-xii.

———. *Terminal Identity: The Virtual Subject in Postmodern Science Fiction*. Duke University Press, 1993.

Burgess, Anthony. *A Clockwork Orange*. 1962. W.W. Norton & Company, 2019.

———. "*A Clockwork Orange* Resucked." 1986. *A Clockwork Orange*. W.W. Norton & Company, 2019.

Cahill, Tim. "The *Rolling Stone* Interview: Stanley Kubrick." 1987. *Stanley Kubrick: Interviews*, edited by Gene D. Phillips. University Press of Mississippi, 2001. 189-203.

———. "Two-Hour Interview with Stanley Kubrick." 1987. Audio Tapes for The *Rolling Stone* Interview. *YouTube*, uploaded by Movie Geeks United. https://www.youtube.com/watch?v=ehQf0LJVOHQ. Accessed May 1, 2022.

Campbell, Joseph. *The Hero with a Thousand Faces*. 1949. New World Library, 2008.

Castle, Allison. *The Stanley Kubrick Archives*. 2005. Taschen, 2016.

Chocrane, Lauren. "*2001: A Space Odyssey*—The Fashion Power of Designer Hardy Amies." *The Guardian*. November 28, 2014. https://www.theguardian.com/fashion/fashion-blog/2014/nov/28/2001-space-odyssey-the-fashion-power-of-designer-hardy-amies. Accessed July 4, 2022.

Christopher, Nicholas. *Somewhere in the Night: Film Noir and the American City*. Henry Holt & Company, 1997.

Ciment, Michel. *Kubrick*. 1980. Holt, Rinehart & Winston, 1983.

Clarke, Arthur C. *2001: A Space Odyssey*. 1968. Roc, 1993.

Cochrane, Lauren. "*2001: A Space Odyssey*—The Fashion Power of Designer Hardy Amies." *The Guardian*. November 28 2014. https://www.theguardian.com/fashion/fashion-blog/2014/nov/28/2001-space-odyssey-the-fashion-power-of-designer-hardy-amies. Accessed December 18, 2023.

Clute, John. "Hitler Wins." *The Encyclopedia of Science Fiction*. May 2, 2022. https://sf-encyclopedia.com/entry/hitler_wins. Accessed May 29, 2022.

———. "Karel Čapek." *The Encyclopedia of Science Fiction*. October 11,

2021. https://sf-encyclopedia.com/entry/capek_karel. Accessed August 14, 2022.

Clute, John and Gary Westfahl. "A.I.: Artificial Intelligence." *The Encyclopedia of Science Fiction*. February 2, 2021. http://www.sf-encyclopedia.com/entry/a_i_artificial_intelligence. Accessed September 1, 2021.

Clute, John, Peter Nicholls, and Brian Stableford. "Definitions of SF." *The Encyclopedia of Science Fiction*. June 15, 2020. https://sf-encyclopedia.com/entry/definitions_of_sf. Accessed November 27, 2021.

Coleridge, Samuel Taylor. "Kubla Khan." 1816. *Romanticism: An Anthology*. Blackwell, 1998. 523-24.

Colombani, Elsa. "Introduction." *A Critical Companion to Stanley Kubrick*, edited by Elsa Colombani. Lexington Books, 2020. 1-19.

Cook, David and Arthur Kroker. *The Postmodern Scene: Excremental Culture and Hyper-Aesthetics*. St. Marten's Press, 1986.

Cook, Roger F. *Postcinematic Vision*. Minnesota University Press, 2020.

Cooke, Elizabeth A. "Understanding the Enemy: The Dialogue of Fear in *Fear and Desire* and *Dr. Strangelove*." *The Philosophy of Stanley Kubrick*, edited by Jerold J. Abrams. University of Kentucky Press, 2009. 9-31.

Cornea, Christine. *Science Fiction Cinema: Between Fantasy and Reality*. Rutgers University Press, 2007.

Csicsery-Ronay Jr., Istvan. "The SF of Theory: Baudrillard and Haraway." *Science Fiction Studies* 18.3 (November 1991): 387-404.

———. *The Seven Beauties of Science Fiction*. Wesleyan University Press, 2008.

"Dark City." *IMDb*. 1998. https://www.imdb.com/title/tt0118929. Accessed April 14, 2022.

Deleuze, Gilles. *Cinema 2: The Time-Image*. 1985. Minnesota University Press, 2003.

———. "The Brain Is the Screen: Interview with Gilles Deleuze on *The Time-Image*." *Discourse* 20.3 (Fall 1998): 47-55.

Deleuze, Gilles and Félix Guattari. *Anti-Oedipus: Capitalism and Schizophrenia*. 1972. Minnesota University Press, 1998.

———. "Capitalism: A Very Special Delirium." *Chaosophy*, edited by Sylvère Lotringer. Semiotext(e), 1995. 53-73.

Dick, Philip K. "Man, Android, and Machine." 1976. *The Shifting Realities of Philip K. Dick: Selected Literary and Philosophical Writings*. Vintage, 1995. 211-32.

———. "The Android and the Human." 1972. *The Shifting Realities of Philip K. Dick: Selected Literary and Philosophical Writings*. Vintage, 1995. 183-210.

Dougherty, Stephen. "Messages from the Stars: *2001: A Space Odyssey* and *His Master's Voice*." *Science Fiction Studies* 48.2 (July 2021): 306-31.

*Dr. Strangelove or: How I Learned to Stop Worrying and Love the Bomb*. Dir. Stanley Kubrick. Hawk Films, 1964.

Duffy, Michael S., Dan North, and Bob Rehak. "Introduction." *Special Effects: New Histories/Theories/Contexts*, edited by Michael S. Duffy, Dan North, and Bob Rehak. BFI, 2015. 1-13.

Emerson, Ralph Waldo. "Nature." 1836. *Selections from Ralph Waldo Emerson*. Houghton Mifflin Company, 1960. 21-56.

Esckilsen, Erik. "The Mechanics of Mistrust: Techno-Antagonism in the Films of Stanley Kubrick." *Critical Insights: Stanley Kubrick*. Salem Press, 2016. 158-75.

Flaxman, Gregory. "Introduction." *The Brain Is the Screen: Deleuze and the Philosophy of Cinema*. Minnesota University Press, 2000. 1-57.

Foote, Bud. "A Conversation with Kim Stanley Robinson." *Science Fiction Studies* 21.1 (March 1994): 51-60.

Frampton, Daniel. *Filmosophy*. Wallflower Press, 2006.

Frederick, Robert B. "Review: *2001: A Space Odyssey*." *Variety*. April 2, 1968. https://variety.com/1968/film/reviews/2001-a-space-odyssey-1200421723. Accessed July 9, 2022.

Freedman, Carl. "*2001* and the Possibility of a Science-Fiction Cinema." *Science Fiction Studies* 25.2 (July 1998): 300-18.

Freud, Sigmund. *Civilization and Its Discontents*. 1930. W.W. Norton & Company, 1989.

Fugue, Lauren. "Fifty Years Later, Scientists Reflect on the Influence of *2001: A Space Odyssey*." *Cosmos*. October 17, 2018. https://cosmosmagazine.com/space/fifty-years-later-scientists-reflect-on-the-influence-of-2001-a-space-odyssey. Accessed July 8, 2022.

Gabbard, Krin and Shailja Sharma. "Stanley Kubrick and the Art Cinema." *Stanley Kubrick's A Clockwork Orange*, edited by Stuart Y. McDougal. Cambridge University Press, 2003. 85-108.

Gaiman, Neil. "Of Time, and Gully Foyle." *The Stars My Destination*. Vintage, 1996. vii-x.

Gelmis, Joseph. "The Film Director as Superstar: Stanley Kubrick." 1970. *Stanley Kubrick: Interviews*, edited by Gene D. Phillips. University Press of Mississippi, 2001. 80-104.

Gibson, William. *Neuromancer*. Ace, 1984.

Gilbert, James. "Auteur with a Capital A." *Stanley Kubrick's 2001: A Space Odyssey—New Essays*, edited by Robert Kolker. Oxford University Press, 2006. 29-41.

Gitlin, Todd. *Media Unlimited*. Metropolitan Books, 2001.

Goddard, James. "Everything Is Science Fiction!" 1970. *The J.G. Ballard Book*, edited by Rick McGrath. The Terminal Press, 2013. 16-31.

Goodhart, Charlotte. "Television through the Ages." *Museum of the Home*. December 11, 2020. https://www.museumofthehome.org.uk/explore/stories-of-home/television-through-the-ages. Accessed August 31, 2022.

Gould, Jonathan. *Can't Buy Me Love: The Beatles, Britain, and America*. Harmony Books, 2007.

Grady, Constance. "*A Clockwork Orange* Author Anthony Burgess: 'Art Is Dangerous.'" *Vox*. June 2, 2018. https://www.vox.com/culture/2018/6/2/17413562/clockwork-orange-author-anthony-burgess-art-is-dangerous. Accessed September 2, 2022.

Grant, Barry Keith. "Of Men and Monoliths: Science Fiction, Gender, and *2001: A Space Odyssey*." *Stanley Kubrick's 2001: A Space Odyssey—New Essays*, edited by Robert Kolker. Oxford University Press, 2006. 69-86.

Graves, Robert and Raphael Patai. *Hebrew Myths: The Book of Genesis*. 1955. Seven Stories Press, 2022.

Grusin, Richard and Jocelyn Szczepaniak-Gillece. "Introduction." *Ends of Cinema.* Minnesota University Press, 2020. vii-xiv.

Harlan, Jan. "Afterword: The Two Masters." *A.I. Artificial Intelligence from Stanley Kubrick to Steven Spielberg: The Vision Behind the Film,* edited by Jan Harlan and Jane M. Struthers. Thames & Hudson, 2009. 148-49.

———. "Blown by a Strong Wind Over the Legal Mountains." *A.I. Artificial Intelligence from Stanley Kubrick to Steven Spielberg: The Vision Behind the Film,* edited by Jan Harlan and Jane M. Struthers. Thames & Hudson, 2009. 8.

Harari, Yuval Noah. *Sapiens: A Brief History of Humankind.* Harper Perennial, 2015.

Houston, Penelope. "Kubrick Country." 1971. *Stanley Kubrick: Interviews,* edited by Gene D. Phillips. University Press of Mississippi, 2001. 108-15.

Hughes, Robert. "A Clockwork Orange: The Décor of Tomorrow's Hell." *Time Magazine.* December 27, 1971. In *Stanley Kubrick's A Clockwork Orange,* edited by Stuart Y. McDougal. Cambridge University Press, 2003. 131-33.

Huxley, Aldous. *The Doors of Perception.* 1954. Flamingo, 1994.

*Iron Sky.* Dir. Timo Vuorensola. Blind Spot Pictures, 2012.

Jafa, Arthur. "My Black Death." *Everything but the Burden: What White People Are Taking from Black Culture,* edited by Greg Tate. Broadway, 2003. 244-57.

Jameson, Frederick. "Progress Versus Utopia; or, Can We Imagine the Future?" *Science Fiction Criticism: An Anthology of Essential Writings.* Bloomsbury, 2017. 211-24.

Jenkins, Greg. *Stanley Kubrick and the Art of Adaptation.* McFarland, 1997.

Kafka, Franz. *The Trial.* 1925. Schocken, 1992.

Kagan, Norman. *The Cinema of Stanley Kubrick.* 1989. Continuum, 2000.

Kellogg, Carolyn. "William Gibson's Cyberpunk Classic *Neuromancer* May Finally Get to Screens." *Los Angeles Times.* May 19, 2011. https://www.latimes.com/archives/blogs/jacket-copy/story/2011-05-19/william-gibsons-cyberpunk-classic-neuromancer-may-finally-get-to-screens. Accessed July 24, 2023.

King, Geoff and Tanya Krzywinska. *Science Fiction Cinema: From Outerspace to Cyberspace*. 2000. Wallflower Press, 2002.

Kirgo, Julie. "Peckinpah, Uncensored and Upgraded." *Los Angeles Times*. August 26, 2002. https://www.latimes.com/archives/la-xpm-2002-aug-26-et-kirgo26-story.html. Accessed August 10, 2022.

Kolker, Robert P. "*A Clockwork Orange* ... Ticking." *Stanley Kubrick's A Clockwork Orange*, edited by Stuart Y. McDougal. Cambridge University Press, 2003. 19-36.

———. "Foreword." *Alien Legacies: The Evolution of the Franchise*, edited by Nathan Abrams and Gregory Frame. Oxford University Press, 2023. vii-viii.

———. *The Extraordinary Image: Orson Welles, Alfred Hitchcock, Stanley Kubrick, and the Reimagining of Cinema*. Rutgers University Press, 2017.

Krämer, Peter. *A Clockwork Orange*. Red Globe Press, 2011.

———. *Dr. Strangelove or: How I Learned to Stop Worrying and Love the Bomb*. BFI, 2014.

———. *2001: A Space Odyssey*. BFI, 2010.

Kubrick, Stanley. *A Clockwork Orange*. Screenplay. 1971. https://www.scriptslug.com/assets/scripts/a-clockwork-orange-1971.pdf. Accessed September 12, 2022.

Lacan, Jacques. "The Signification of the Phallus." 1958. *Écrits*. W.W. Norton & Company, 1977. 281-91.

Landy, Marcia. "The Cinematographic Brain in *2001: A Space Odyssey*." *Stanley Kubrick's 2001: A Space Odyssey—New Essays*, edited by Robert Kolker. Oxford University Press, 2006. 87-104.

Latham, Rob. "'Lack of Respect, Wrong Attitude, Failure to Obey Authority': *Dark Star, A Boy and His Dog*, and New Wave Cult SF." *Science Fiction Double Feature: The Science Fiction Film as Cult Text*. Liverpool University Press, 2021. 205-19.

Lennon, John and Paul McCartney. "With a Little Help from My Friends." *Sgt. Pepper's Lonely Hearts Club Band*. EMI, 1967.

Lobrutto, Vincent. *Stanley Kubrick: A Biography*. Da Capo Press, 1999.

Mainar, Luis M. García. *Narrative and Stylistic Patterns in the Films of*

*Stanley Kubrick.* Camden House, 1999.

McBride, Joseph. *Steven Spielberg: A Biography.* University Press of Mississippi, 2010.

McLuhan, Marshall. *Understanding Media: The Extensions of Man.* 1964. Ginko Press, 2017.

McQuiston, Kate. "Value, Violence, and Music Recognized: *A Clockwork Orange* as Musicology." *Stanley Kubrick: Essays on his Film and Legacy.* McFarland, 2007. 105-22.

Metz, Christian. "*Trucage* and the Film." *Critical Inquiry* 3.4 (Summer 1977): 657-75.

Mikics, David. *Stanley Kubrick: American Filmmaker.* Yale University Press, 2020.

*Minority Report.* Dir. Steven Spielberg. 20th Century Fox, 2002.

Morris, Nigel. "*A.I. Artificial Intelligence*: Eyes Wide Open." *The Cinema of Stephen Spielberg: Empire of Light.* Wallflower Press, 2007. 299-315.

Mulvey, Laura. "Visual Pleasure and Narrative Cinema." 1975. *Media and Cultural Studies: Keyworks.* Blackwell Publishing, 2001. 393-404.

Naremore, James. *On Kubrick.* 2007. BFI, 2023.

Ndalianis, Angela. "Baroque Façades: Jeff Bridges's Face and *Tron: Legacy.*" *Special Effects: New Histories/Theories/Contexts,* edited by Dan North, Bob Rehak, and Michael S. Duffy. BFI, 2015. 154-65.

Nelson, Thomas Allen. *Kubrick: Inside a Film Artist's Maze.* 1982. Indiana University Press, 2000.

Newitz, Annalee. "The First Cyborg and the First Singularity." *The Clockwork Man.* 1923. HiLo, 2013. 11-16.

Nicholls, Peter. "Sex." *The Encyclopedia of Science Fiction.* September 20, 2020. https://sf-encyclopedia.com/entry/sex. Accessed June 8, 2022.

Nietzsche, Friedrich. *Ecce Homo.* 1908. Penguin, 2004.

———. *On the Genealogy of Morals.* 1887. Penguin, 2013.

Nordern, Eric. "*Playboy* Interview: Stanley Kubrick." 1968. *Stanley Kubrick: Interviews,* edited by Gene D. Phillips. University Press of Mississippi, 2001. 47-74.

North, Dan. *Performing Illusions: Cinema, Special Effects, and the Virtual Actor.* Wallflower Press, 2008.

Orris, Scott. "Empty Space: The Depersonalization of the Future in *2001: A Space Odyssey.*" *Film Matters* 9.1 (Spring 2018): 109-16.

Orwell, George. *Nineteen Eighty-Four.* 1949. Signet, 1977.

Pezzotta, Elisa. *Stanley Kubrick: Adapting the Sublime.* University Press of Mississippi, 2016.

Phillips, Gene D. "Introduction." *Stanley Kubrick: Interviews,* edited by Gene D. Phillips. University Press of Mississippi, 2001. vii-xii.

———. "Stop the World: Stanley Kubrick." 1973. *Stanley Kubrick: Interviews,* edited by Gene D. Phillips. University Press of Mississippi, 2001. 140-58.

Proyas, Alex. "Real Alex Proyas." *Facebook.* April 9, 2022. https://www.facebook.com/RealAlexProyas. Accessed April 10, 2022.

*Psycho.* Dir. Alfred Hitchcock. Paramount, 1960.

Rabinowitz, Peter J. "'A Bird of Like Rarest Spun Heavenmetal': Music in *A Clockwork Orange.*" *Stanley Kubrick's A Clockwork Orange,* edited by Stuart Y. McDougal. Cambridge University Press, 2003. 109-30.

Raphael, Rebecca. "The Doomsday Body, or, *Dr. Strangelove* as Disabled Cyborg." *Golem: Journal of Religion and Monsters* 1.1 (Spring 2006). http://www.golemjournal.org. Accessed August 15, 2022.

Rasmussen, Randy. *Stanley Kubrick: Seven Films Analyzed.* McFarland, 2001.

Reucher, Gaby. "Beethoven as Nazi Propaganda." *Deutsche Welle.* April 5, 2020. https://www.dw.com/en/beethoven-as-nazi-propaganda/a-53262640. Accessed September 10, 2022.

Rice, Julian. *Kubrick's Story, Spielberg's Film: A.I. Artificial Intelligence.* Rowman & Littlefield, 2017.

*Rocky IV.* Dir. Sylvester Stallone. MGM, 1985.

Rogers, Jude. "'She Made Music Jump into 3D': Wendy Carlos, the Reclusive Synth Genius." *The Guardian.* November 11, 2020. https://www.theguardian.com/music/2020/nov/11/she-made-music-jump-into-3d-wendy-carlos-the-reclusive-synth-genius. Accessed September 7, 2022.

Schmerheim, Philipp. "Film, Not Sliced Up into Pieces, or: How Film Made Me Feel Thinking." Review of *Filmosophy,* by Daniel

Frampton. *Film-Philosophy* 12.2 (September 2008): 109-23.

Scrivner, Joyce. "Madness." *The Greenwood Encyclopedia of Science Fiction and Fantasy: Volume 2*. Greenwood Press, 2005. 485-87.

Servitje, Lorenzo. "Of Drugs and Droogs: Cultural Dynamics, Psychopharmacology, and Neuroscience in Anthony Burgess's *A Clockwork Orange*." *Literature and Medicine* 36.1 (Spring 2018): 101-23.

Shakespeare, William. *Hamlet*. 1601. W.W. Norton & Company, 2011.

Shelley, Mary. *Frankenstein*. 1818. W.W. Norton & Company, 2012.

Sikora, Joshua. "The Everlasting Moment: Enchantment and Myth in *A.I.* and *2001: A Space Odyssey*." *A Critical Companion to Stanley Kubrick*, edited by Elsa Colombani. Lexington Books, 2020. 263-76.

Siskel, Gene. "Candidly Kubrick." 1987. *Stanley Kubrick: Interviews*, edited by Gene D. Phillips. University Press of Mississippi, 2001. 177-88.

Slusser, George. *Science Fiction: Toward a World Literature*. Lexington Books, 2022.

Sobchack, Vivian. "Love Machines: Boy Toys, Toy Boys and the Oxymorons of *A.I.: Artificial Intelligence*." *Science Fiction Film and Television* 1.1 (2008): 1-13.

———. *Screening Space: The American Science Fiction Film*. Rutgers University Press, 1998.

*Stanley Kubrick: A Life in Pictures*. Dir. Jan Harlan. Warner Brothers, 2001.

Struthers, Jane M. "Part 1: The Arrival." *A.I. Artificial Intelligence from Stanley Kubrick to Steven Spielberg: The Vision Behind the Film*, edited by Jan Harlan and Jane M. Struthers. Thames & Hudson, 2009. 30-59.

———. "Part 2: The Journey." *A.I. Artificial Intelligence from Stanley Kubrick to Steven Spielberg: The Vision Behind the Film*, edited by Jan Harlan and Jane M. Struthers. Thames & Hudson, 2009. 60-119.

———. "Part 3: The Discovery." *A.I. Artificial Intelligence from Stanley Kubrick to Steven Spielberg: The Vision Behind the Film*, edited by Jan Harlan and Jane M. Struthers. Thames & Hudson, 2009. 120-47.

———. "The Birth of A.I." *A.I. Artificial Intelligence from Stanley*

*Kubrick to Steven Spielberg: The Vision Behind the Film,* edited by Jan Harlan and Jane M. Struthers. Thames & Hudson, 2009. 10-25.

Suvin, Darko. *Metamorphoses of Science Fiction.* 1977. Peter Lang, 2016.

*The Fifth Element.* Dir. Luc Besson. Gaumont, 1997.

*The Matrix.* Dir. Lana and Lilly Wachowski. Warner Brothers, 1999.

Tryon, Chuck. "*Iron Sky*'s War Bonds: Cult SF Cinema and Crowd-sourcing." *Science Fiction Double Feature: The Science Fiction Film as Cult Text,* edited by J.P. Telotte and Gerald Duchovnay. Liverpool University Press, 2021. 115-29.

*2001: A Space Odyssey.* Dir. Stanley Kubrick. Stanley Kubrick Productions, 1968.

*2001: The Making of a Myth.* Dir. Paul Joyce. Journeyman Pictures, 2001.

Vint, Sherryl. *Science Fiction.* MIT Press, 2021.

Vitale, Christopher. "*Cinema 1: The Movement-Image*: The Deleuzian Notion of the Image, or Worldslicing as Cinema Beyond the Human." *Networkologies.* n.d. https://networkologies.wordpress.com/2011/04/04/the-deleuzian-notion-of-the-image-a-slice-of-the-world-or-cinema-beyond-the-human. Accessed October 30, 2021.

Youngblood, Gene. "Lolita." *Criterion.com.* September 24, 1992. https://www.criterion.com/current/posts/836-lolita. Accessed November 28, 2021.

Walker, Alexander. *Stanley Kubrick Directs.* Harcourt Brace Jovanovich, 1971.

Welles, Orson and Peter Bogdanovich. *This Is Orson Welles.* Da Capo Press, 1998.

Wessman, Colin. "How the Synthesizer Changed the Way We Listen to Movies." *Collider.com.* February 14, 2022. https://collider.com/synthesizer-movie-scores-history-explained. Accessed September 6, 2022.

Williams, Madison Mae. "'Violence Is a Very Horrible Thing': Brechtian Alienation Effect in Kubrick's *A Clockwork Orange.*" *A Critical Companion to Stanley Kubrick,* edited by Elsa Colombani. Lexington Books, 2020. 151-63.

Wolfe, Tom. "Pornoviolence." 1967. *Mauve Gloves and Madmen, Clutter and Vine.* Farrar, Straus & Giroux, 1988. 178-87.

Worthen, Meredith. *Sexual Deviance and Society: A Sociological Examination.* Routledge, 2016.

Žižek, Slavoj. *Looking Awry: An Introduction to Jacques Lacan through Popular Culture.* 1992. The MIT Press, 1998.

# INDEX

# STRANGELOVE
# COUNTRY

## OTHER BOOKS BY D. HARLAN WILSON

**NOVELS**
*Outré*
*Primordial: An Abstraction*
*The Kyoto Man*
*Codename Prague*
*Dr. Identity, or, Farewell to Plaquedemia*
*Blankety Blank: A Memoir of Vulgaria*

**THEORY-FICTION**
*The Psychotic Dr. Schreber*
*Peckinpah: An Ultraviolent Romance*

**DRAMA**
*Jackanape and the Fingermen*
*Three Plays*

**AUTO/BIOGRAPHIES**
*Nietzsche: The Unmanned Autohagiography*
*Douglass: The Lost Autobiography*
*Freud: The Penultimate Biography*
*Hitler: The Terminal Biography*

**FICTION COLLECTIONS**
*Natural Complexions*
*Battle without Honor or Humanity: Volume 2*
*Battle without Honor or Humanity: Volume 1*
*Diegeses*
*They Had Goat Heads*
*Pseudo-City*
*Stranger on the Loose*
*The Kafka Effekt*

**SCIENCE FICTION STUDIES**
*The Stars My Destination* | Palgrave SFF: A New Canon
*Minority Report* | Constellations
*J.G. Ballard* | Modern Masters of Science Fiction
*They Live* | Cultographies
*Technologized Desire: Postcapitalist Science Fiction*

**D. HARLAN WILSON** is an American novelist, scholar, editor, playwright, and college professor. He is the author of over thirty book-length works of fiction and nonfiction, and hundreds of his stories, essays, and plays have appeared in magazines, journals, and anthologies throughout the world in over ten languages. Wilson serves as editor-in-chief for Anti-Oedipus Press and reviews editor for *Extrapolation*; he is also a cohost on the Dickheads Podcast, devoted to life and writing of Philip K. Dick.